FUNDAMENTALS OF FAMILY FINANCE

Living *Joyfully* within your Means

FIRST EDITION

E. JEFFREY HILL, PhD
BRYAN L. SUDWEEKS, PhD

   BYU SCHOOL OF FAMILY LIFE

Fundamentals of Family Finance:
Living Joyfully Within Your Means

E. Jeffrey Hill and Bryan L. Sudweeks

First Edition Credits

Managing Editor: Kent Minson
Project Lead: Ashley LeBaron
Lead Editor: Kayci Treu
Head Teaching Assistants: Alex Gunnerson, Matt Judd

All images licensed through dollarphotoclub.com (now Adobe Stock) except the following:
pp. 1–2, 197 image 1 courtesy Jeff Hill; p. 3 image 1, courtesy Brian Sudweeks; pp. 4, 6, 196, courtesy lds.org; p. 202 image 1, © 2016 Jaren Wilkey/BYU Photo, used by permission.

Copyright © 2016 School of Family Life, Brigham Young University Academic Publishing

We want the helpful principles of this book to be widely distributed and so we encourage use of these materials under the fair use clause of the 1976 Copyright Act (See Section 107 of Chapter 1 of the Copyright Law of the United States of America). Unless otherwise noted, text and images in this book are available for nonprofit and educational purposes, such as research, teaching, and private study. For these limited purposes, these materials may be reproduced without prior permission. Use of the material in this book for other purposes, including commercial purposes, requires prior written permission. The content of this book may be protected by U.S. copyright law (Title 17, U.S.C.) and/or by the copyright or neighboring-rights laws of other nations. Additionally, the reproduction of some materials may be restricted by privacy and/or publicity rights. Unless otherwise indicated, this book is copyright (c) School of Family Life, Brigham Young University Academic Publishing, and is shared with you under the terms of the Creative Commons Attribution-Noncommercial-Share Alike license. This work is not an official publication of The Church of Jesus Christ of Latter-day Saints. The views expressed herein are the responsibility of the authors and do not necessarily represent the position of the Church or Brigham Young University.

Text ISBN: 9781611650235 (BYU Academic Publishing)
Trade ISBN: 9781611661095 (Y Mountain Press)

For more information or permission to use material from this text contact:
BYU Academic Publishing
3995 WSC
Provo, UT 84606
Tel. (801) 422-6231
Fax (801) 422-0070
Academic publishing@byu.edu

To report ideas or text corrections email:
jeff_hill@byu.edu

Acknowledgments

We are deeply indebted to many other individuals who worked so diligently to make this book possible: Ashley LeBaron's creative team: Alex Gunnerson, Nick Jones, Jarna Knickerbocker, Travis Spencer, Carly Schmltz, Kayci Treu, and Christina Rosa; Kayci Treu's editing team: Leah Jennings, Tiana Cole, Sydney Cobb, and Jessica Kirkham; Dr. Hill's students in SFL 260, Family Finance; and Dr. Sudweeks students in FIN 418, Financial Planning.

To my wife
Tammy
And to our children:
Sarah, Jeffrey (and Jenny), Aaron (and Jenny), Abigail (and James), Jordan, Hannah (and Joshua), Heidi, Emily (and Ben), Amanda (and Nathaniel), Ryan, Seth, Cam, and Maddy
And to our 23 (and counting) grandchildren!
May they all abide these principles and live joyfully within their means!
EJH

To my wife:
Anne
And to our children and grandchildren:
Kimberly (and Lane, Logan and Ryan Adrich), Natalie (and Taylor, Halle and Dylan Barrett), Laura (and Devin Dearden), Clinton, Emilee, Ashley and Kaili
BLS

Contents

Introduction
Fundamentals of Family Finance . . . 1

Chapter 1
Time Value of Money (TVM) 15

Chapter 2
Budgeting, Net Worth, and More . . 25

Chapter 3
Cash Management and More 43

Chapter 4
Credit and Loans 51

Chapter 5
Tax Planning 71

Chapter 6
Risk Management and Insurance . . 87

Chapter 7
Understanding and Financing Major Family Purchases: Buying a Car   103

Chapter 8
Understanding and Financing Major Family Purchases: Buying a Home   111

Chapter 9
Investing for the Long Term 123

Chapter 10
Retirement Planning. 141

Chapter 11
Tips for Frugal Living 151

Chapter 12
Work and Family 161

Chapter 13
Marriage and Money 173

Chapter 14
Children and Money. 183

Chapter 15
Consecration 195

Glossary 207

Introduction

Fundamentals of Family Finance

Living Joyfully Within Your Means

Dr. E. Jeffrey Hill

This is a book about the fundamentals of family finance. It's about the very basic principles of how to manage money in your home so that family relationships are strengthened instead of destroyed. It is about the day-to-day things you do with your material resources so that you can claim the blessing of living joyfully within your means.

As an initial introduction I, Dr. E. Jeffrey Hill, would like to get personal and briefly share some things I have learned over my lifetime about family finances and joyful living. A long, long time ago, Juanita Ray and I met while attending BYU. We played racquetball together, courted for a time, and were married in the temple. As newlyweds, we had no money. We lived in a tiny two-room apartment with low ceilings, we bought clothes from Deseret Industries, and we ate her family's food storage. We drank disgusting powdered milk for a year, but we had each other, we had our love, and we had the gospel. It was a good year. We learned that money doesn't buy happiness.

I graduated and got a good job. (We started drinking whole milk—heavenly!) I had been taught to pay 10 percent to the Lord, save at least 10 percent to invest, and live on the rest. Juanita and I followed those principles as we created our family budgets over the years. We were fruitful, and after twenty-five years we had a bunch of kids and had paid for our home. We had solid investments. We learned that if you consistently save a little money and invest it in a broad, diversified stock market fund, it grows through the miracle of compound interest.

Then came the hard part. Though Juanita and I were financially set for a long life together—we anticipated many missions, lots of travel, and lots of grandkids—life didn't go as planned. Juanita got cancer. She fought valiantly, but cancer won. I learned that there are many things that matter more than money, and I learned that "you can't take it with you."

After Juanita died, I was a lonely, single dad. I couldn't sleep. I got angry easily. I didn't eat well. To compensate for my feelings, I spent a lot of money. Juanita had always helped me constrain my spending, and with her gone I bought lots of things and traveled lots of places. I learned through personal experience how foolish it is to spend money when you are hungry, angry, lonely, and tired.

Then a miracle happened. God sent me an amazing, beautiful widow named Tammy Mulford. It was so fun to be dating again (and to have money this time)! Tammy and I fell in love and were married for time in the Bountiful Utah Temple. What pure joy! And what a good woman! It takes a remarkable person to marry a stuffy BYU professor with so many kids. I am eternally grateful!

Tammy and I have learned that money makes important things possible. It is never easy to join two families, but money proved useful for us when blending a large family, especially one that includes twelve children, six in-laws, and twenty-three grandchildren.

Money also made it possible for Tammy to go to graduate school. She now blesses many lives as an excellent marriage and family therapist and an adjunct professor at BYU. This was only an option because we had the financial resources to do it.

In this book I want to share the fundamentals of family finance so that you can experience the peace that comes from joyfully living within your means. I want to help you discover how money management can make important things possible for you and your family, and I'll tell a few more stories along the way.

I, Dr. Bryan L. Sudweeks, would also like to share a few personal items about our family and a few of the lessons we have learned about family finances and the joy of living within our means. I was born in an LDS family, served a mission, graduated from BYU, and worked for a few years. At age 28 (I was a menace to society for many years) I met my future wife at family home evening in the Stanford Singles Ward. We were married, and immediately moved to Washington D.C. to pursue a Ph.D. as guided by my patriarchal blessing. Before we left, we had a father's blessing in which we were promised that if we did the things we should, the Lord would bless us to be able to work "beyond our natural abilities." That blessing was realized.

While earning the Ph.D., we lived very simply, including inexpensive apartments, used cars, particle board shelves, and a door on four chimney flues as a desk. We had our first child halfway through the program and a second right after. We watched our finances carefully and even graduated with a little money in the bank. We set our goals as a family and worked to achieve them. We worked in two different startup asset management companies, paid cash for our cars, and saved more than 20 percent of our salary every month for retirement and children's missions and education. We also learned the importance of giving: that God shovels it to us, and we shovel it back (and God has a bigger shovel). We learned to sacri-

Dr. Bryan L. Sudweeks

fice what we wanted now for what we wanted most, which was "family happiness in this life and eternal life in the life to come." We tried hard to do these things and still make memories for our children. We created two family mottos: "no empty chairs" to emphasize the importance of family, and "we can do hard things" to emphasize the importance of choice.

We moved from Washington to California, and the children continued to come (our seventh child and sixth daughter was born in Walnut Creek, CA). We tried to have a balanced view of life: we tried to do well in our family, occupation, and service to the Lord (all were very busy). We found that when we had the Lord's help (and balance), we could accomplish so much more.

Anne and I had a goal that when I turned 45 we would retire, pay off our home, have a specific amount of money saved, and come back and teach at Brigham Young University, not because we had to, but because we wanted to. In addition, we felt the Lord had given us these wonderful experiences in the finance area, and that by coming back, we could share what the Lord had blessed us with. My 45th birthday was my last day of work and we had achieved each of our goals.

The person teaching personal finance in the Marriott School of Management at BYU retired at the same time that we came back to BYU, so I took that class. It has been a great opportunity to share the things we have learned from our experiences, work and in our family. The single most important lesson has been the importance of bringing Christ into our personal and family finances.

We worked with other BYU Faculty to create a personal finance website (www.personalfinance.byu.edu) to help individuals and families become more financially self-reliant. When Jeff and I met, it was an amazing experience to meet someone who was trying to do the exact same thing I was trying to do, which was to teach people to have faith in Jesus Christ and be unified with their spouses in the stewardship of their financial resources. Jeff is an amazing teacher, professional, example and friend, and I appreciate the opportunity he has given me to participate with him in this wonderful project. Let's get started!

Introduction

Every semester hundreds of BYU students enroll in SFL 260: Family Finance. This book is used as a textbook in that course. Oddly enough, the purpose of that course, and this book, is *not* to teach you how to get rich or accumulate wealth. Its purpose is to teach you to magnify your financial **stewardship** and use prudent financial management so you can more fully bless yourself, your family, and others. You will learn how to use financial resources to joyfully strengthen your family and build up the kingdom of God on the earth.

I love to teach family finance because it is one of the most practical things you will ever study. You will use almost everything you learn from this book for the rest of your life. You will acquire skills that will guide you in preparing budgets, managing debt, filing taxes, making

stewardship

An ethic that embodies the responsible planning and management of resources.

home and auto purchases, finding insurance, acquiring investments, and improving marriage and family relationships.

The best way to learn something is to teach it. I highly recommend that you find someone with whom you can share what you learn in this book. That person could be your spouse, a roommate, a friend, a parent, a child, a sibling, or anyone else you choose. As you share your newfound knowledge and skills, you will etch into your mind and your heart what you need to know to be financially successful.

At the beginning of each semester at BYU, I ask my students to remember three things:

1. Life is hard . . . but you can do hard things. With the help of the Lord, you can do anything He wants you to do—even balance a budget or invest in a mutual fund.

2. When life doesn't go as planned, don't get frustrated; make the best of it. Most of the time things don't go as planned—especially in financial matters—and if we don't make the best of our lives, we'll spend a lot of our time feeling frustrated.

3. TTT: Things Take Time. The best things in life take time. In fact, the best financial plan is the "get rich slowly" plan, where you safely and systematically invest to acquire resources that can be used to bless God's children.

Managing money can be tricky. We are told to save and invest money for our mortal future, and yet the scriptures counsel us to also "lay up for [our]selves treasures in heaven."[1] It is not so difficult to accomplish your monetary and spiritual goals if you build your finances upon a firm foundation: the gospel of Jesus Christ. If you do this, then as the rains of recessions descend, floods of lay-offs come, and winds of high interest rates blow and beat upon your house, it will not fall, for it is founded upon the rock of Christ.[2]

Family finance can generally be viewed in two ways, either from an eternal perspective or from the world's materialistic perspective. The eternal perspective assumes all material resources are owned by God and that we are stewards over those resources so that we may bless His children. The world's materialistic perspective is any other perspective that takes God out of the equation. The perspective you choose will make a big difference in the way you manage your money and your life. Perhaps family finance, from an eternal perspective, is simply the temporal application of spiritual principles.

In this chapter, we will share an eternal perspective on the "why's," "what's," and "how's" of family finance. We will highlight inspired financial doctrines, profound financial principles, practical financial applications, and a few interesting stories to help you put your financial house in order. Success is essential. How you choose to consecrate your material resources is at the core of your purpose in life. Let's embark!

Why? What? How?

The Why's

In order to answer the question "Why should I learn about family finance?" you must reflect on inspired doctrine.

1. SPIRITUAL:

   To bring you to Christ

The ultimate purpose of everything God does is to bring us to Christ. If God's work and

glory is to bring to pass the "immortality and eternal life of man,"[3] and if the only way you can have eternal life is through Jesus Christ,[4] then the purpose of all God does, including encouraging you to wisely manage your finances, is to bring you to Christ.

2. TEMPORAL:

To help you become a wise steward

The Lord said, "For it is required of the Lord, at the hand of every steward, to render an account of his stewardship, both in time and in eternity. For he who is faithful and wise in time is accounted worthy to inherit the mansions prepared for him of my Father."[5] It may be that the way you magnify your financial stewardship in mortality will be indicative of the stewardships you will receive in the eternities.

3. INDIVIDUAL:

To accomplish your divine mission

You have a sacred mission to perform here on earth, magnifying your "divine nature and destiny."[6] Your mission will require material resources. As you fulfill your financial stewardship faithfully, you can acquire resources to consecrate to the work God has for you to do.

4. FAMILY:

To return with your family back to Heavenly Father's presence

An eternal perspective of home finances strengthens your eternal marriage and is a conduit for positive parenting. President David O. McKay reminded us that "No other success can compensate for failure in the home."[7] You will be disappointed in life if you gain the riches of the world and lose your spouse and family in the process.[8]

The What's

The second important question for you to consider is, "What are the profound principles upon which this stewardship perspective is based?"

PRINCIPLE 1: OWNERSHIP

The Psalmist wrote: "The earth is the Lord's, and the fullness thereof; the world, and they that dwell therein."[9] We know from scriptures that the Lord is the creator of the earth;[10] the creator of worlds, men, and all things;[11] the giver of our knowledge;[12] the supplier of our breath; the giver of our life;[13] and the Giver of all we have and are. Nothing you have is your own—it is all God's. Therefore, you should not feel proud because of the things you acquire.

PRINCIPLE 2: STEWARDSHIP

Because God owns everything, you have a responsibility to use your resources for His purposes. You should first meet the needs and appropriate wants of your family and then consecrate the rest to bless God's other children. Being blessed with material things in life should not only be seen as a blessing but also as a responsibility, for "unto whom much is given much is required."[14]

PRINCIPLE 3: AGENCY

Your financial stewardship enables you to make choices. President David O. McKay wrote, "Next to the bestowal of life itself, the right to direct that life is God's greatest gift to man."[15] The blessing of **agency** is an unconditional gift from God. The choices you make with money are at the heart of mortality's test. Will you choose to waste your resources upon transitory pleasures, or will you choose to serve others and build up the kingdom of God? Will you choose to act on impulse and burden yourself with debt, or will you act prudently so that money becomes a tool for family joy instead of a cause of stress and worry? The way you use the gift of financial resources shows what you truly believe and how much you really love God and His Son, Jesus Christ.

PRINCIPLE 4: ACCOUNTABILITY

The Lord counseled, "For it is required

Ownership
The right to possess or own something.

Agency
The ability to choose.

of the Lord, at the hand of every steward, to render an account of his stewardship, both in time and in eternity."[16] The first three principles outlined above are God's gift to you. The fourth principle of **accountability**, if followed wisely, can be your gift back to God. You will be required to give Him an account of your stewardship over the blessings you have received.

The How's

Finally, you should consider the *"how's"* of family finance, found by answering this question: "How can I practically apply family finance in my life?" An eternal perspective will help you know how to apply family finance principles. You must build your financial house upon the rock of the gospel of Jesus Christ. Fortunately, prophets, seers, and revelators—Christ's representatives on the earth—have given clear financial guidance.[17]

1. Pay the Lord first in tithes, fast offerings, and other contributions

Tithing is the primary law upon which financial blessings are predicated. If you pay a full tithing (10 percent of your income or increase) and are generous with offerings, the windows of heaven will be opened to you.[18] If you have a regular monthly income, making out the first check of each month to the Church for tithing is a reflection of your faith.

Contributing a generous **fast offering** enables you to share your material blessings with those in need. Though the minimum amount offered is the value of the two meals not eaten during the fast, President Spencer W. Kimball counseled: "I think we should be very generous and give, instead of the amount we saved by our two meals of fasting, perhaps much, much more—ten times more where we are in a position to do it."[19]

Contributions to the Church beyond tithing and fast offerings should be considered. Elder Jeffrey R. Holland taught, "Be as generous as circumstances permit in your . . . humanitarian, educational, and missionary contributions."[20] As you make these contributions to the Lord consistently, you will begin to see blessings pour into your life.

2. Create, use, and update a budget

Every person of every age should create, use, and update a personal or family **budget**. If you don't have one already, this book will help you create one. A budget is simply a plan for how you are going to spend the money that is available to you. To create a budget, you determine your spendable income and allocate it to different categories of expenses. Then you track your actual spending against your budget. It is acceptable to go over in some categories if you are under by the same amount in others. A budget is a living document that is modified as conditions warrant.

> Elder Robert D. Hales taught, "We help our children learn to be provident providers by establishing a family budget. We should regularly review our family income, savings, and spending plan in family council meetings. This will teach our children to recognize the difference between wants and needs and to plan ahead for meaningful use of family resources."[21]

Budgets can vary in complexity. I suggest that every budget should include at least a 10 percent allocation to tithes and offerings. Most budgets should also include at least a 10 percent allocation to long-term savings. You can find sample budgets on numerous Internet sites, such as the Marriott School's excellent website personalfinance.byu.edu[22] and lds.org,[23] and on many apps, such as mint.com.[24]

Accountability
The obligation to account for one's actions or to accept responsibility.

Tithing
The act of paying a tithe, which is a portion (in the LDS Church, a tenth) of a person's income, to support religious institutions.

Fast Offerings
The term used in The Church of Jesus Christ of Latter-day Saints to denote money or usable commodities donated to the Church, which are then available to provide financial help for those in need.

Budget
A plan for how you are going to spend the money that is available to you.

Budgets generally include categories for food, housing, utilities, clothing, transportation, medical, recreation, debt reduction, and miscellaneous expenditures. It is often this last budget category, the miscellaneous category, that gets overlooked. Unexpected expenses always come up that don't fit neatly into your budget categories: a car repair or a root canal, perhaps an engagement ring or even a wedding.

In a marriage relationship, it is important that both the husband and the wife have a say in budget creation, and that they help each other live within their means and claim joy. In many marriages, one partner is a saver, and the other partner is a spender. Both play an important role. Early in a marriage, it is a great blessing when the saver can help the spender stay within the budget. Elder Robert D. Hales poignantly illustrated this point in the following story:

> We were newly married and had very little money. I was in the air force, and we had missed Christmas together. I was on assignment overseas. When I got home, I saw a beautiful dress in a store window and suggested to my wife that if she liked it, we would buy it. Mary went into the dressing room of the store. After a moment the salesclerk came out, brushed by me, and returned the dress to its place in the store window. As we left the store, I asked, "What happened?" She replied, "It was a beautiful dress, but we can't afford it!" Those words went straight to my heart. I have learned that the three most loving words are "I love you," and the four most caring words for those we love are "We can't afford it."[25]

> *I have learned that the three most loving words are 'I love you,' and the four most caring words for those we love are 'We can't afford it.'*
> —Elder Robert D. Hales

The spender can also play an important role in the marriage. If the family is financially stable for a period of time, the spender can help the saver see the wisdom in setting goals and planning for some special expenditures in the budget: maybe a nice second honeymoon, a boat, a camping trailer, or a sports court. All of these could strengthen family relationships through wholesome family recreation.

Learn to appreciate both the savers and the spenders in your relationships. Whether you are married or single, I invite you to create, use, and update some form of budget for the rest of your life.

3. Minimize and eventually eliminate debt

We have repeatedly been counseled to avoid debt wherever possible. In a recent First Presidency message, President Thomas S. Monson taught, "We encourage you . . . [to look] to the condition of your finances. We urge you to . . . discipline yourselves in your purchases to avoid debt. Pay off debt as quickly as you can, and free yourselves from this bondage. Save a little money regularly to gradually build a **financial reserve**."[26]

President Monson may have chuckled as he wrote, "Many more people could ride out the storm-tossed waves in their economic lives if they had a supply of food and clothing and

Financial Reserve
Cash or other liquid assets held to cover 3–6 months of emergency expenses.

8 Chapter Introduction: Fundamentals of Family Finance

were debt-free. Today we find that many have followed this counsel in reverse: they have a supply of debt and are food-free."[27]

President Monson probably *wasn't* chuckling when he quoted President J. Reuben Clark: "Once in debt, interest is your companion every minute of the day and night; you

cannot shun it or slip away from it; . . . and whenever you get in its way or cross its course or fail to meet its demands, it crushes you."[28]

So is any debt legitimate? The counsel of Church leaders on debt was recently summarized by Elder Robert D. Hales: "Some debt incurred for education, a modest home, or a basic automobile may be necessary to provide for a family."[29] Necessary debt for a BYU education usually pays off: recent study revealed that the cost of a BYU education had the highest return on investment of any university in Utah.[30]

debt worth 10 percent of your income, reducing the amount you can afford for a house payment. Unfortunately, some forget to include tithing in their calculations. Please treat 10 percent of your income as a debt when considering how much of a house payment you can afford.

We also recommend that you avoid home-equity loans. When property values go down, home equity loans can leave you upside-down in your home. This doesn't mean you are standing on your head in your living room; it means you cannot sell your home for what you owe on it. When that happens, you become a prisoner in your home because you can't sell it. Worse yet, many people in this situation have lost their homes because they couldn't afford the payments when financial challenges occurred. Be very careful when considering a home equity loan.

Many people do not realize that you can

> *Some debt incurred for education, a modest home, or a basic automobile may be necessary to provide for a family.* —Elder Robert D. Hales

Sign up for a fifteen-year mortgage instead of a thirty-year home mortgage.

Here I would like to interject what I believe is the biggest financial mistake made by recent BYU graduates: buying a house that is beyond their means, then paying large monthly mortgage payments for decades. There is a reason for this problem. When you apply for a mortgage loan, you are asked about your debts. Tithing represents a

actually pay off a home mortgage. One way to accomplish this is by signing up for a fifteen-year mortgage instead of a thirty-year mortgage. The interest rate is lower, and you can save hundreds of thousands of dollars in interest.

If you already have debts, adding a "debt repayment" category to your budget helps you pay them off. The money allocated to this category is applied each month as an extra pay-

ment to the debt with the highest interest rate until it is eliminated. Again, personalfinance.byu.edu has excellent advice on this topic.[31]

4. Prepare for emergencies and build a reserve

Your family will have greater peace of mind and greater insulation from unexpected financial difficulties if you build a financial reserve to act as a cushion for rough times. Most financial planners recommend three to six months' worth of living expenses be set aside in a savings or checking account. These emergency funds should be held in reserve for major unexpected needs—lost job, hospital or medical bills, major home or car repairs, travel to a funeral, etc. In addition to preparing a cash

reserve, it is also important to build up appropriate food storage and assemble 72-hour kits, first-aid kits, and other emergency essentials to prepare against times of need.

5. Invest early, consistently, and wisely

Concurrent with building a reserve, you should begin saving for short- and long-term goals. Some short-term goals may include purchasing a newer vehicle, upgrading a cell phone, getting a new outfit, taking a trip to Disneyland or buying furniture. It is gratifying to save and sacrifice for these short-term goals.

Some long-term goals to save for include paying cash for a car or making a down payment on a home. You may also be saving for missions, education, weddings, large philanthropic contributions, funeral expenses, and retirement.

I would now like to briefly share some investing advice related to retirement. After graduating from BYU, you and your spouse should decide to save at least 10 percent of your income for retirement and understand your available options. If your employer offers a matching contribution to a 401(k), you should always contribute enough to get the full match. There is no other safe investment that yields a 100 percent return the first year! If your employer does not offer a 401(k), then consider investing in a personal IRA (Individual Retirement Account). 401(k)'s and IRAs are tax-advantaged retirement plans set up by the government to encourage retirement savings. We'll explore the ins and outs of these plans in Chapter 8.

We would also like to caution you against a few investment options. First, avoid **speculation**. Speculation is any investment that promises a greater-than-market-rate return. Most of these are scams or extremely high-risk ventures. In a letter from the First Presidency, members of the Church were warned about "those who use relationships of trust to promote risky or even fraudulent investment and business schemes."[32]

Second, it is important to realize that

Speculation
Any investment that promises a greater than market-rate return.

the only way to get greater-than-market-rate returns is to take greater-than-market-rate risks. This means if you put money into investments that promise large returns, you likely stand to lose a lot of money. It is much better to take the "get rich slowly" approach and invest wisely for the long term.

6. Protect yourself and your family through adequate insurance

Without insurance, major financial setbacks could wipe out decades of savings. Adequate insurance that protects major investments provides a family peace of mind. Elder Marvin J. Ashton counseled:

> Appropriately involve yourself in an insurance program. It is most important to have sufficient medical, automobile, and homeowners insurance and an adequate life insurance program. Costs associated with illness, accident, and death may be so large that uninsured families can be financially burdened for many years.[33]

Once you have someone who is depen-

dent upon you for income, you have a responsibility to get life insurance. You should have enough insurance to replace your income for long enough to raise your children and for your spouse to be financially self-sufficient. Some financial planners recommend 10–15 times your gross salary. In general, term life insurance is less expensive than whole life insurance to obtain this coverage. In addition, be sure to have adequate health, auto, disability, and homeowners/renters insurance.

Because of the Affordable Care Act, almost everyone in the United States is required to have health insurance. In general, if you have little need for health services, you are better off to have a high-deductible plan with lower monthly payments. However, if you interact with health services more than average, it is usually better to have a lower deductible and higher monthly payments.

7. Share finances as equal partners in your marriage

You and your spouse must stand as equal

financial partners in your marriage. You must both be involved in creating, implementing, and modifying the family budget. You must be open and transparent in your financial communication with your spouse. Both you and your spouse should have knowledge of family income, expenses, investments, and debt. You should not hide liabilities or assets from one another.

Regarding finances in marriage, Elder Marvin J. Ashton wrote: "Management of family finances should be full and equal and mutual between a husband and a wife. Control of the money by one spouse as a source of power and authority causes inequality in a marriage and is inappropriate."[34]

Unfortunately, many couples are not successful in managing their finances, and the resulting conflict compromises their marriages. Indeed, research shows that financial difficulties are often associated with marital stress[35] and divorce.[36] Dr. Bernard Poduska reflected, "The saying 'married for better or worse, until *debt* do us part' seems to reflect today's marital realities more accurately than does the traditional vow."[37] A word of advice for those seeking an eternal mate (you know who you are): An important criterion for a future spouse is the way they handle money.

8. Teach your children and family about finances

You must teach your children to manage money well. Elder Joseph B. Wirthlin taught, "Too many of our youth get into financial difficulty because they never learned proper principles of financial common sense at home. Teach your children while they are young. Teach them that they cannot have something merely because they want it. Teach them the principles of hard work, frugality, and saving." [38]

Teach your children to set and achieve goals, and let them see you doing the same. Teach them the principles of financial management, and show them how you apply those principles in your life. Involve them in creating their own budgets and in creating the family budgets. Teach the principles of hard work,

frugality, and saving, and stress the importance of obtaining as much education as possible. Teach by example.

Summary

Remember this: With every dollar you spend, you choose which perspective you will take— either the eternal perspective or the world's materialistic perspective. The sooner you understand that managing your finances is part of living the gospel of Jesus Christ, the greater your motivation will be to obey the commandments and get your financial house in order. God has promised He will not give us a commandment unless He prepares a way for us to fulfill it.[39] We know that this includes the commandments relating to our finances. Understanding the why's, what's, and how's—the doctrines, principles, and applications—of family finance is critical. With an eternal perspective, we can be laying up for ourselves true

"treasures in heaven"[40] while simultaneously planning for our careers and supporting our families.

Notes

1. Matthew 6:20
2. Matthew 7:25
3. Moses 1:39
4. John 14:6
5. D&C 72:3–4
6. "The Family: A Proclamation to the World," (Oct. 2004), https://www.lds.org/topics/family-proclamation?lang=eng.
7. David O. McKay, *Conference Report*, (Apr. 1935), 116.
8. Matthew 16:26
9. Psalms 24:1
10. John 1:3
11. D&C 93:10
12. Moses 7:32
13. Mosiah 2:21
14. D&C 82:3
15. David O. McKay, *Conference Report*, (Apr. 1950), 32.
16. D&C 72:3

17. The following are excellent references for a gospel perspective of family finances:

    N. Eldon Tanner, "Constancy Amid Change," (Oct. 1979), https://www.lds.org/ensign/1979/11/constancy-amid-change?lang=eng.

    Marvin J. Ashton, "One for the Money," (Sept. 2007), https://www.lds.org/ensign/2007/09/one-for-the-money?lang=eng.

    Robert D. Hales, "Becoming Provident Providers Temporally and Spiritually," (April 2009), https://www.lds.org/ensign/2009/05/becoming-provident-providers-temporally-and-spiritually?lang=eng.

    Joseph B. Wirthlin, "Earthly Debts, Heavenly Debts," (April 2004), https://www.lds.org/ensign/2004/05/earthly-debts-heavenly-debts?lang=eng.

    "Teachings: Heber J. Grant Chapter 13: Principles of Financial Security," https://www.lds.org/manual/teachings-heber-j-grant/chapter-13?lang=eng.

    Dieter F. Uchtdorf, "Providing in the Lord's Way," (Oct. 2011), https://www.lds.org/ensign/2011/11/providing-in-the-lords-way?lang=eng.

    L. Tom Perry, "If Ye Are Prepared Ye Shall Not Fear," (Oct. 1995), https://www.lds.org/ensign/1995/11/if-ye-are-prepared-ye-shall-not-fear?lang=eng.

    Ezra Taft Benson, "Prepare for the Days of Tribulation," (Oct. 1980), https://www.lds.org/ensign/1980/11/prepare-for-the-days-of-tribulation?lang=eng.

    The Church of Jesus Christ of Latter-day Saints, Conference Reports of The Church of Jesus Christ of Latter-Day Saints (The Church of Jesus Christ of Latter-day Saints, Salt Lake City, 1880, 1938), http://archive.org/details/conferencereport1938a.

    Joe J. Christensen, "Greed, Selfishness, and Overindulgence," (April 1999), https://www.lds.org/ensign/1999/05/greed-selfishness-and-overindulgence?lang=eng.

    Franklin D. Richards, "Personal and Family Financial Preparedness," (April 1979), https://www.lds.org/ensign/1979/05/personal-and-family-financial-preparedness?lang=eng.

18. Malachi 3:10
19. Spencer W. Kimball, *Conference Report*, (April 1974), 184.
20. Jeffrey R. Holland, "Are We Not All Beggars?" (Oct. 2014), https://www.lds.org/ensign/2014/11/saturday-afternoon-session/are-we-not-all-beggars?lang=eng.
21. Robert D. Hales, "Becoming Provident Providers Temporally and Spiritually," (April 2009), https://www.lds.org/general-conference/2009/04/becoming-provident-providers-temporally-and-spiritually?lang=eng.
22. The BYU Marriott School of Management's Personal Finance website at http://personalfinance.byu.edu is a tool to help students, individuals, and families become wiser financial stewards over the resources the Lord has blessed them with. It includes much valuable information on many levels, from beginning to advanced.
23. https://www.lds.org/bc/content/shared/english/pdf/callings/welfare/72727_FamilyBudgetWorksheet_pdf.pdf
24. https://www.mint.com/budgeting-3/keep-track-of-your-finances-with-a-free-budget-template
25. Robert D. Hales, "Becoming Provident Providers Temporally and Spiritually," (April 2009), https://www.lds.org/ensign/2009/05/becoming-provident-providers-temporally-and-spiritually?lang=eng.
26. The Church of Jesus Christ of Latter-day Saints, "All Is Safely Gathered In: Family Finances," (Salt Lake City, UT: Intellectual Reserve, Inc., 2007), https://www.lds.org/bc/content/shared/content/english/pdf/language-materials/04007_eng.pdf.
27. Thomas S. Monson, "Are We Prepared?" (Sept. 2014), https://www.lds.org/ensign/2014/09/are-we-prepared?lang=eng.
28. J. Reuben Clark Jr., *Conference Report*, (April 1938), 102–109, https://archive.org/details/conferencereport1938a (as cited in Thomas S. Monson, "Constant Truths for Changing Times" (April 2005), https://www.lds.org/ensign/2005/05/constant-truths-for-changing-times?lang=eng.)
29. See 26 above.
30. Emma Penrod and Deseret News, "BYU Offers Highest Return in Educational Investment in the State of Utah, Rankings Say," DeseretNews.com, http://www.deseretnews.com/article/865579636/BYU-offers-highest-return-in-educational-investment-in-the-state-of-Utah-rankings-say.html?pg=all.
31. http://personalfinance.byu.edu
32. Ben Winslow and Deseret News, "Leaders Warn LDS against Money Scams," DeseretNews.com, http://www.deseretnews.com/article/695261200/Leaders-warn-LDS-against-money-scams.html?pg=all.

33. Marvin J. Ashton, "Guide to Family Finance," (April 2000), https://www.lds.org/liahona/2000/04/guide-to-family-finance?lang=eng.
34. Marvin J. Ashton, "One for the Money," (Sept. 2007), https://www.lds.org/ensign/2007/09/one-for-the-money?lang=eng.
35. Clinton G. Gudmunson et al., "Linking Financial Strain to Marital Instability: Examining the Roles of Emotional Distress and Marital Interaction," Journal of Family and Economic Issues 28, no. 3 (September 2007): 357–76, doi:http://link.springer.com/journal/volumesAndIssues/10834.
36. Jeffrey Dew, Sonya Britt, and Sandra Huston, "Examining the Relationship Between Financial Issues and Divorce," Family Relations 61, no. 4 (October 2012): 615–28, doi:10.1111/j.1741-3729.2012.00715.x.574 couples
37. Bernard Poduska, "Till Debt Do Us Part: Balancing Finances, Feelings, and Family," (Salt Lake City, Utah: Shadow Mountain, 2000).
38. Joseph B. Wirthlin, "Earthly Debts, Heavenly Debts," (April 2004), https://www.lds.org/general-conference/2004/04/earthly-debts-heavenly-debts?lang=eng.
39. 1 Nephi 3:7
40. Helaman 5:8

1

Time Value of Money (TVM)

Blessing Your Family with the Eighth Wonder of the World

In past centuries, articles of fine clothing such as silk scarves and dresses were very valuable. Wealthy Europeans would use them to store financial value, carefully packing away the clothing in cedar chests for future financial security. However, there was an enemy to this financial strategy: *Tineola bisselliella,* as scientists call it today. In those days, it was known as the clothes moth.[1] This moth can lay up to one thousand eggs, each of which can hatch into a larva with a voracious appetite, eating virtually anything organic. Imagine the disappointment of someone planning to retire who, upon opening his chest, is greeted by a cloud of moths and discovers his retirement investments have been devoured by thousands of caterpillars!

"Lay not up for yourselves treasures upon earth, where moth and rust doth corrupt"
(Matthew 6:19)

Likewise, today there is an enemy to savers who do not understand the time value of money and do not invest their money wisely: inflation. I will demonstrate this with a very graphic illustration. Reader discretion is advised; this is not for the faint of heart!

Imagine that you want to ensure a comfortable retirement and carefully calculate that you will need $500,000 when you turn seventy in fifty years. You work very hard, scrimp and save, and put one hundred crisp $100 bills ($10,000) away in a cedar chest

LEARN

- That the value of your family's money is always changing due to inflation and interest

- About the power of the eighth wonder of the world—compound interest

- Basic family finance terminology associated with TVM

- To set family financial goals using TVM

"Moth and Rust Doth Corrupt" https://www.youtube.com/watch?v=lcf5G0FxJfw

Time value of money (TVM)

How the value of money changes over time due to inflation and interest.

Avoid letting your money be eaten away by inflation like the plague!

Inflation

Decrease in the purchasing power of money.

Interest

Remuneration for investing or loaning money.

every New Year's Day for fifty years. Imagine your disappointment when at age seventy you open the cedar chest and, because of inflation,[2] discover that your retirement fund of five thousand crisp $100 bills ($500,000) will only purchase the equivalent of $70,356![3] Now you are going to have to work forever. You will never have a comfortable retirement!

Inflation can wreak as much havoc with your retirement savings as the larvae of the clothes moth did with fine clothing. You can prevent this havoc by understanding and applying the time value of money.

Of the many principles of family finance, the key mathematical principle you should master is the **time value of money (TVM)**. This principle basically states that the value of the dollar is not stagnant. As time passes, your dollars do one of two things: they either grow in value due to interest earned, or they decline due to the corrosive effect of inflation. The key to successful financial planning and investing is to create a situation where the interest you receive is significantly greater than the rate of inflation. The purpose of this chapter is to give you a conceptual overview of the time value of money.

Inflation and Interest

First, let's compare and contrast inflation and interest. **Inflation** represents an increase in the price your family will pay for goods and services over time. Because of inflation, your family's dollars will buy less in the future (future value) than they will today (present value). The overarching economic reason for inflation is an increase in the supply of available money in relation to the supply of available goods and services. The more money is printed and sent cycling through the economy, the more producers can ask for their goods and services. Although inflation is a healthy byproduct of economic growth, too much inflation is not healthy for your family's long-term financial situation.

Avoid letting your money be eaten away by inflation like the plague!

Inflation negatively impacts your family's investments. Although the amount of money you are saving now will have the same *nominal* value in the future ($1000 will still be $1000), your family will not be able to buy as much with that money because the purchasing power of the money has eroded. Inflation makes it necessary to save more and invest money because your currency will be worth less in the future.

During the past fifty years, the annual inflation rate in the United States has ranged from a low of –0.4 percent in 2009 to a high of 13.5 percent in 1980.[4] For family financial planning, various experts suggest assuming a long-term annual inflation rate between 2.5 percent and 4 percent. The United States inflation rate for 2014 was 1.6 percent. See www.usinflation.org for more information on the current and past inflation rates, as well as an inflation calculator to help you realistically determine investment goals for the future.

Although inflation decreases your purchasing power, **interest** helps your money grow. In this broad sense, interest pertains to any use of your money that results in a return on investment. The return is generally positive (your money grows), but with some risky investments, the return can be negative (your money diminishes or disappears altogether). Some examples of how you might invest your money to gain interest include checking and savings accounts, certificates of deposit, government and corporate bonds, stocks, commodities (such as gold), and real estate.

Try thinking of it this way: Interest is similar to rent. Just as tenants pay rent to landlords in exchange for the use of an apartment or house, people and institutions will pay you interest in exchange for the temporary use of your money. You can either invest your money yourself, or you can lend it to others who will then invest your money and pay you an agreed-upon rate. We will explore the topic of investing in much greater detail in Chapter 8.

Here's another way to look at inflation and interest: A dollar in hand today is worth more than a dollar received in the future. Infla-

tion is one of the main reasons you pay interest when you borrow money (for credit cards, mortgages, etc.). A dollar in hand today really is worth more than a dollar received in the future because you can invest that dollar today and begin earning interest on it. The sooner your money can earn interest, the faster your interest can earn interest, and the more money you will have.

> Elder Joe J. Christensen said in the April 1999 General Conference, "There are those with average incomes who, over a lifetime, do amass some means, and there are those who receive large salaries who do not. What is the difference? It is simply spending less than they receive, saving along the way, and taking advantage of the power of compound interest."[5]

We will now introduce you to a real "marvelous work and a wonder"[6] related to your family's financial future. Albert Einstein is thought to have said that "Compound interest is the eighth wonder of the world."[7] **Compound interest** means that not only is your initial investment earning interest, your interest is earning interest! Compounding refers to the number of periods in which interest is calculated during the year. Interest can be compounded annually, quarterly, monthly, and even daily. The shorter the compounding period, the more money from interest you will earn, and the faster your money will grow. Using compound interest can bless your family greatly. The following example about compound interest demonstrates how understanding the time value of money is crucial to making wise investments for your family's financial future.

Imagine there are four twenty-year-old BYU students, each with $10,000 to invest now in preparation for retirement in 2065. Let's compare different investment options, assuming similar returns to the past few decades.[8]

The first student does not trust the financial system, and he puts the money under his bed in a strongbox. In fifty years, he still has $10,000. And, alas, because of inflation (assuming a 4 percent long-term inflation rate) the $10,000 will only have the purchasing power of $1,407.

The second student puts her money in a savings account, which averages about 2.5 percent annual return. Because of compound interest, it doubles every twenty-five years. She has $40,000 when she retires, but because of inflation, it will only be worth $4,904.

The third puts his money in a safe government bond mutual fund, which averages about 4.5 percent annual return. It doubles every fifteen years. By 2065, the $10,000 has become almost $100,000, but because of inflation, it will only be worth $13,294. At least it beat inflation!

The fourth puts her money in a broad, diversified stock market fund, which averages about 10 percent return. It doubles every seven and a half years. In fifty years, it doubles nearly seven times, and the $10,000 has become more than $1,000,000! And even when inflation is accounted for, the $10,000 has grown in purchasing power to $204,553!

That is the miracle of compound interest! When you consistently and wisely invest like the fourth student, you have the peace of mind that comes from knowing you will be able to conquer the moth of inflation that threatens your financial security. You will be able to have a financial reserve you can count on. You will be able to retire and serve missions without a financial care in the world! Wow! Isn't time value of money amazing!?!

▶ Time Value of Money: https://www.youtube.com/watch?v=ASP6LGHfjow

Compound interest
Interest earned on interest.

Financial Terms and Definitions

Investment
A current commitment of your money in the expectation of reaping future returns.

Present value (PV)
Current value of money.

Principal
The original amount of money borrowed or invested (generally synonymous with present value).

Interest rate (I)
The rate you will receive for investing at a specified compounding period for a specified period of time (generally expressed in percent per year).

Nominal return
The return on an investment before the impacts of inflation and taxes are taken into account.

After-tax return
The return on an investment after the impact of federal, state, and local taxes has been taken into account.

Real return
The rate of return on an investment after the impacts of taxes and inflation are taken into account.

Compounding periods (N)
The frequency with which interest is applied to an investment.

Let's take a look at some financial terms and definitions. An **investment** is a current commitment of your money in the expectation of reaping future financial returns. Examples of major financial investments include checking and savings accounts, certificates of deposit, government and corporate bonds, stocks, commodities (such as gold), and real estate.

In this book, references will be made to other important investments such as education and relationships. It is important that we have a broader view of what an investment is so that we recognize those investments that are of most worth—those that bring true joy in this life and in the life to come. You should have priorities when it comes to investments, and the most important investments you will make involve your family, your religion, and your relationship with God. The Book of Mormon prophet Jacob wisely counseled, "Wherefore, do not spend money for that which is of no worth, nor your labor for that which cannot satisfy."[9]

Present value (PV) refers to the original amount of money borrowed or invested, i.e. the current value of a future sum of money. It is also the initial **principal** of a loan or investment. When paying off a mortgage, a certain amount of each payment goes toward paying off the principal and a certain amount goes toward paying interest.

The annual **interest rate (I)**, in investment terms, is the rate you will receive for investing at a specified compounding period for a specified period of time, expressed as a percentage per year. It can be a specific, fixed rate (as is the case with a bank account or a bond) or it can be a projected rate (like in a stock-based mutual fund). More specifically, this can refer to the nominal, after-tax, or real return. **Nominal return** is the return on an investment before the impact of inflation and taxes is taken into account. **After-tax return** is the rate of return on an investment (interest earned) after the impact of federal, state, and local taxes are taken into account. **Real return** is the return on an investment after accounting for impact of taxes and inflation.

Compounding periods (N) refer to the frequency with which interest is applied to an investment. As mentioned previously, interest may be compounded daily, monthly, quarterly, or annually. A key relationship exists between time and interest rate. The shorter the compounding period, the higher the effective annual interest rate (the actual rate you are earning on your investment after taking the effect of compounding into account). For example, if interest is compounded daily, the investment will grow faster than if the interest is compounded monthly, quarterly, or annually.

Payment (PMT) is a periodic amount invested or received during the life of the investment. For example, in a car loan it would be the amount you pay per month as you bring the principal down from the initial loan value (Present Value or PV) to the final loan value of zero (Future Value or FV).

Future value (FV) is the monetary value of an investment at some point in the future after taking into account the present value

(the principal), the annual interest rate (I), the number of compounding periods (N), and any payments (PMT) along the way. For a loan, the FV is always zero.

A **lump sum** is a one-time payment or investment. The example of the four BYU students used earlier demonstrates a lump sum investment. Lump sum problems utilize present value (PV), future value (FV), number of periods of compounding (N), and interest rate (I) functions in a financial calculator. These are lump sum events, meaning they occur only once.

Annuity is the disbursement of money on a periodic basis—a series of equal payments which are made at a specific time (for example, at the end of a month or year). The example earlier in the chapter of investing $10,000 every year is an example of an annuity. Annuity problems also utilize the payment (PMT) function on a financial calculator in addition to PV, FV, N, and I. This disbursement (or payment) may either be money received by you (monthly allowance, bimonthly paycheck, annual stock dividend, etc.) or money leaving you (quarterly deposit into savings, monthly loan payment, etc.). When money is received by you, the sign of this amount in a financial calculator is positive. When money is leaving you, the sign of this amount in a financial calculator is negative.

Purchasing power is the value of monetary funds based on the amount of goods or services that one unit of money can buy. The purchasing power of a dollar changes over time because of inflation. For example, due to inflation, you would need to make a much higher wage than your grandfather did fifty years ago to have the same purchasing power that he did then.

Opportunity cost is the potential loss or gain that occurs when one financial option is chosen over another. For example, when you consider leaving your employment to go to college, you must consider the value of the wages that you will lose during the years you study to get your degree. In making the decision, this opportunity cost would be measured against the higher wages that you hope to earn after you receive your college degree. As another example, the opportunity cost of buying a boat is not only the dollar amount of the purchase, but also everything you are giving up that you could have bought with that same money.

Opportunity cost applies to more than just finances. Choosing to invest time on your education or career that could have been spent with your family carries with it a certain cost. It is important to regularly evaluate how you are using your resources so that your opportunity cost can be in harmony with your family's eternal goals. We will explore this more in Chapter 12.

Family Financial Goals

"For which of you, intending to build a tower, sitteth not down first, and counteth the cost, whether he have sufficient to finish it?" (Luke 14:28)

Once you have an eternal perspective on wealth and understand the importance of the time value of money, the next important step is

Payment (PMT)
A periodic amount invested or received during the life of the investment (e.g., monthly payment, annual disbursement, dividend, etc.).

Future value (FV)
The monetary value of an investment at some point in the future.

Lump sum
One payment at a specific time.

Annuity
The disbursement of money on a periodic basis—a series of equal payments which are made at a specific time.

Purchasing power
The value of monetary funds based on the amount of goods or services that one unit of money can buy.

Opportunity cost
The potential loss or gain that occurs when one financial option is chosen over another.

> "I am so thoroughly convinced that if we don't set goals in our life and learn how to master the techniques of living to reach our goals, we can reach a ripe old age and look back on our life only to see that we reached but a small part of our potential. When one learns to master the principles of setting a goal, he will then be able to make a great difference in the results he attains in this life."
> —M. Russell Ballard[10]

to begin your Family Financial Plan (FFP) and set family goals. Ezra Taft Benson counseled:

> Plan for your financial future. As you move through life toward retirement and the decades which follow, we invite all . . . to plan frugally for the years following full-time employment. Be even more cautious . . . about "get-rich" schemes, mortgaging homes, or investing in uncertain ventures. Proceed cautiously so that the planning of a lifetime is not disrupted by one or a series of poor financial decisions. Plan your financial future early; then follow the plan.[11]

Financial planning is the process of planning how to wisely use your available resources to achieve your personal and family goals. It will help you determine where you are, where you want to be, and how you will get there. While financial planning may not help you make more money (although it likely will), it will help you make better choices and become better stewards over the things you have been blessed with.

We encourage you and your family to write down your wishes, transform them into goals, and accomplish them. Setting goals is not simply writing a list of things you would "like" to accomplish. Rather, it is a process of understanding yourself and your family—your aspirations, desires, and values—and then trying to understand what God wants you to accomplish. Once you have determined these things, you must combine them to form a plan of action that will help you attain your potential as a unified family.

Financial planning is not easy. Motivation, diligence, and time are required to complete a successful family financial plan. However, like most things that take time, family financial planning is well worth the effort. Marvin J. Ashton commented, "True happiness is not made in getting something. True happiness is becoming something. This can be done by being committed to lofty goals. We cannot become something without commitment."[12]

Creating Your Family Financial Plan

We recommend a six-step process for putting together your Family Financial Plan.

Step 1:

Decide What You Are About

Deciding what you are about establishes what kinds of things are important to you. It expresses your family's core values and beliefs. What is truly important to you? What do you feel Heavenly Father wants you to do or be? How would you like to be remembered when you leave this life? What do you want to accomplish with your life? These are probably the most important questions you will ever ask and answer, and discussing these things as a family strengthens relational bonds.

Step 2:

Evaluate Your Financial Health

Evaluating your financial health helps you determine where you are financially. If you don't know where you are, how can you determine how to get to where you need to be? You will learn more specifically how to evaluate your financial health in the next chapter. Determine where you are financially right now—are you financially healthy? Are you solvent (do you have sufficient cash in your wallet or in your checking account to pay your bills)? How much debt do you have? How much are you saving each month and year? You will learn more about this in Chapter 2.

Step 3:

Define Your Family Goals

Once you know what is important to you and where you are financially, it is critical to define your family goals. The first step is to write your goals down. Attach a cost to each goal. Remember, there are more costs than just financial costs. What are the true costs of your goals in terms of time, money, and effort? There is no difference between financial and personal or family goals. Financial goals are personal goals with a monetary cost attached.

It is also important to determine potential obstacles. By identifying the obstacles early in the analysis, you increase your ability to plan for, avoid, and overcome those obstacles. Set a date for when your goals are to be completed. In what time frame can the goal be reasonably accomplished? Make your goals SMART: specific, measurable, attainable, relevant, and time-bound. Then, share them with others so they may hold you accountable for your goals. Family goals are strong when you help each other remember and stick to them. We will learn more about how to define and apply your goals to a family budget in Chapter 2.

Step 4:

Develop a Plan of Action

Think long term: consider your family's future needs. Develop a budget, and use it wisely. Plan for big-ticket purchases, such as houses and cars. Plan for managing debt, and remember that debt is the enemy to growth. Plan for insurance, and protect yourself. Determine and write your investment plan, and follow that plan. Plan for the expenses of children, missions, and college. Plan for retirement. Most importantly, plan your financial future early and then live your plan. This book will help you know how to develop that plan.

Step 5:

Implement Your Plan

Once you have your plan, implement it. Use common sense and moderation in the things you do. Set wise goals and work toward them each day. Stay positive. Remember that your family plan is a goal to set your sights on, not a stick to beat yourselves with. Realize that detours will come, but also realize that you can get back on track. We all encounter detours,

but good things come to those who hang in there!

Step 6:

Revise Your Plan as Necessary

Ongoing revision is an important part of your plan. Remember that people and goals change—you need to account for this. Review your goals annually at a minimum, and make sure your plan still matches your goals. If necessary, fine-tune your plan. Remember, your plan is etched in paper, not in stone. In the weeks ahead, you will probably change your financial plan quite a bit as you identify critical areas and learn more about financial decisions.

An Eternal Perspective of Family Goals

Think about how the following poem by Jessie B. Rittenhouse relates to your family goals:

> I bargained with Life for a Penny,
>   and Life would pay no more,
> However I begged at evening,
>   when I counted my scanty store.
> For Life is a just employer,
>   He will give you what you ask,
> But once you have set the wages,
>   why, you must bear the task.
> I worked for a menial's hire,
>   only to learn, dismayed,

SMART principle

Family goals should be

Specific
Measurable
Attainable
Relevant
Time-bound

That any wage I had asked of Life,
  Life would have willingly paid.[13]

Too many of us do not think about what we want to get out of life. Instead, we wander aimlessly through life and forget who we are. We set our wages too low—settling for just a single penny. Unless we make some changes, we will be disappointed with the penny we receive from life.

Ezra Taft Benson said:

Every accountable child of God needs to set goals, short- and long-range goals. A man who is pressing forward to accomplish worthy goals can soon put despondency under his feet, and once a goal is accomplished, others can be set up. Some will be continuing goals . . . Now there is a lifetime goal—to walk in His steps, to perfect ourselves in every virtue as He has done, to seek His face, and to work to make our calling and election sure.[14]

As you follow the teachings of Jesus Christ, you will receive direction that can help you put your family's most important priorities first. The scriptures tell us: "Be thou humble, and the Lord thy God shall lead thee by the hand, and give thee answer to thy prayers."[15] As we come to understand ourselves, our goals, and our desires, and as we learn to do God's will, He will help us understand the direction our lives should take.

What is God's ultimate goal for His children? The scriptures reveal that His ultimate goal is for us to achieve eternal life. Our most important goal, therefore, is to obtain eternal life with our families. The rest of our goals should help us achieve this overarching goal. A wise philosopher said, "We are not human beings having a spiritual experience. We are spiritual beings having a human experience" (Pierre Teilhard de Chardin). The key, then, is to balance both the spiritual and the temporal in our personal and family goals.

Temporal goals relate to the temporal measures of success that we hope to accomplish. These goals relate to money, title, or fame; influence, rank, or power; and assets, investments, or possessions. We must be vigilant; temporal goals are generally the easiest to measure and are the most visible of our goals, which may lead us to work on them more than some of the more important, eternal goals. Achieving temporal goals may also lead to trade-offs, such as working longer hours, spending less time with family, or taking assignments inconsistent with personal values due to "extenuating circumstances." If we are not careful, life can easily become an "unending stream of extenuating circumstances."[16] Remember to balance your temporal goals with your eternal goals.

As you continue studying this book, create and revise your own family goals, both financially and in all aspects of life. The time value of money is a wonderful tool you can use to help your family accomplish your long-term financial goals.

Conclusion

Time value of money is the mathematical and conceptual basis for much of what we will learn about in subsequent chapters. In this chapter, we learned that the value of money is always changing due to inflation and interest. We learned about the power of compound interest and how it is key to your family's financial success. We learned basic family finance terminology that will act as a foundation as you continue to learn throughout this course. We also learned about the importance of family financial goals and how to set them. Through all of this, we stressed how essential your financial stewardship is to your family and how it reflects a consecrated life.

Other Resources

- www.personalfinance.byu.edu/beginning
- www.usinflation.org
- www.youtube.com/watch?v=ASP6LGHfjow
- "Moth and Dust Doth Corrupt" Animation: https://www.youtube.com/watch?v=lcf5G-0FxJfw
- "Time Value of Money" Animation: https://www.youtube.com/watch?v=ASP6LGHfjow

Notes

1. http://www.todayifoundout.com/index.php/2013/11/moths-really-eat-clothes/.
2. http://www.calculatorsoup.com/calculators/financial/investment-inflation-calculator.php.
3. http://usinflation.org/us-inflation-rate-calculator/.
4. http://usinflation.org/us-inflation-rate/.
5. Joe J. Christensen, "Greed, Selfishness, and Overindulgence," (April, 1999), https://www.lds.org/general-conference/1999/04/greed-selfishness-and-overindulgence?lang=eng.
6. Isaiah 29:14.
7. http://www.telegraph.co.uk/sponsored/finance/premier-asset-management/11257819/compound-interest-investment.html; http://www.quotesonfinance.com/quote/79/Albert-Einstein-Compound-interest.
8. http://www.homesteadfunds.com/.
9. 2 Nephi 9:51.
10. M. Russell Ballard, *Preach My Gospel,* (Intellectual Reserve, Inc., 2004), 146, https://www.lds.org/manual/preach-my-gospel-a-guide-to-missionary-service/how-do-i-use-time-wisely?lang=eng.
11. Ezra Taft Benson, "To the Elderly in the Church," (Oct. 1989), 4, https://www.lds.org/general-conference/1989/10/to-the-elderly-in-the-church?lang=eng.
12. Marvin J. Ashton, "The Word Is Commitment," *Ensign* (Nov. 1983), 61, https://www.lds.org/general-conference/1983/10/the-word-is-commitment?lang=eng.
13. Quoted in *Think and Grow Rich* by Napoleon Hill, (New York: Fawcett Books, 1960), 40.
14. Ezra Taft Benson, "Do Not Despair," *Ensign* (Nov. 1974), 65, https://www.lds.org/general-conference/1974/10/do-not-despair?lang=eng.
15. D&C 112:10.
16. Clayton M. Christensen, "How Will You Measure Your Life," *Harvard Business Review* (July–Aug. 2010).

2

Budgeting, Net Worth, and More

Measuring Your Family's Financial Health and Planning for Future Success

LEARN

- To record your family's important personal and financial information
- How to document your family's financial past with a family income and expense statement
- To calculate your family's present financial health with a family net worth statement
- How to plan your family's future finances by developing and implementing a successful family budget

As we learned in the previous chapter, understanding the time value of money is an essential tool in meeting family needs and satisfying appropriate wants of family members. Indeed, providing for the needs and wants of your home is a God-given responsibility, and planning for the future, both temporally and spiritually, is part of God's eternal plan. Elder Robert D. Hales taught,

> All of us are responsible to provide for ourselves and our families in both temporal and spiritual ways. To provide providently, we must practice the principles of provident living: joyfully living within our means, being content with what we have, avoiding excessive debt, and diligently saving and preparing for rainy-day emergencies. When we live providently, we can provide for ourselves and our families and also follow the Savior's example to serve and bless others.[1]

Part of planning for your family's financial future includes evaluating and monitoring your financial health. Family financial statements are very important in this process. In this chapter, we will examine several different kinds of family financial statements: an income and expense statement as a record of the past; a net worth statement as a snapshot of the present; and a budget as a plan for the future. A family income and expense statement shows categorized cash inflows and outflows over a specific period of time, generally a month or a year. A family net worth statement is calculated periodically (usually at the end of a month, quarter, or year) by subtracting a snapshot of your family's liabilities (what you owe) from a snapshot of your family's assets (what you own). A family budget forecasts planned spending within the constraints of your expected income on a monthly or annual basis. Each of these family financial statements is essential for financial health.

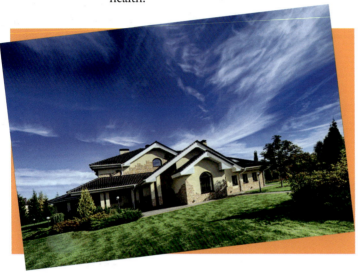

familysearch.org

Just as company executives use financial statements to help manage their businesses to achieve specific financial goals, families can also use financial statements to understand their current financial health and help them meet their family goals. Financial statements are important tools that help us provide the necessities of life for our families.[2] Learning how to track your income, expenses, assets, and liabilities, as well as learning how to budget effectively will help you and your family maintain good financial health and, consequently, good spiritual health. Let's embark on this adventure!

Family Financial Record Keeping

The Church of Jesus Christ of Latter-day Saints is a "house of order."[3] Prophets and apostles have asked us to have this same order in our homes, including in our personal record keeping. We are asked to keep journals, record stories and important dates, and update family history information so that our descendants know about us and our lives. We are encouraged to gather and post our ancestors' information as well. Keeping our personal records in order simplifies the process of documenting where we have been, where we are, and where we hope to be. Keeping our financial records in order does the same for our financial lives.

"Behold, there shall be a record kept among you . . ." (D&C 21:1)

Habitually keeping your family's important personal and financial records organized will contribute to your family's financial success. Well-kept records help you track how your money is being spent, which will help you create and stick to a budget. Additionally, organized record keeping helps you easily find the information you need to file your taxes. Should an emergency arise, family members and legal representatives may need to access your financial information, and an organized set of records will help them easily find the necessary information.

The way we keep family financial records has changed dramatically in recent years. Families used to keep paper copies of all their records, usually filling several filing cabinets in a den, office, closet, or garage. Inside these innumerable, carefully labeled folders were canceled checks, bank statements, pay stubs, bank deposit slips, credit card statements, loan coupons, household receipts, donation slips, tax returns, and on and on and on. Nearly everyone kept a paper copy of almost every financial transaction, holding on to them for years. What a mess!

Today, most record keeping can be done electronically and then safely saved in the Cloud. In many cases, keeping a physical paper trail is no longer possible unless you print your records yourself. For example, most employers require your salary to be deposited electronically, so there are no pay stubs to file away. Most banks no longer provide physical copies of canceled checks, so those are unnecessary as well. Often, the physical records you need to keep may be limited to just a few folders in one file drawer. You are blessed to live in this day and age!

Although most financial transactions are recorded electronically today, it is still important that they be well-organized so that pertinent information can be retrieved in a timely manner. Some documents must be kept as hard copies, including birth certificates, marriage licenses, and passports. You should keep these items together in a safe place.

You should also know how long certain records should be kept. Let's review some family records.

Family Income and Expense Statement

A family **income and expense statement** is a record of your family's past cash inflows and outflows over a specified period of time—usually the previous month or year. It can give

Family Records

Records to keep forever:
- Adoption papers
- Birth certificates
- Citizenship papers
- Death certificates
- Divorce decrees
- Education records (diplomas, transcripts, etc.)
- Marriage licenses
- Military discharge papers
- Passports (even expired passports)
- Safe deposit box key
- Social security cards

Records to keep forever, updating as needed:
- Advance directives (living wills)
- Family and personal journals
- Family and personal photos, videos, and audio recordings
- Household inventory
- Life histories
- Password list
- Powers of attorney
- Safe deposit box inventory list
- Social security statement (current year)
- Vaccination records
- Wills

Records to keep as long as they are in force or as long as you are the owner:
- Contracts
- Home purchase and improvement records
- Life insurance policies (often in the Cloud)
- Loan documents
- Real estate deeds
- Receipts for items under warranty
- Receipts for large purchases
- Service contracts and warranties
- Stock and bond certificates (often in the cloud)
- Vehicle titles

Records to keep for at least seven years:
- Income tax returns
- Anything needed to document income tax returns
  - Access to bank statement documenting tax information
  - Access to credit card statements documenting tax information
  - Contribution receipts
    - LDS – Yearly contribution summary
    - DI donation receipts
  - Medical receipts
  - W-2 forms
  - 1099 and other tax forms

Family Income: Cash Inflows

Cash inflows include income that is available to be used for the expenses of the family. This money is usually deposited in the family checking account. Sources of income usually include net wages and salaries from employment (after taxes, health care costs, retirement, etc. are deducted). Inflows can also include tips, interest, dividends, royalties, gifts, tax returns, scholarships, and refunds. In a dual-income family, cash inflows should include income from both husband and wife. In some cases, children may also contribute to the family income.

Family Expenses: Cash Outflows

Cash outflows include all the expenses of the family. If there are sufficient cash inflows, the expenses are generally paid out of the family checking account, either directly or indirectly by paying off credit cards each month. However, if cash outflows exceed cash inflows, the difference is made up by taking on debt, usually in the form of high-interest credit cards.

There are two kinds of expenses: fixed expenses and variable expenses. **Fixed expenses** are expenses over which you do not have any direct control. There is no wiggle room with fixed expenses because you are obligated to pay a certain amount every month or every year. Examples of fixed expenses include tithing, rent, home mortgage, car payment, insurance payments, college loan payments, tuition, and property taxes.

Variable expenses are those expenses over which you have a greater measure of control. For example, food is a variable expense. Though you need to eat, you can choose to eat dinner at a restaurant or make dinner at home. What you choose to eat greatly affects the level of expense. Other examples of variable expenses include clothing, entertainment, vacations, and home maintenance.

To create an income and expense statement, you first record net income received. This includes any deposits into the family checking account and could include income, refunds, gifts, etc. Then you track and categorize every expense—everything going out of the family checking account. Here is a sample of the categories an income and expense statement might include. (See Table 2.1.)

Expenses can be tracked manually or electronically. One way to accurately track your expenses is to make sure every expense is paid for with a check, credit card, or debit card. Then the transactions can be noted and categorized from the bank and credit card statements. An easy way to automate this is with an online app such as www.mint.com or www.creditkarma.com. These aggregate all transactions in real time, allowing you to have an up-to-the-minute view of your expenses. These apps will be explained in greater detail in the budgeting portion of this chapter.

After you have categorized every income and expense transaction, you sum up the totals and complete the family income and expense statement.

Example

Joseph and Vanessa are a young married couple who graduated from BYU last year. Joseph received his master's degree in marriage and family therapy and Vanessa received a bachelor's degree in English. Last year Joseph earned $50,000 (net income after taxes and deductions) as a marriage and family therapist, and Vanessa earned $75,000 net income editing family finance textbooks. Over the course of the year, this $125,000 was deposited in their family checking account. They kept all 1,434 receipts for their expenses during the year and manually categorized and entered them into a spreadsheet. Amazingly, every expense category total was a precise multiple of one thousand! This is what their annual income and expense statement looked like.

(See Table 2.2.)

Income and expense statement

A record of your family's past cash inflows and outflows over a specified period of time.

Cash inflow

Family income.

Cash outflow

Family expenditures.

Fixed expenses

Expenditures that your family has little direct control over and that do not often change from month to month.

Variable expenses

Expenditures that your family controls and that may vary from month to month.

Table 2.1 Blank Income and Expense Statement

Income (Cash Inflows)		Expenses (Cash Outflows)	
After Tax Income		Tithing/Donations	
Job 1		Long-term Savings	
Job 2		Debt Payments	
Job 3		Housing (rent/mortgage)	
Other Income		Utilities	
Interest		Food	
Dividends		Clothing	
Capital Gains		Transportation	
Refunds		Medical/Dental	
Gifts		Recreation/Entertainment	
Other		Gifts	
		School Expenses	
		Miscellaneous	
		Mad Money	
Total Income		Total Expenses	

Total Income – Total Expenses = Cash Surplus <or Deficit>

Table 2.2 Example Income and Expense Statement

Income (Cash Inflows)		Expenses (Cash Outflows)	
After Tax Income		Tithing/Donations	$15,000
Therapist	$50,000	Long-term Savings	$15,000
Editor	$75,000	Debt Payments	$5,000
Job 3		Housing (rent/mortgage)	$15,000
Other Income		Utilities	$5,000
Interest		Food	$5,000
Dividends		Clothing	$4,000
Capital Gains		Transportation	$6,000
Refunds		Medical/Dental	$5,000
Gifts		Recreation/Entertainment	$4,000
Other		Gifts	$1,000
		School Expenses	
		Miscellaneous	$5,000
		Mad Money	$5,000
Total Income	$125,000	Total Expenses	$90,000

$125,000 (Total Income) – $90,000 (Total Expenses) = $35,000 (Cash Surplus)

Family Net Worth Statement

While an income and expense statement is a record of your family's *past* financial history and a budget is your family's financial plan for the *future*, a **net worth statement** is a snapshot of your family's *present* financial situation. Commonly referred to as a balance sheet, a family net worth statement is calculated by subtracting the monetary value of your family's **liabilities** from the monetary value of your family's **assets**. This statement can be very helpful in determining your family's financial health and in making financial decisions. In addition, a net worth statement may be required when applying for credit, such as a home mortgage. Since these are important matters, net worth should be calculated carefully and at regular intervals, such as at the end of every month, every quarter, or every year. Net worth can be calculated for the family as a whole or for each individual in the family.

Family Net Worth Equation

Family Net Worth =
Family Assets – Family Liabilities

Family Assets

Put simply, family assets are the monetary value of what your family owns that could be turned into cash. These assets come in many forms, including the following:

- Monetary assets: cash, savings accounts, checking accounts, certificates of deposit (CDs), etc.
- Investment assets: stocks, bonds, mutual funds, etc.
- Retirement assets: company pensions, IRAs, 401(k) plans, etc.
- Real estate: land, homes, rental properties, etc.
- Vehicles and other personal property: cars, trucks, recreational vehicles, boats, furniture, clothing, electronic equipment, jewelry, etc.

To determine the total dollar value of your family's assets, find the sum of the **current market value** of all assets. The current market value is the price at which your asset could be sold in the present market environment. There are various ways to calculate the current market value. To calculate a vehicle's value, you can look up the low book listing for your make and model in the Kelley Blue Book on www.kbb.com. To calculate your home's current market value, you can refer to www.zillow.com or www.realtor.com for an estimate. When calculating investment assets, you can use the most current market price as listed in any of the following sources: *The Wall Street Journal* (www.wsj.com), *Barron's* (www.barrons.com), *USA Today* (www.usatoday.com/money/), or other financial periodicals. When calculating the value of personal property, be sure to use the estimated price you could sell the item for, not what you paid for it when it was new. This often equates to a thrift store, garage sale, www.craigslist.org, or www.ksl.com price.

Family Liabilities

Family liabilities are synonymous with debt and can be categorized into current liabilities and long-term liabilities. Current liabilities are those debts which are due on the short-term, or within one year. Two examples of current liabilities are your current credit card balance (even if you pay off the balance every month) and unpaid utility bills. Long-term liabilities are debts that are repaid over

---

Net worth statement
A snapshot of your family's total assets minus your total liabilities on a particular day.

Liabilities
Synonymous with debt, calculated by adding up the outstanding balances on any current and long-term family debts.

Assets
The monetary value of what your family owns that could be turned into cash.

Current market value
The price at which your family's asset could be sold in the present market environment.

a period longer than one year. Three common examples of long-term liabilities are student loans, auto loans, and home mortgages.

You can calculate your liabilities by adding up the outstanding balances on any current and long-term debts. Note that your outstanding balance is not your monthly payment but rather the total amount, or principal, you still owe as of the date on your net worth statement. If your debt has accrued interest, such as with credit card debt, this should be calculated as part of that liability. Note that rent or tuition is not considered a debt unless it is overdue.

Calculating Your Family Net Worth

Remember, your family net worth is a snapshot of your total assets minus your total liabilities on any particular day. For example, a net worth of $1,350 indicates that you have $1,350 more in assets than in liabilities. In other words, if you were to sell everything you had at its current market value, you would have $1,350 left after paying off all of your debts.

Many liabilities have a counterbalancing asset. For example, a liability of $200,000 for a home mortgage loan might be more or less "balanced" by the current market price of the home, an asset worth $260,000.

Tables 2.3 and 2.4 are two examples of net worth statements. The first shows a college student's possible net worth statement; the latter shows a statement for a couple who graduated from BYU ten years ago and now has a family with four children.

Notice that the college student's net worth is significantly less than the family's. In fact, many students have a negative net worth, with more liabilities than assets. This is normal, particularly when student loans have been acquired. A student loan is a unique form of debt because although the counterbalancing

Table 2.3 Net Worth of a College Student

Assets	Current Market Value	Liabilities	Total Dollar Amount
Cash	$47.88	Credit card balance	$847.45
Savings account	$1,292.30	Student loans	$5,500
Checking account	$415.66	Loan from Dad	$1,000
Mutual fund	$500		
Car	$3,500		
Clothing	$400		
Electronic equipment	$300		
Jewelry	$50		
Total Current Value of Assets	$6,505.84	Total Amount of Liabilities	$7,347.45

Total Assets − Total Liabilities = <$841.61> (Net Worth)

Table 2.4 Net Worth of a Couple with Four Children

Assets	Current Market Value	Liabilities	Total Dollar Amount
Cash	$255	Credit card balance	$458
Savings account	$10,432	Student loans	$23,000
Checking account	$4,918	Mortgage loan	$152,000
Bonds	$9,500	Car loans	$6,400
Stocks	$167,461		
401(k) plan	$129,993		
Home	$380,000		
Cars	$23,500		
Clothing	$700		
Furniture	$3,000		
Electronic equipment	$2,000		
Jewelry	$3,000		
Total Assets	**$734,759**	**Total Amount of Liabilities**	**$181,858**

$734,759 (Total Assets) − $181,858 (Total Liabilities) = $552,901 (Family Net Worth)

---

asset—the knowledge and preparation you gain in college—is of great value, it is not easily quantified and does not count in the net worth calculation. Therefore, a student loan of $5,500 shows up as a liability on the balance sheet with no offsetting asset. In reality, the "asset" is your increased earning power in the future, but that cannot be shown on the balance sheet.

As people get older and start families, buy houses, build retirement investments, etc., it is common for both the total liabilities and the total assets to grow, but financially healthy couples continually build greater net worth by both increasing their family's assets and decreasing their family's liabilities.

Budgeting

Now that you have documented your past spending (family income and expense statement) and evaluated your current financial situation (family net worth statement), the next thing to do is plan for your financial future by creating a family **budget**. Simply stated, a family budget is a spending plan to meet future needs and wants in harmony with available family income. It is perhaps the most important thing families can do to keep their financial houses in order and minimize financial difficulties. President Spencer W. Kimball taught,

> Every family should have a budget. Why, we would not think of going one day without a budget in this Church or our businesses. We have to know approximately what we may receive, and we certainly must know what we are going to spend. And one of the successes of the Church would have to be that the Brethren watch these things very carefully, and we do not spend that which we do not have.[4]

Effective budgeting is an ongoing and interactive process that involves five repeating steps:

1. Set goals to address family needs and wants, and determine financial resources needed to meet those goals.

2. Categorize your current income and

Budget
A spending plan in which family income is allocated to specific categories of expenditures.

spending (family income and expense statement).

3. Develop your family budget by allocating income to budget categories that will meet your family's goals.

4. Implement your budget by tracking income and expenses against your budget.

5. On a regular basis (usually monthly), compare your budget to your actual expenses and make changes to your budget when necessary to achieve your goals.

Step 1

Set goals to address family needs and wants, and determine the financial resources needed to meet those goals.

The Book of Mormon prophet Jacob wrote: "Wherefore, do not spend money for that which is of no worth, nor your labor for that which cannot satisfy."[5] The purpose of a budget is to make a plan to use your financial resources for those things of worth, your true needs and worthy wants. As we expend the fruits of our labor on these things, we feel a great sense of satisfaction. It is not enough just to want to save money—you should know what you are saving for. Basic needs, such as food, clothing, shelter, and transportation should take first priority. After needs are taken care of, the worthy wants of family members should be considered.

The acronym **SMART** is a good way to describe your family goals. They should be Specific, Measurable, Attainable, Relevant, and Time-bound. Your family goals should also be written down, because, "A goal not written down is merely a wish."[6] It may also be useful to place these goals in a place where your family will see them often. This may help to remind you of your purpose and bring about more success.

Let's look at the example of George and Tara. George and Tara got married as juniors, had a baby, and both graduated from BYU last year. George got a good job as an engineer earning $80,000 per year. They expect to have several more children in the next decade or so. They set a goal to buy a used late-model minivan in three years without going into debt. They figure they'll need it to fit all their children and their children's car seats. They determine it will cost about $18,000 to realize that goal. Knowing this, they create a budget in which they will save $500 per month to put toward that goal. After saving $500 per month for 36 months they will have the money they need to pay cash for a nice Honda Sienna. It is much easier for George and Tara to save and sacrifice when they know what they are saving and sacrificing for.

Many families have not set goals together nor have they determined what their true needs and worthy wants are. They spend money on many different things in an attempt to find out what makes them happy. They engage in impulse buying. As a result, they find little satisfaction in their family financial stewardship. Your family can be different!

Once you understand what is important to you, write down your goals, and begin working toward those goals, you will find that spending money on things that really matter becomes a lot easier. This kind of financial living allows you to control your money rather than letting your money control you. A budget is not worth much if it does not help your family accomplish your family goals.

SMART principle

Family goals should be

Specific
Measurable
Attainable
Relevant
Time-bound

Step 2

Categorize your current income and spending in categories.

The next step is to categorize your current income and spending. Gather all of your financial transactions over some period of time (usually a month or year), put them in categories, and sum a total for each category. This is most easily done when all of your income goes into one account, usually the family checking account, and then all expenses are paid for from this account. Online apps such as www.mint.com and www.creditkarma.com can do most of this automatically. A family net worth statement can also be a great tool in assessing your current financial health and how you are using your money. Analyzing your past cash flow patterns can help you create a realistic budget.

Step 3

Develop your family budget by allocating income to budget categories that will meet your family's goals.

Based on family goals to meet needs and wants, and the information in the family income and expense statement, the next step is to intelligently allocate available income to budget categories. To be effective, family budgeting should be guided by the following principles:

- Spend less than you earn (income should exceed expenses)
- Keep good records for spending, taxes, and other purposes
- Use a budgeting method that meets your individual and family needs and circumstances

BUDGET CATEGORIES

There are limitless budget categories that you can choose from to help keep track of your spending, because families spend money on an endless list of things. Some families who appreciate (and can handle) more flexibility use fewer, broader categories, while families who need more structure use many small categories. Again, it is up to you to decide which categories fit best in your family budget, but here are a few of the most popular categories.

Budget Categories

- Income 1, income 2, etc.
- Tax return
- Savings
- Mortgage/rent
- Tithing
- Charitable donations
- Utilities
- Groceries
- Fast food/eating out
- Credit card payments
- Insurance (different types)
- Phone bill
- Car payment
- Education
- Food
- Fun
- Miscellaneous
- Mad money
- Clothing
- Pocket cash
- Car expenses
- Travel

The **miscellaneous** section is one of the most important sections in your budget. It's highly unlikely you will ever create a budget

---

Miscellaneous

One of your budget's most important, but often neglected, categories; a generous catch-all category for those unexpected expenses which find the holes in your budget.

that will perfectly match all your expenses. There are many unforeseen expenses which tend to pop up that may not fit the categories within your budget. It is always a great idea to have a generous catch-all miscellaneous category for those unexpected expenses which find the holes in your budget.

Avoid not having a miscellaneous category in your budget like the plague!

"**Mad money**" is a certain amount of funds allocated to each spouse, for which they are not responsible to the other spouse. For example, you and your spouse might have $50 per month each of "mad money" that you can spend however and whenever you wish (as long as it legal and moral). This can strengthen marriages and give each spouse some personal freedom, while still helping the couple stick to a budget.

Remember to budget for your family's short- and long-term goals. Purposefully spend your money on what you value. Invest your money in what matters most, such as budgeting for weekly date nights to strengthen your marriage. The easiest way to work toward goals and make them happen is to allocate money toward them each month.

If your family is struggling to spend less than you earn, it may be helpful to rethink your fixed expenses and your variable expenses previously discussed in this chapter (see family income and expense statement). Remember, expenditures that you may have thought of as fixed expenses are in fact variable, and can often be either reduced or eliminated as needed. For example, you might sell a car with a $500 per month car payment, and then purchase a less expensive vehicle. You may also choose to eliminate your $100 monthly cable bill for a time. Differentiating between needs and wants is a valuable skill, especially in times when money is tight.

Table 2.5 is an example budget of a young couple who have recently graduated from college and started working and do not have children yet.

Table 2.5 Example Budget

	Budget	Actual	Difference
Income			
Wages/salaries (after taxes)	$2,500	$2,400	<$100>
Other income	$200	$250	$50
Total income	$2,700	$2,650	<$50>
Expenditures			
Tithing/Donations	$325	$318	<$7>
Long-term savings	$405	$398	<$7>
Short-term savings	$70	$70	$0
Food	$300	$320	$20
Mortgage or rent	$600	$600	$0
Utilities	$300	$325	$25
Transportation	$180	$165	<$15>
Debt payments	$50	$50	$0
Insurance	$150	$150	$0
Medical	$40	$40	$0
Clothing	$150	$100	<$50>
Miscellaneous	$100	$75	<$25>
Mad money	$30	$30	$0
Total expenditures	$2,700	$2,641	<$59>
Income minus Expenditures	$0	$9	$9

Mad money
A certain amount of funds allocated to each spouse, for which they are not responsible to the other spouse.

Budgeting the Better Way

Many families determine how much they will save according to how much money is left at the end of each month. They receive their paychecks, pay their tithes and expenses, and then save what they do not spend during the rest of the month.

Always have a miscellaneous category in your budget.

Income – Tithing – Expenses =
Available for Savings and Family Goals

This is an ineffective pattern for budgeting monthly income because families are paying themselves last. It also creates the feeling that your family budget is a ball and chain that is restricting you.

Avoid not budgeting the better way like the plague!

There is a better pattern. After you have paid your tithes and offerings to the Lord, pay yourselves a predetermined amount or percentage directly into savings, then budget and live on the remaining income.

Income – Pay the Lord – Pay Yourselves
(savings and goals) – Expenses =
Other Savings

Using this pattern will help you keep your priorities in order and create more positive feelings about your family budget. L. Tom Perry suggested something similar to this new pattern for budgeting when he wrote,

> After paying your tithing of 10 percent to the Lord, you pay yourself a predetermined amount directly into savings. That leaves you a balance of your income to budget for taxes, food, clothing, shelter, transportation, etc. It is amazing to me that so many people work all of their lives for the grocer, the landlord, the power company, the automobile salesman, and the bank, and yet think so little of their own efforts that they pay themselves nothing.[7]

Budgeting Methods

Different families use different budgeting methods (or a combination of several methods) because each family has unique preferences for how to track their money. Whatever method your family chooses to use should accomplish the principles you learned earlier in this section.

Consider the timeline you want for your

budget. How you create your budget may depend on whether it is for the short-term (weekly or monthly), intermediate-term (quarterly or yearly), or long-term (several years to a decade). It would be a good idea to have a set budget for each term, and you might decide to use different methods for each term. However, a monthly budget is the most common because so many payments are due on a monthly basis. Here are a few of the most common budgeting methods:

Online Internet Services

To use this method, you create an account on a financial tracking service such as www.mint.com or www.creditkarma.com. You provide this service access to all of your financial accounts (bank accounts, credit cards, investment accounts, etc.) and set up a monthly budget allocating a set amount per month to different categories. Then, in real time, the service tracks credit card, debit card, and check activity.

As long as you deposit all of your income into one account and always use a credit card, debit card, or check for every expenditure, you will always have a perfect record of your income and expenses. Using this method, you can always check the status of your budget. You can also opt to receive automatic alerts if you start spending more than you have allocated. Another benefit to using online internet services is that they provide your credit score free of charge.

Some have worried about the security issues that can arise from giving all of your personal financial information to online service providers such as those mentioned above. It appears that these two service providers have equivalent security measures as secure as the financial institutions themselves. This type of service is free. The service providers make their money by offering you financial options (e.g., credit cards, loans, etc.) based on your financial data and credit score, but you do not have to purchase any of these offers to use the service for free.

Spreadsheets/Written

This method is mostly self-explanatory. If you are good with Excel or another spreadsheet software, then this may be the method for you. There are endless ways to set up your personal spreadsheet, but you might list take-home pay (money you earn after taxes and other deductions) at the top. You then determine spending by categories (rows) and dates (columns), and prepare a budget for each category. As bills come in, you pay the bills and input the spending on each date (column) and category (row). Be sure to allocate adequate amounts for a financial reserve and for long-term goals. This method can be useful if it is updated regularly and reviewed often.

Computer Software Methods

This method can be a little more expensive than other methods, but there are many

options available. Two of the most popular budgeting software currently available are Quicken and Mvelopes. Much like the spreadsheet method, most software programs assist you in determining spending categories, tracking your expenses in those categories, and setting up saving and spending goals. There are even budgeting apps that can be of great help. If set up correctly, this method can save significant time and effort while helping your family achieve your goals.

The Envelope Method

This method requires you to physically take the money your family plans to spend that month or week out of the bank and divide the cash into different envelopes that are marked as different expense categories (like rent, food, entertainment, etc.). Once a category's envelope is empty, you cannot spend any more money in that category until the time period is over, at which time you go to the bank and get cash for the next period. For those who find living within a budget difficult, this may be the most straightforward method.

Zero-Based Budgeting

This method is centered on the idea that every cent of money you earn already has a place for it to go even before you receive it. This means allocating all of your income into different categories, leaving very little wiggle room for going over budget in any category or having extravagant spending binges. This method can help you increase the amount of money in your savings account.

DNAH-ial Methods (Do Nothing and Hope) or "It's All in My Head" Budgeting

This is the method used by most individuals, and it is the cheapest and least time-consuming. It requires nothing. Individuals simply deny responsibility and hope things work out. They only respond when things get so bad that they have to act. The downside is that there is no planning, no preparation for long-term goals and objectives, and likely no savings.

Avoid the "Do Nothing and Hope" budget like the plague!

Although you have to determine yourself which method is best for you, the best methods are those that have the following attributes:

1. Low cost and relatively easy to use
2. Allow downloading of bills from banks and credit card companies—makes data entry easier
3. Allow adequate categorization of spending for income, spending, reporting and tax purposes
4. Minimize the time spent on finances

Step 4

Implement your budget by tracking income and expenses against your budget.

Now that you have set up an effective family budget, give it a try. Record all income and expenses in their proper categories; accurate record keeping is a crucial part of good budgeting. Add up all the amounts listed in each category, and make a note of how much you have left over in each category at the end of each week.

Adjust your plan as necessary to make it work for you. Try to be financially prudent—don't buy things you don't need or haven't budgeted for. Following the **HALT principle** can help with this. Strive to avoid buying things when you are feeling Hungry, Angry, Lonely, or Tired. It's easy to try to make ourselves feel better by spending money, but in the end it will hurt your family budget and increase your stress. Use each month as a learning experience to help you do better the next month.

Avoid making purchases or financial decisions when you are Hungry, Angry, Lonely, or Tired like the plague.

HUNGRY

ANGRY

LONELY

TIRED

While you are in the implementation stage of your budgeting, take time to assess how well you are doing. Here are a few introspective questions that you can ask to see how well your budget is being implemented in your family:

HALT principle

Avoid making purchases or financial decisions when you are

Hungry
Angry
Lonely
Tired

 Avoid the "Do Nothing and Hope" budget like the plague!

HALT video
http://bcove.me/davyf55y

 Avoid making purchases or financial decisions when you are Hungry, Angry, Lonely, or Tired like the plague!

- Do you know how much money you have in your accounts right now?
- Do you know how much you can spend when you go grocery shopping?
- How often do you check your budget?
- Do you adjust your budget every month?
- Are you prepared for unexpected financial setbacks by having a section of your budget devoted to savings?
- Is your budget realistic?
- Is your budget personalized to you and your spending?
- Do you have a miscellaneous section in your budget?
- Do you view your current budgeting practices as helpful?
- (If married) Do you and your spouse have "mad money" in your budget?
- (If married) Do you and your spouse have time set aside weekly to go over your budget together?
- (If married) Do you feel that you and your spouse are on the "same page" financially?
- (If married) Are there any unresolved financial issues between you and your spouse that could be solved through sitting down together and going over your family budget? (For example, have you or your spouse been angry with one another for spending too much money?)
- (If married, with children) Are you including your children in the family budgeting process?

Step 5

Compare your budget to your actual expenses and make changes where necessary to achieve your goals.

The fifth step in creating an effective budget is comparing your budget to your actual

Online Budget Help

For further help, you can look online for sample budgets. There are good resources on websites like:

- www.mint.com
- www.personalfinance.byu.edu
- www.daveramsey.com

Even a Google search will give you plenty of sample budgets.

spending. As necessary, adjust the amounts you have budgeted for different expenses to create a more effective budget. As you make adjustments, don't reduce payments to God or to yourself.

Creating a budget is a learning experience. You will likely never create a perfect budget because life situations change. Every month may require different spending needs. Assessing and editing your budget each month for different expenses that come with different situations is a healthy habit to establish.

Budgeting Advice for Couples

Elder Robert L. Simpson taught,

Each husband and wife needs to reason together about the family budget on a regular basis. If downward adjustments need to be made in the family spending habits, it is far better to do what needs to be done now rather than build up to an impossible

financial crisis later on—a crisis that too often leads to the divorce courts.[8]

Budgeting can be a big stress on a couple's relationship. Here are a few tips to help manage that stress and learn to budget together:

- Decide who would be the best, or the main person, in charge of budgeting
- Mutually agree to monthly budget amounts
- Discuss finances early and often (weekly) to resolve misunderstandings
- Be flexible and forgiving with each other—compromise
- Be willing to adapt

Overall, remember that if you don't control your money, it will control you. As Marvin J. Ashton stated,

> Some claim living within a budget takes the fun out of life and is too restrictive. But those who avoid the inconvenience of a budget must suffer the pains of living outside of it. The Church operates within a budget. Successful business functions within a budget. Families free of crushing debt have a budget. Budget guidelines encourage better performance and management.[9]

Commit to healthy, successful budgeting for the rest of your life!

Financial Ratios

> *"But if ye do not watch yourselves, and your thoughts, and your words, and your deeds, and observe the commandments of God…ye must perish. And now, O man, remember, and perish not."*
> (Mosiah 4:30)

Financial ratios are another way to measure your family's financial health. Using ratios can help you better understand how you are managing financial resources by pointing out areas of strength and areas of weakness. Analyzing these ratios over time can help you identify trends and compare your financial standing to recommended target ratios.

Ratios to Remember

Table 2.6 shows some of the more common ratios.

Conclusion

In this chapter we have explored several essential ways to measure your family's financial health and to plan for future financial success. We have taught about the importance of regularly and accurately recording your family's personal and financial information. You learned to document your family's financial past with a family income and expense statement. You documented all of your family's

Table 2.6 Common Ratios

Ratio	Calculation	Example	Interpretation	Recommended Guidelines
Debt Ratio	Liabilities divided by net worth	$25,000/$50,000 = 0.5	Shows relationship between debt and net worth	A low debt ratio is best
Current Ratio	Liquid assets divided by current liabilities	$4,000/$2,000 = 2	Indicates $2.00 in liquid assets for every $1.00 of current liabilities	A high current ratio is desirable to have cash available to pay bills
Liquidity Ratio	Liquid assets divided by monthly expenses	$10,000/$4,000 = 2.5	Indicates the number of months in which living expenses can be paid if an emergency arises	A high liquidity ratio is desirable
Debt-payments ratio	Monthly credit payments divided by take-home pay	$540/$3,600 = .15	Indicates how much of a person's earnings goes for debt payments (excluding a home mortgage)	Most financial advisers recommend a debt/payments ratio of less than 20 percent
Savings ratio	Amount saved each month divided by gross income	$648/$5,400 = .12	Shows relationship between amount saved and income earned	Financial experts recommend monthly savings of 5–10 percent

financial assets and liabilities in order to calculate a family net worth statement. And finally, you developed and implemented a family budget. We wish you well as you take your family's financial health into your own hands and move purposefully toward your family goals.

Other Resources

- www.barrons.com
- www.creditkarma.com
- www.daveramsey.com
- www.kbb.com
- www.ksl.com
- www.mint.com
- www.personalfinance.byu.edu
- www.realtor.com
- www.usatoday.com/money
- www.wsj.com
- www.zillow.com
- HALT Video: http://bcove.me/davyf55y

Notes

1. Elder Robert D. Hales, *Becoming Provident Providers Temporally and Spiritually* (Apr. 2009), https://www.lds.org/general-conference/2009/04/becoming-provident-providers-temporally-and-spiritually?lang=eng.
2. "The Family: A Proclamation to the World," (Oct. 2004), https://www.lds.org/topics/family-proclamation?lang=eng.
3. D&C 88:119
4. "Finances," *Eternal Marriage Student Manual*, https://www.lds.org/manual/eternal-marriage-student-manual/finances?lang=eng.
5. 2 Nephi 9:51
6. Sean Covey, *The 7 Habits of Highly Effective Teens* (New York, NY: Simon and Schuster, 1998), 59.
7. L. Tom Perry. *Becoming Self-Reliant* (Oct. 1991), https://www.lds.org/general-conference/1991/10/becoming-self-reliant?lang=eng.
8. Robert L. Simpson, "A Lasting Marriage," *Conference Report* (Apr. 1982), https://www.lds.org/general-conference/1982/04/a-lasting-marriage?lang=eng.
9. Marvin J. Ashton, "It's No Fun Being Poor," (Sep. 1982), https://www.lds.org/ensign/1982/09/its-no-fun-being-poor?lang=eng.

3

Cash Management and More

Introducing Your Family to Banks and Other Financial Institutions

LEARN

- The importance of saving money in an emergency fund
- About several cash management alternatives
- About different types of financial institutions
- To compare financial institutions based on their convenience, cost, consideration, security, and gain

Cash management deals with how to effectively manage your family's monetary assets. **Monetary assets** are financial resources that are legal tender (cash) or can be converted to legal tender very quickly. They are very low risk. Some examples of monetary assets are the currency in your wallet, coins in a pickle jar, checking and savings accounts, certificates of deposit (CDs), and money market accounts. Things like houses, cars, washing machines, stamp collections, apartment buildings, gold, silver, bonds, art collections, baseball teams, stocks, and children are not considered monetary assets because they cannot be turned into cash very quickly (if at all) or they are not low-risk. The goals of effective cash management include convenience (easy-to-access services without travel or hassle), cost (you are not charged fees and/or penalties), consideration (you can get personal help when you need it), security (low risk of losing any money), and gain (you are paid some interest from those who use your cash).

Because everyone receives and spends money, cash manage-

Chapter 3: Cash Management and More

Goals of effective cash management:

- convenience
- cost
- consideration
- security
- gain

Cash management

How to effectively manage your family's monetary assets.

Monetary assets

Financial resources that are legal tender (cash) or can be converted to legal tender very quickly.

Liquidity

The immediate accessibility of money.

Emergency Fund

Liquid financial resources to meet unexpected and immediate needs; this should total at least 3–6 months of living expenses.

Importance of an Emergency Fund

Perhaps the most important role of cash management is to save sufficient monetary assets to build an **emergency fund** for your family. Your family's emergency fund is a resource you can use to meet unexpected, immediate needs for money caused by job loss, car problems, an emergency surgery, or myriad other disasters. Even if you escape these calamities, just knowing that you have an emergency fund will give you and your family peace of mind.

ment is an essential part of your family's financial strategy. Cash and cash-like assets provide your family needed financial protection and flexibility because of their high liquidity. **Liquidity** refers to how quickly and easily you can access your money. Funds that are more liquid are immediately accessible for both ordinary and urgent family needs. Long-term assets are not considered very liquid because they are often impossible to access immediately, and may have substantial penalties for access on short notice. For example, suppose you own a piece of property that could be sold in 180 days for $500,000. If you need the money in two weeks, you may be forced to have a "fire sale" and only receive $400,000 for it. Having sufficient liquid funds on hand provides you and your family peace of mind and is an important component of financial health and security.

Although it is essential for your family to have enough cash reserves to meet immediate and emergency needs, it is also very important to have long-term investments. A couple who invests all of their retirement contributions into a savings account at a bank will find in 40 years that much of their financial wardrobe would have been mercilessly devoured by the clothes moth of inflation. Monetary assets generally have returns less than the rate of inflation, so the wise family will generously invest in tax-advantaged, diversified, primarily stock-based mutual funds as well. This is necessary to unleash the eighth wonder of the world: the miracle of compound interest.

The general rule of thumb for an emergency fund is to have sufficient liquid assets to cover three to six months of family expenses. If you want to be even more prepared, you may want to substitute the term "expenses" with the term "income" because your income should be higher than your expenses. Keeping three to six months of income in your emergency fund means there is a greater chance you will not need to tap into long-term savings to meet short-term cash needs.

Some might ask, "Is it still necessary to have an emergency fund in this world of credit

cards and home equity loans?" The answer is yes, absolutely! It may even be more necessary than it was in the past. Credit cards and home equity lines of credit may be canceled if you lose your job or have a debilitating accident. Secure, available funds that can be accessed quickly provide peace of mind in a troubling world.

President Gordon B. Hinckley taught the importance of having an emergency fund: "May the Lord bless you . . . to set your houses in order. If you have paid your debts, if you have a reserve, even though it be small, then should storms howl about your head, you will have shelter for your wives and children and peace in your hearts."[1]

Cash Management Options

There are many options available to help you manage your family's monetary assets, and each has its own costs and benefits. Some cash-management alternatives include cash on hand, checking accounts, savings accounts, certificates of deposit, and money market accounts. Gaining a basic understanding of each of these cash management options can be helpful as you decide where to put your money.

An important attribute to keep in mind when comparing cash-management options is liquidity. In general, the higher the liquidity of a cash management option is, the lower the interest rate will be for that option.

Emergency Fund Story

The story of Brett's family illustrates the importance of having an emergency fund and an emergency food supply.

After returning from a mission, Brett married his sweetheart and received an engineering degree from BYU. He obtained a good-paying job in his field and distinguished himself as a top performer. He provided well for his family that now included three growing children (ages 11, 13, and 15).

Brett and his wife Mary were financially responsible. Not only did they pay their tithing and set aside 10 percent for long-term savings, they also saved a six-month emergency fund and a one-year food supply. They could easily afford the payments on their modest country home with its acre of land and a few fruit trees. They seemed set.

One day, Brett came home from work and calmly announced to the family, "Our company doesn't exist anymore; I'm without a job and without an income." Though this was a complete surprise for everyone, Brett told his family they did not need to worry. They had prepared for this emergency by preparing a one-year supply of food and an emergency supply of money that could probably last about a year. They would have to be frugal, but they could make it until he found another job, a hunt he estimated would take about one year.

The family pulled together to deal with this financial trial. They reduced expenses to a minimum. In family prayers, they specifically asked that Dad might find a job. In the meantime, looking for a job became Brett's new full-time job. He spent 30–40 hours per week job hunting, which was much less than the 50–60 hours per week he had been working. Brett used this newfound discretionary time to engage in more family activities. They chose inexpensive recreation such as camping and backpacking. Brett would later say, "Losing my job was the best thing that ever happened to my family. We really connected!"

After nine months of searching, Brett finally found another good job in a different state. This time, he chose a job that demanded fewer hours with slightly lower pay because he wanted more family time.

Since this family was prepared with an emergency supply of money and food, the trial of unemployment became a period of growth and unity.

Cash On Hand

The most basic cash management option is to store real currency on your person or somewhere in your home (under your mattress, in a home safe, in the cookie jar, etc.). This option has the advantage of being totally accessible with a guarantee of no fees. However, it doesn't offer interest earned and carries the risk of theft and loss.

FDIC

Federal Deposit Insurance Corporation. The government agency which insures deposits at most commercial banks for up to $250,000 per depositor. Joint depositors are insured for up to $500,000.

Avoid bouncing checks like the plague!

Checking Accounts

Checking accounts are perhaps the most common cash management option because most paychecks are deposited directly into a checking account. They are also among the most liquid of all cash management alternatives. Checking accounts provide you with immediate access to your funds anywhere that accepts checks or debit cards. Money held in a checking account can be conveniently withdrawn by writing checks, accessing automated teller machines, using debit cards, and authorizing automatic withdrawals.

The high liquidity of checking accounts also means they have very low interest rates and sometimes garner no interest at all. For example, in late 2015, the standard rate of interest on a checking account at Zions First National Bank was 0.05 percent per year.[2] That means that on a $3,000 average balance, over one year you would earn exactly $1.50, just enough for a soda in the Cougar Eat once a year! For this reason, you should limit your checking account balance to the liquidity you actually need for current expenses and deposit the rest where you can earn higher interest.

Unlike credit cards, purchases made with checks and debit cards cannot exceed the amount available in the consumer's checking account without incurring a substantial fee. When this happens, it is called overdrawing, or "bouncing" a check. Because a penalty occurs every time a payment exceeds the amount in the account, overdrawing can be very costly and should be avoided through careful budgeting practices. As of 2015, the average cost of the first bounced check is $30.47.[3] One way to avoid bouncing checks is to link your checking account to a mobile app like mint.com so that you always know what your checking balance is.

Avoid bouncing checks like the plague.

Knowingly writing a bad check, or writing the check even though you know there are insufficient funds in your account to cover the check, is a crime. Bad checks are also known as NSF checks, rubber checks, or bounced checks. You can go to jail and receive stiff fines for writing bad checks. Depending on the state, this may be called fraud, forgery, and, in some cases, embezzlement. Don't take a chance. Always know that you have money in your account before writing a check or using a debit card.

Checking accounts are extremely safe and are generally insured by the **Federal Deposit Insurance Corporation** (FDIC). The FDIC was a result of the Great Depression. During the 1930s, many depositors lost confidence

in the banking system and withdrew their savings. This run on the banks caused many banks to fail and exasperated the financial crisis. By insuring deposits, the government hopes to avoid a repeat of the financial catastrophe of the Great Depression. The FDIC insures deposits at most commercial banks for up to $250,000 per depositor. Joint depositors are insured for up to $500,000. Simply put, if the bank fails, you get your money back.

In credit unions, checking accounts are called share draft accounts. They have slightly higher interest rates. The **National Credit Union Administration** (NCUA) insures deposits at credit unions for up to $250,000 per depositor or $500,000 for joint depositors, the same amount that the FDIC insures at banks.

Savings Accounts

Money in a savings account is deposited with a financial institution. To use it, you must either go to the bank and withdraw it, or transfer it to a checking account where it may be accessed by check, ATM, or debit card. Because money in a savings account is slightly less liquid than money in a checking account, savings accounts have a slightly higher interest rate. As of the writing of this textbook, interest rates on savings accounts are extremely low. For the past 50 years, annual interest on savings accounts has generally been between 2 percent and 6 percent.[4] In late 2015, the standard rate of interest on a statement savings account at Zions Bank was 0.06 percent per year.[5] That means that on a $3,000 average balance, over one year you would earn exactly $1.80! Savings accounts are extremely safe and are generally insured by the Federal Deposit Insurance Corporation (FDIC).

Certificates of Deposit (CDs)

Certificates of deposit (CDs) pay you a fixed interest rate for keeping your funds in the account for a fixed period of time. Interest rates are fixed for the life of the deposit, and the longer the term of the deposit, the higher the interest rate. For example, in late 2015 the interest rates at Zions Bank ranged from 0.25 percent on a one-year CD to 0.80 percent on a five-year CD.[6] CDs are less liquid than other cash-management alternatives because the money must be deposited for a certain amount of time before it can be withdrawn without penalty. They are, however, FDIC or NCUA insured when deposited in banks or credit unions.

Money Market Accounts (MMAs)

A **money market account** (MMA) is similar to a savings account, but instead of having a fixed rate of interest, its interest rate varies with the current level of market interest rates. MMAs generally have higher interest rates and a higher required minimum balance. For example, in late-2015 the interest rates at Zions Bank ranged from 0.10 percent on an MMA account with a minimum balance of $1,000 to 0.18 percent on an MMA account with a minimum balance of $1,000,000.[7] MMAs are also insured by the FDIC or NCUA when deposited in banks or credit unions.

In today's market of historically low interest rates, the rate of return among all these and other alternatives varies little. As we will see in the next section, the determining selection criteria in these days lie with the convenience and fees charged by the different financial institutions.

Financial Institutions

As you explore different cash management alternatives, you must also consider the differ-

NCUA

National Credit Union Administration. Government agency which insures deposits at credit unions for up to $250,000 per depositor or $500,000 for joint depositors.

CD

Certificate of Deposit. Pay a fixed interest rate for keeping your funds in the account for a fixed period of time.

MMA

Money Market Account. This is similar to a savings account, but instead of having a fixed rate of interest, its interest rate varies with the current level of market interest rates.

ent types of financial institutions that offer those alternatives. Here we will consider three of the most common alternatives: commercial banks, online banks, and credit unions.

Commercial Banks

Also known as brick and mortar banks, commercial banks generally compete by offering the widest variety of support and services. They usually have employees who can help you face-to-face with financial situations: a bank president, loan officers, customer service representatives, tellers, etc. For some, it is comforting to have a banker who knows them by name and sends them a Christmas card. Commercial banks also offer on-site services such as safe deposit boxes, fax service, cashier's checks, cookies, coffee, and (in Utah) hot chocolate. Because they have to cover the cost of the building and of these services, they usually do not offer the highest interest rates on deposits or the lowest interest rates on loans. With today's very low interest rates, there are not many differences among different commercial banks, unless you are saving large amounts of money. Some common banks near BYU include Wells Fargo Bank, Zions Bank, U.S. Bank, Chase, and AmericanWest Bank.

Online Banks

Online or Internet banks are electronic banks that do not have traditional brick-and-mortar branches. Because they have fewer branches, employees, and capital expenditures than traditional banks, they can generally pay higher interest rates on deposits and charge less for loans than traditional banks do. However, they do not have anyone you can sit down with face-to-face. Everything is done electronically. Obviously, they do not offer the onsite services that commercial banks and credit unions offer. Some common online banks include Ally Bank, Nationwide Bank, Discover Bank, Capital One 360, and ING.

Credit Unions

Credit unions are similar to banks, but they are not-for-profit organizations and are owned by their members. The members are those who invest in and borrow from the credit union. Since credit unions do not need to make a profit, they often offer slightly higher rates on savings accounts and lower rates on loans. Credit unions offer many of the same benefits that commercial banks offer. Some common credit unions around BYU include Utah Community Credit Union (UCCU), Mountain America Credit Union (MACU), Deseret First Credit Union (DFCU), and University Federal Credit Union (UFCU).

> Remember—a positive attitude, a well-thought-out plan, and consistent self-discipline can help us improve our circumstances. Applying these keys in our daily work will help produce more income, and practicing them in our homes will help reduce expenses. When we combine these principles with keeping the commandments of God, we can learn to become better managers of our time and resources and become financially secure.
> —M. Russell Ballard[8]

Criteria for Comparing Financial Institutions

There are five simple criteria that can make the process of selecting one or more financial institutions easier: convenience, cost (and fees), consideration, security, and gain. Here are some questions to ask about each.

Convenience

How convenient is it for you to work with the institution? What is the availability of branches and ATMs? Are they close to your home and work? Will you have to travel much? What are the direct deposit options? Can you deposit a check with your phone? Does the institution offer overdraft protection, safety deposit boxes, credit cards, etc.?

Cost (and fees)

How much will it cost to do business with this bank? What are the monthly fees associated with checking and savings accounts? Are there minimum balances required? What happens if you fall below the minimum balance? Are there per check fees or balance-dependent scaled fees? What fees are associated with overdrafts or insufficient funds? What interest rates are charged on loans?

Consideration

Does the institution offer personalized financial advice and give attention to detail? How important is it that a bank officer remembers your name and is happy to work with you? Do you have an unusual financial situation that would be better handled by a person than a rule?

Security

Are your accounts insured by FDIC or NCUA? Do you have more than $250,000 in one account? (Amounts above $250,000 are not insured.)

Gain

Is interest paid on your checking account? On your savings account? What are the interest rates? What is the effective annual yield (the "actual" amount of interest paid on the account)? One place to compare interest rates for cash management is www.bankrate.com.[9]

In today's market of extremely low interest rates and competitive services, the most important criterion is often convenience, especially when it comes to the location of the bank and ATM machines. With a convenient bank you save time and out-of-network fees. Cost and fees would probably be the second most important criterion, especially if you have a knack for overdrawing your checking account.

Summary

In this chapter, you learned about cash management and how to effectively manage your family's monetary assets. This is an important component of your overall financial

The $30.59 Gatorade

It was a hot summer's afternoon. Jeremy was riding his new road bike from Provo to Vivian Park. By the time he got to Will's Pit Stop at the mouth of Provo Canyon, he needed some Gatorade®. He didn't have any cash with him, but he did have his Wells Fargo debit card. As he stood before the ATM he knew he had a low balance but wasn't quite sure how much that balance was. He thought, "Well, if I don't have the money in there, the ATM will decline my card, right?" Wrong! Because of courtesy fees on his debit card, this Gatorade® cost Jeremy a bundle.

Jeremy really only had $12.15 in his checking account. He withdrew $20 from the Zions Bank ATM at Will's Pit Stop and bought a $1.59 liter of Gatorade®. The ATM honored his transaction but assessed a $25.00 courtesy fee. In addition, since the ATM was out-of-network he paid $2.00 to Wells Fargo and $2.00 to Zions Bank. The Gatorade® quenched Jeremy's thirst, but the total cost was $30.59! The moral of the story: Make sure you have money in your checking account to cover ATM or debit card transactions. Also, when you sign up for your debit card, decline the "courtesy fees" option. Then your card will be declined if you don't have the money.

strategy. You learned about the importance of having an emergency fund on which you could survive for three to six months. You learned about several cash management alternatives, including checking accounts, savings accounts, CDs, and Money Market Funds. You also became familiar with three kinds of financial institutions: commercial banks, credit unions, and online banks. Finally, you learned five criteria for evaluating institutions and cash management alternatives: cost, convenience, consideration, security, and gain. As you have learned by now, "The temporal is intertwined with the spiritual. God has given us this mortal experience and the temporal challenges that attend it as a laboratory where we can grow into the beings Heavenly Father wants us to become. May we understand the great duty and blessing that come from following and providing in the Lord's way."[10]

Now we are ready to move on to credit and loans!

Notes

1. President Gordon B. Hinckley, "To the Boys and to the Men," (Nov. 1998), 51.
2. https://www.zionsbank.com/personal/comparison-table/checking/#checking.
3. http://www.bankrate.com/finance/checking/5-cities-with-highest-bounced-check-fees-1.aspx.
4. http://swanlowpark.co.uk/savingsinterestannual.jsp.
5. https://www.zionsbank.com/personal/comparison-table/checking/#money-market-savings.
6. https://www.zionsbank.com/personal/comparison-table/checking/#cd-ira.
7. https://www.zionsbank.com/personal/comparison-table/checking/#money-market-savings.
8. M. Russell Ballard, "Providing For Our Needs," (April 1981), https://www.lds.org/general-conference/1981/04/providing-for-our-needs?lang=eng.
9. www.bankrate.com.
10. Dieter F. Uchtdorf, "Providing in the Lord's Way," (Oct. 2011), https://www.lds.org/general-conference/2011/10/providing-in-the-lords-way?lang=eng.

4

Credit and Loans

How to Minimize and Eliminate Family Debt

LEARN

- The role of a credit score in your family's financial health

- The benefits and dangers of credit cards, and know how to appropriately use them to build your family's credit

- About different types of consumer loans

- Effective strategies to eliminate debt

John and Jennifer got married in the Provo Utah Temple in 2004 when John was a sophomore majoring in mechanical engineering and Jennifer was a junior majoring in accounting at BYU. They were deeply in love and decided to have children right away. They walked together when they graduated in April 2007, each holding a young child in a cute, tiny graduation robe, complete with miniature cap. Everyone ooohed and aaaaahed when this beautiful family walked across the stage in the Marriott Center. They graduated with about $10,000 in student loans, which they considered to be a good investment.

John got a great engineering job in Seattle with Brown and Caldwell, and they bought a nice home in Puyallup with room for their growing family. Jennifer enjoyed being a stay-at-home mom and did some accounting work on the side. Their house payment stretched them a bit, but they managed it. They faithfully paid their tithing, paid off their credit cards every month before the grace period expired, and always paid their house payment on time.

After having their third child, they decided to wait a little while before having any more kids. However, nine months later they were (unexpectedly) expecting again, and they realized that they would need a larger vehicle to fit their growing family. The time had arrived to become a true Mormon family and buy a minivan!

They didn't like going into debt for a vehicle and had already saved about $6,000. After doing some research, they decided to purchase a 2007 Honda Odyssey for about $12,000. They would get a modest two-year loan and pay back about $250 per month. Then they would start saving for their next car.

At the Honda dealership, all the used vans looked well used. ☺ The salesman noticed they weren't too excited and asked to see John's driver's license. The salesman disappeared for a few minutes and then came back with a big grin. "Did you know your credit score is 795? That's excellent! I'd like to show you what we can do for you." He guided them to the new 2016 Odyssey, which had every feature imaginable and some they had never imagined. "You are so fortunate to have been responsible with your credit; now you are able to qualify for such a vehicle," said the salesman. They took a test drive and loved every acceleration, turn, and stop.

Upon returning to the sales office, the salesman took $2,000 off the price just because he liked them. He told them that because of their outstanding credit score, he could offer a very low interest rate (3.8 percent) for sixty months to lower their payments. He also offered to defer the first payment until after New Year's Day so that the purchase wouldn't impact their Christmas spending. The final price would be only $34,000. Their payments would be about $500 a month. They thought for a few minutes and felt they could swing it. A little voice quietly prompted Jennifer, "You should sleep on this and pray about it," but John was so excited that she didn't mention it to him.

In the end, they both signed for the minivan and drove this heavenly vehicle off the lot. On the way home, Jennifer felt a strong kick from the growing baby inside her. At first, Jennifer thought the baby kicked her because he was so excited about the minivan. Later on, she thought the baby must have kicked her because they had been so stupid to spend all that money! But they enjoyed the Christmas season and their new minivan. They drove in comfort to the ward Christmas party and to church every week. Everyone asked about their beautiful van. They even drove to Bellingham to visit Jennifer's parents for Christmas. The normally onerous trip was like a comfortable dream.

Then the dream ended and turned into a nightmare. In January, the payments started. John and Jennifer had to really scrimp and save to pay the $500 car loan each month in addition to their mortgage payment and student loans. They cut their dating budget in half and shaved off other expenses. They were making it until the new baby came eight weeks early. He needed surgery to correct a congenital defect and was in intensive care for a week. Fortunately, they had good insurance, and of the $280,000 medical bill, they only had to pay about $8,000. Still, despite their best efforts, it became impossible to make ends meet every month. For the first time, they didn't pay off their credit cards. One thing led to another and soon they had a $10,000 credit card debt (on which they were paying 18 percent interest) on top of the other debts they already had. They started arguing about finances nearly every day, making more poor financial decisions in their anger. All of this put a real strain on their temple marriage. Soon, they were considering divorce.

It is true that credit can be a wonderful tool and that it has enabled many families to meet important needs that they could not have met otherwise: a college degree, a home, a car. Church leaders have said that "debt incurred for education, a modest home, or a basic automobile may be necessary to provide for a family."[1]

However, unwise debt has also been the financial downfall of many good people, such as John and Jennifer. President J. Reuben Clark, Jr. warned, "Once in debt, interest is your companion every minute of the day and night; you cannot shun it or slip away from it . . . and whenever you get in its way or cross its course or fail to meet its demands, it crushes you."[2]

Once in debt, interest is your companion every minute of the day and night; you cannot shun it or slip away from it . . . and whenever you get in its way or cross its course or fail to meet its demands, it crushes you.

Debt can crush families by driving a wedge between husband and wife, contributing to marital conflict. Indeed, research shows that financial difficulties, often based in excessive debt, are associated with marital stress[3] and even divorce.[4] Elder Marvin J. Ashton quoted a study by the American Bar Association that indicated that "89 percent of all divorces can be traced to quarrels and accusations over money."[5] Dr. Bernard Poduska reflected: "The saying 'married for better or worse, or until *debt* do us part' seems to reflect today's marital realities more accurately than does the traditional vow."[6]

Many of these financial problems come upon us because we do not have the self-control to wait until we can afford what we want. Instead, we borrow to get what we want right now. We have not sufficiently developed the virtue of patience.[7] Benjamin Franklin must have chuckled when he wrote, "Tis against some men's principles to pay interest, and it seems against others' to pay the principal."

President Thomas S. Monson also highlighted how debt can negatively affect family relationships: "Feelings become strained, quarrels more frequent and nerves frayed when excess debt knocks on the door. Resources channeled to make payment on debts do not put one crumb on the table, provide one degree of warmth in the house, or bring one thread into a garment."[8]

Credit cards can become a particularly destructive financial instrument if not carefully watched and controlled. When credit card debt gets out of control, it not only contributes to financial troubles but to personal and relational heartache as well. President Gordon B. Hinckley said, "Debt can be a terrible thing. It is so easy to incur and so difficult to repay. Borrowed money is had only at a price, and that price can be burdensome."[9] President Ezra Taft Benson was equally as pointed: "Let us avoid debt as we would avoid a plague; where we are now in debt, let us get out of debt; if not today, then tomorrow."[10]

Avoid unnecessary debt like the plague.

The purpose of this chapter is to provide basic financial information about credit so that you can use credit wisely to meet basic needs while working to minimize and eventually eliminate your family's financial debt. Your family should ultimately aim to be debt free without credit card debt, student loans, consumer loans, a car payment, or a mortgage. Unfortunately most families do not become debt free until they retire, if at all. That said, you can be different! By wisely managing your credit and using the principles learned in this book class, many of you could be totally debt free by your forties or earlier. We invite you to learn these principles well so that credit is a blessing to you and so that debt never crushes you.

Avoid unnecessary debt like the plague!

I readily concede that it's important to have sufficient money for our needs, but beyond that, money has little to do with true happiness. Often it is the work and sacrifice one experiences in obtaining money for a worthwhile purpose that produces the most satisfaction. —W. Eugene Hansen[11]

Credit and Debt

What is credit, and why should you care about it? According to *Investopedia,* **credit** is "A contractual agreement in which a borrower receives something of value now and agrees to repay the lender at some date in the future, generally with interest. The term also refers to the borrowing capacity of an individual or company."[12]

The key phrase in this definition is "generally with interest." Because you pay back with interest when you borrow to buy something on credit, you almost always pay more than you would have had you saved and paid cash for the same item. My dad used to always tell me, "There are two kinds of people in the world: those who *pay* interest and those who *understand* interest." It's true. If you understand interest, you will do everything you can to minimize and eventually eliminate **debt**. Although you would think that reasonable people would stay out of debt, most do not. In fact, debt load is growing at every level. Let's take a quick look at some revealing statistics about debt in the United States.

Credit
A contractual agreement in which a borrower receives something of value now and agrees to repay the lender at some date in the future, generally with interest; the term also refers to the borrowing capacity of an individual or company.

Debt
Something owed to someone else.

The Growth of Consumer Debt

The debt problem in the United States has grown dramatically over the past few decades. Between 1970 and 2010, the median family income in America increased 509 percent in *nominal* terms (before taxes) but only 10 percent in *real* (or purchasing power) terms. During the same time period, total consumer debt per capita increased 1,109 percent in *nominal* terms and 119 percent in *real* terms.

If you want a sobering picture of debt in the United States (and if you like numbers), go to www.usdebtclock.org, which projects debt in the United States in real time.[13] Don't go there if you are susceptible to heart problems, because what you will see is truly heart-stopping! I visited the site on April 2, 2016 at about 10:00 PM, and this is what I saw:

- Total Student Loan Debt: $1,342,118,261,657
- Total Credit Card Debt: $933,030,632,454
- Total Mortgage Debt: $13,898,813,892,145
- Total Personal Debt: $17,464,075,322,093

As I viewed this continually updating screen, I saw the total personal debt increase by thousands of dollars every second. Personal debt is rapidly exceeding 17 *trillion* dollars (a trillion is a million millions). That's a lot! This amount translates into $54,021 of personal debt for each of the 323,281,052 people living in the United States.

The United States national debt is also growing to astronomical proportions. As of April 2, 2016, it was $19,230,732,482,257, which translates into $59,486 for each person in the United States. Fortunately, interest rates on Treasury bills (or T-bills), which finance our debt, are very low right now. The government only pays about $400 billion in interest on the national debt each year.[14] The rest of the world likes to invest in our Treasury bills, helping to finance the debt, because they are so safe and are backed by the "full faith and credit" of the United States. Altogether, foreign governments hold about $6 trillion of our national debt. So if you combine personal debt with the national debt, there is enough debt for more than $113,000 for each person in the United States.

We are truly a nation of debtors—both in Washington, DC and in our own homes. There are many downsides of debt; however, credit can be a blessing if used responsibly. In fact, credit is a necessity for your family's financial health. Let's learn more about why.

Some debt—such as for a modest home, expenses for education, perhaps for a needed first car—may be necessary. But never should we enter into financial bondage through consumer debt without carefully weighing the costs. —Joseph B. Wirthlin

Building good credit is very important for your family because of the need to borrow for legitimate family needs. Church leaders, while generally discouraging debt, have indicated that borrowing is often needed for three things: a modest home, basic transportation, and education. Elder Joseph B. Wirthlin summarized this oft-repeated counsel about debt: "Some debt—such as for a modest home, expenses for education, perhaps for a needed first car—may be necessary. But never should we enter into financial bondage through consumer debt without carefully weighing the costs."[15] Let's now look at five characteristics that lenders look for when you apply for a loan.

The 5 Cs of Credit

In order to use credit, you must meet the criteria of the lender. Lenders often use the following five Cs of credit to judge loan applicants: character, capital, capacity, collateral, and conditions.

Character is demonstrated by your honesty and reliability, your willingness to pay, and your record of financial accountability. When you set up a budget and maintain your household in a business-like manner, you demonstrate your commitment to the integrity of your financial matters. For many lenders, a good reflection of your character is your credit score.

Capital is measured by your assets—housing equity, automobiles, personal property, savings, emergency fund, investments, and life insurance. Lenders will often have you demonstrate your capital with a family net worth statement.

Capacity is your ability to repay the debt from your family's income. This is a measure of your earned income, both present and expected, and a measure of your current debt payments.

Collateral is an asset that can be pledged against the loan (meaning that if you can't pay

Character
The amount of integrity you demonstrate.

Capital
The worth of all your assets.

Capacity
Your ability to repay the debt from your family's income.

Collateral
An asset that can be pledged against a loan.

Conditions

The economic state of the nation or community at the time of a loan request.

Credit score

A three-digit number that is used by banks, insurance companies, and other financial institutions to determine how likely it is that you will be creditworthy and pay your debts on time.

Credit bureaus

Private companies that collect and report your financial information from creditors, public records, and various institutions.

Credit reports

Files of information that credit bureaus compile about specific individuals.

back the loan, this asset is forfeited to pay off the loan). Lenders will be more likely to make a loan for a car than for a Caribbean cruise. However, if you were to pledge a CD (certificate of deposit) against the loan for a cruise, the lender would probably make the loan. If you cannot repay the loan on a car, the lender repossesses the car (the collateral). If you could not pay back the loan for a cruise, the lender cannot take the cruise (you've probably already returned from it anyways), but if you use the CD as collateral, the lender can take the CD. Loans without collateral generally have higher interest rates while loans with collateral have lower interest rates.

The economic **conditions** of the nation or community at the time of the loan request may also affect the lender's loan decisions. If the local economy is in a nosedive and massive layoffs are expected, the lender may not be willing to make a loan—even to a borrower who meets the other four Cs. For example, it was very difficult to get a loan during the great recession of the late 2000s.

Your Credit Score

Maintaining a high credit score is important to your family's financial health. A **credit score** is a three-digit number used by banks, insurance companies, and other financial institutions to determine how likely it is that you will be creditworthy and pay your debts on

time. When you apply for a home mortgage, credit card, car loan, student loan, or automobile insurance, lenders will use your credit score to decide whether or not to loan you the money and what interest rate to charge. When a couple applies for a mortgage, the credit scores of both husband and wife are checked. That's why it is important to include both husband and wife on all credit cards and loans.

Personal financial information that is used to establish your credit score is gathered by credit bureaus. **Credit bureaus** are private companies that collect and report information from creditors, public records, and various institutions. There are many different credit bureaus, but the three major ones are Equifax, Experian, and TransUnion.

Credit reports are files that report the information gathered by credit bureaus. Most individuals who have any type of credit (credit cards, checking accounts, loans, etc.) have a credit report. This report is extremely detailed and contains personal demographics such as

age, social security number, employment history, criminal convictions, and information about your credit history.

Be aware that the information gathered by credit bureaus is not always correct. In fact, almost half of all credit reports contain incorrect or obsolete information. If you are ever denied a line of credit, you can request a free copy of your credit report from each of the credit bureaus. Additionally, you can request a free copy once a year from each of the three major credit reporting agencies by going to annualcreditreport.com.

You should review your credit report annually to ensure its validity. Even simple mistakes can lower your credit score, which may prevent you from getting a mortgage or a consumer loan, or increase the cost of your auto insurance.

If you think there are mistakes on your credit report, you need to have them investigated. If an investigation does not clear up a mark on your credit report, but you still disagree with it, you can add a personal statement of up to 100 words to your credit report explaining what happened with a specific creditor. When you apply for credit, potential lenders can see your explanation of what happened and consider it when they make their lending decisions.

Credit evaluation is the process of turning the information in your credit report into a three-digit number—your credit score. A credit score is like a GPA: it is a specific number that is used to easily group individuals.

Your credit score determines whether or not you deserve to get a loan and what interest rate you will pay on the credit offered. Generally, the higher your credit score, the lower the interest rate you will have to pay.

For example, consider the variance in interest rate on an auto loan for those with varying credit scores:

FICO® score	APR [?]	Monthly payment
720-850	3.399%	$558
690-719	4.572%	$571
660-689	6.308%	$591
620-659	10.865%	$645
590-619	15.320%	$700
500-589	17.173%	$724

What Is a FICO Score?

The most common type of credit score is the **FICO score**. Lenders usually base your interest rate on your FICO score, which can range from 300 to 850. The higher the score, the better. Generally, a score less than 620 is considered poor, between 620 and 679 is fair, 680 to 719 is good, and 720 and above is considered excellent credit. You can purchase a copy of your FICO credit score from www.myfico.com or purchase credit scores from other credit scoring and reporting companies such as Experian, TransUnion, and Equifax. In addition, you can get your credit score for free at www.creditkarma.com and www.mint.com and from a variety of credit card companies.

How Is Your Credit Score Determined?

There are a number of different institutions that calculate credit scores. Since the FICO score is the most common, this chapter will discuss how your credit score is determined based on the FICO scoring methodology.

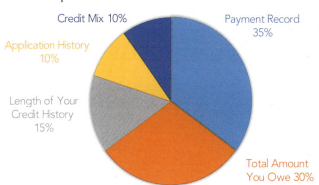

Managing Your Credit Score

You must take an active role in managing your credit score. Ideally, you should review your credit score monthly on a free service like mint.com or creditkarma.com and review your credit reports annually. Do these things more often if you are planning to take out a loan for a house within the next 12 months. By plan-

Credit evaluation

The process of turning the information in your credit report into a three-digit number to determine whether or not you deserve to be given credit.

FICO score

The most common type of credit score.

Table 4.1 Understanding and Manage Your Credit Score

Percentage	Component	Questions to consider	Strategies to improve your credit score
35 percent	Payment record	Do you pay your bills on time?	Pay your bills on time. Paying even one bill late one time will reduce your credit score. Avoid late payments by paying off your credit card the day the bill comes, instead of waiting until the day it is due.
30 percent	Total amount you owe	What percent of your available credit or *credit limit* do you still owe? This is calculated based on the amount owed the day your credit score pulled, even if you pay off your credit cards every month.	Try to borrow less than 15 percent of your available credit limit. Pay off your credit cards several times a month to keep this ratio low. Ask to increase your credit limit on your cards, even if you have no intention of using the higher limits.
15 percent	Length of your credit history	How long have you held a credit account?	It is better to not close credit card accounts. If you don't want to use it anymore, cut up the card but don't close the account. Keeping your oldest accounts open shows you have learned to manage credit over a long period of time. A good rule of thumb is to rotate active use among two or three credit cards at a time.
10 percent	Application history	How many times and how often have you applied for credit?	Do not apply for credit too often but having enough credit is also important. Apply for a new credit card about once every one or two years.
10 percent	Credit mix	Do you have a variety of sources of credit?	You do not want to have too many of the same kind of card (ex. having a Sears' card and a Kohl's card). Cards for retail stores that offer a 10–20% discount on your first purchase can have a negative effect on your credit score.

Always manage your credit score carefully.

ning ahead, you can resolve any inaccuracies on your credit report before you apply for a loan; planning ahead can help you get the highest credit score (and the lowest interest rate) possible.

Avoid careless management of your credit score like the plague.

Credit Scores and Marriage

Elder L. Whitney Clayton said, "Husbands and wives make all decisions about finances together, and both have access to all information."[16] When you apply for credit cards, make your spouse a joint account holder. When you apply for loans, cosign on the loan together. Although spouses have separate credit scores, both will be considered when applying for loans. Because of this, it is very important for both spouses to have a strong credit score.

Credit card
A form of open credit that allows you to borrow money up to a specific limit with no collateral, with the expectation that you will pay back the money at a specific interest rate and with specific terms.

Credit Cards

Obtaining and appropriately using credit cards is an important part of building credit and using it to its full advantage. A **credit card** is a form of open credit that allows you to borrow money up to a specific limit with no collateral. It is expected that you will pay back the money at a specific interest rate and with specific terms. Generally, the interest rate is comparably high because the loan is unsecured by collateral. You are required to make a mini-

mum payment each month but are allowed to carry the balance and pay interest on the balance from month to month.

Most credit cards have a **grace period**. If you pay the balance in full within the grace period, the interest is forgiven. If you do not pay back within the grace period, you are liable for all the interest charged from the moment you made the purchase. The key principle to make credit cards useful for your family is to pay them off before the grace period expires, every month without fail. In fact, we encourage you to pay your credit card bill the day you get it. This helps you avoid interest and actually helps your credit score. The rest of this section will address some important concepts that will help you use a credit card effectively.

Eligibility

To be eligible for a credit card, you must be eighteen or older. If under the age of twenty-one, you must either have a steady income (the wage amount to qualify varies by credit card issuer) or cosign with an individual who is at least twenty-one years old. If you are twenty-one or older, you must either have a steady income or have "reasonable access" to a partner's steady income either through a shared

account or through proof of regular transfers made by the partner to your account. If you are married, both partners should be account holders so that the wise use of the credit card will improve the credit scores of both partners.

Before applying for a credit card, it is recommended that you conduct your own honest self-assessment to gauge whether or not you consider yourself qualified to be a responsible credit card holder. Credit card debt can be devastating to your family's financial health. Remember that although buying on credit means a delayed payment, you still have to pay it off. Furthermore, if you do not pay off your cards on time, you will have to pay the full amount plus large amounts of interest. It is almost always unwise to purchase anything with a credit card that you cannot pay off before the grace period expires. If you need to borrow money, it is better to get a loan with collateral so that you are saved from the high interest rates of credit cards.

Avoid not paying off your credit card balance each month like the plague.

Think of your credit card as a more convenient version of cash: don't spend money you don't have. Pay it off regularly, perhaps the day you get the bill. Keep track of your spending to ensure you stay within your family budget. Using a financial app like mint.com can help you track credit card expenditures in real time. Those who cannot use a credit card in a responsible way should delay obtaining one until they can live by these principles.

Evaluating Credit Cards

Once you have decided that getting a credit card is right for you, you must decide which one will best suit your family.

If you carry a **balance** on your credit card (meaning that you *do not* pay off the balance

Grace period
The period of time between a payment due and penalties.

Always pay off your credit card balance each month.

Balance
The total amount owed on a credit card at a specific time.

Evalutating Credit Cards

The following should be considered when evaluating credit cards:

- Annual fee (ranging from zero to about $95)
- Perks (frequent flyer miles, cash back, etc.)
- Grace period (no interest is charged on new purchases if you pay your bill in full on time each month)
- APR (Interest rate charged on outstanding balances expressed as an annual percentage rate)
- Method of determining the interest rate (i.e. discount rate plus five percentage points, prime rate + 3.75 points, etc.)
- Minimum payment required

Credit limit
The available credit given to a specific account holder.

due each month), you should select a credit card with the lowest possible annual percentage rate. Whether or not the card has a grace period is irrelevant because a grace period only applies if you pay the full balance each month. If you pay your credit card bill in full each month, you should choose a card with a grace period and a low annual fee. The APR is irrelevant because you never carry a balance. Financial websites like creditkarma.com and mint.com provide great resources for evaluating credit cards. Creditcards.com also provides useful information.

A good rule of thumb to maximize your credit score is to not apply for more than one credit card per year. Generally, we recommend having about two or three credit cards in active use at a time. When you stop using a card it is usually better to leave the account open because even though you don't use it, having the credit line open will strengthen your credit score. However, if your card has a large annual fee, it may be better to cancel the card and take a small hit to your credit score.

It is often difficult to obtain your first credit card. If you are denied, you could have a parent cosign for you. You could also get a secured credit card. With this option, you have a low **credit limit** and make a security deposit for the amount of the limit. After you establish a history of paying off your loans, the security deposit is refunded.

Appropriate Card Uses (Benefits and Drawbacks)

Although some popular financial advisors advocate not having a credit card at all, there are several benefits for having at least one credit card.

- *Emergencies*: Credit cards can be useful when you don't have cash on hand and need to pay for something immediately, such as an auto repair or an insurance co-payment.

- *Reservations*: Credit cards can be used to guarantee hotel rooms, rental cars, and other rental items. This is especially important if you travel frequently.

- *Convenience*: With a credit card, you can buy things over the phone or on the Internet. Credit cards make purchasing things very easy. They also provide you with a record of everything you spend, an important bookkeeping benefit.

- *Cash flow and timing*: If something is on sale and you know you have the cash coming in a week, you can actually buy the item before you pay for it. In this way, you can take advantage of sales. (But remember, you do not save money by spending money.)

- *Free services*: Often, credit cards offer rewards such as extended warranties, travel insurance, airplane miles, gasoline rebates, and cash rebates, which can reduce the overall cost of some items.

- *Credit score*: As mentioned previously, buying on credit and paying off your credit cards regularly is important to building a strong credit score. It demonstrates to lenders that you are responsible and capable of paying off loans. Even if you do not have a large budget, making your purchases (groceries, clothing, textbooks, etc.) via credit card will build your credit over time. Then when you go to get a mortgage loan, you will have a lower interest rate because of your good credit score.

There are also some important drawbacks to be aware of when using credit cards.

- *Increased spending:* You may not take as much time to think about how much you are spending when you use a credit card. Research has shown that, on average, people spend more with a credit card than they do with cash—sometimes as much as 100 percent more.[17]

- *Losing track of spending*: It's easy to lose track of what you spend with your credit card. It requires discipline to track the charges you make.

- *Interest and other costs*: Interest charges can range anywhere from 8 percent to 25 percent. In addition to these interest charges, you must take into account compounding periods, annual fees, and other miscellaneous fees, such as cash advance fees and balance transfer fees. Because of these fees, the cost of using credit cards is often double or triple the cost of using other types of loans.

- *Obligations on future income:* Most importantly, when you use credit cards, you put obligations on future income. As you take on more debt, you not only obligate future income but you also limit future flexibility you may need if emergencies arise.

Danger Ahead!

It is vital to handle credit appropriately because credit abuse can very quickly get out of hand. An alcoholic or smoker may think that one drink or one cigarette will not hurt. But soon it is two, then three, then a pack.

Avoid becoming a **credit-holic** *like the plague.*

Elder L. Tom Perry warned:

The current cries we hear coming from the great and spacious building tempt us to compete for ownership in the things of this world. We think we need a larger home, with a three-car garage, a recreational vehicle parked next to it. We long for designer clothes, extra TV sets, all with VCRs, the latest model computers, and the newest car. Often these items are purchased with borrowed money, without giving any thought to providing for our future needs. The result of all this instant gratification is overloaded bankruptcy courts and families that are far too preoccupied with their financial burdens.[18]

Should any of the following danger signals occur, get your financial life together so that you can again be the effective financial steward that the Lord wants you to be.

1. Are total consumer credit payments over 20 percent of your monthly budget?
2. Is an increasing portion of your income going to debt repayment?
3. Are your credit cards at or near their limit?
4. Are you always late on one or more bills?
5. Are you borrowing to pay for things you used to pay for with cash?
6. Have you taken out a new loan to repay an old loan?
7. Is your net worth decreasing?
8. If you lost your job, would you make it for 3–6 months?
9. Are creditors threatening to repossess?

If you responded "yes" to any of the above danger signals, take a moment to consider what you could do today to help yourself get back on track. If not corrected, credit-holic symptoms can quickly spiral out of control, resulting in serious financial consequences for you and your family.

As an additional suggestion, review the above checklist with your spouse and discuss and resolve any problems together. If done in

Credit-holic

Someone who is addicted to credit and whose financial life is out of control.

Avoid becoming a credit-holic like the plague!

a spirit of kindness, this will strengthen your relationship as well as your finances!

If you find yourself becoming addicted to the lure of buying on credit but still want to build your credit score, don't cancel your accounts. Perform "**plastic surgery**" on your credit cards by cutting them up with scissors or running them through the shredder. That way, you won't be using the cards anymore, and keeping your account open will still build your credit score slowly over time.

Plastic surgery
Cutting up a credit card, making it unusable, but still keeping the account open.

Additional Questions to Consider

The following section addresses two questions: What do I do if I lose my credit card? and What is the difference between a credit card and a debit card?

What do I do if I lose my credit card?

You have probably heard horror stories about credit card fraud. Here is some critical information to limit the damage in case your credit cards are lost or stolen.

1. First, inform your credit card company of the loss or theft immediately. You will then have no liability for fraudulent use. It is a good idea to have the toll-free number handy so you know whom to call. They will immediately cancel the cards you have and re-issue new cards, often sending the replacement cards the next day.

2. If your credit cards were stolen, immediately file a police report in the jurisdiction where the theft occurred. This proves to credit providers that you were diligent, and it is a first step toward a possible investigation.

3. Most importantly, call the three national credit reporting organizations (Equifax, Experian, and TransUnion) immediately to place a fraud alert on your name and social security number. This alert notifies any company checking your credit that your credit cards were stolen, and they have to contact you by phone to authorize new credit.

What is the difference between a credit card and a debit card?

When you use a credit card you create a loan that will be paid off later, preferably before the grace period expires. Money actually leaves your account weeks after you make credit card purchases. When you use a debit card the money for the transaction is withdrawn immediately from your bank account. In this way, debit cards are like checks—you must have sufficient money in your account when you use a debit card, or else the transaction may be declined. Debit cards can also be used to withdraw cash at network ATMs without fees (in the United States). When you use a credit card to withdraw cash out of an ATM you may incur substantial fees. Debit cards

offer less protection in case of fraud than credit cards and usually do not offer reward points.

Consumer Loans

A **consumer loan** is "an amount of money lent to an individual (usually on a non-secured basis) for personal, family, or household purposes. Consumer loans are monitored by government regulatory agencies for their compliance with consumer protection regulations such as the Truth in Lending Act."[19] It is called a "consumer loan" because that which is purchased decreases in value and is eventually consumed. Such items include electronics, automobiles, furniture, and recreational vehicles. Consumer loans are expensive, with high interest rates, and should rarely be used. These loans encourage you to buy now rather than to save for the future.

Committing future earnings to today's consumption may keep you from achieving more important long-term personal goals. Consumer loans also reduce the amount of money your family can save for your goals because they require you to pay interest with money you might otherwise have saved and invested. Most importantly, consumer loans are almost always unnecessary.

If you find yourself tempted to obtain a consumer loan to buy a new dining room table or bedroom set or ski boat or something else, ask yourself the following questions:

1. Do we really need to make this purchase? Is this a need or a want? Separate these two categories. Consumer loans should not be used to finance wants. In rare occasions it may be appropriate to use consumer loans to finance needs. A ski boat is not a need.

2. Is this item in our budget or in our financial plan? Could we wait, sacrifice, save, and buy this item in the future without borrowing money? You should save rather than borrow to buy most items.

3. What is the total cost of this item if financed by a consumer loan (including fees and interest)? What is the difference in cost between buying this item with cash and buying this item on credit with high interest? Compare these two alternatives.

4. What would be the impact of this purchase on our other goals? Can we maintain sufficient liquidity and still achieve our other goals? Choose wisely.

5. Will this purchase bring us closer to our family goals or take us further away from them? If the purchase brings you closer to your goals, including your goal of obedience to God's commandments (such as the commandment to minimize and eventually eliminate debt), make the purchase. If the purchase takes you further away from your family goals, don't make it.

If you answer these questions honestly, it will be much easier to determine whether you should take out a consumer loan or not. Usually, the answer is not.

Different Types of Consumer Loans

It is important to understand that there are different types of consumer loans which have different characteristics. Some of the different types of loans include single-payment and installment loans, secured and unsecured loans, variable-rate and fixed-rate loans, and convertible loans.

Single-payment loans are also known as

Consumer loans

An amount of money lent to an individual for personal, family, or household purposes.

Single-payment loans

A type of short-term lending repaid in one lump sum that may be used to temporarily finance a purchase until permanent, long-term financing can be arranged.

Chapter 4: Credit and Loans

Installment loans
Loans that are repaid at regular intervals.

Secured loans
Loans which use one of your assets as collateral to guarantee that the lending institution will get the amount of the loan back even if you fail to make payments.

Unsecured loans
Loans which do not require collateral and are generally offered only to borrowers with excellent credit histories.

Fixed-rate loans
Loans that maintain the same interest rate for the duration of the loan.

Variable-rate loans
Loans which have an interest rate that is adjusted at different intervals over the life of the loan.

Convertible loans
Loans in which the interest-rate structure can change.

Loan contract
A document which describes what the lender requires of your family once you are granted the loan.

balloon loans. Normally, these loans are used for short-term lending of one year or less. They may also be used to temporarily finance a purchase until more permanent, long-term financing can be arranged; this is why these loans are also sometimes called bridge or interim loans. This type of loan is repaid in one lump sum, including interest, at the end of the specified term—for example, at the end of one year.

Installment loans are loans that are repaid at regular intervals—for example, every month. Each payment includes part of the principal and some interest. An installment loan amortizes over the length of the loan, which means that with each monthly payment you make, more of your payment goes toward paying off the principal and less goes toward paying for interest. Installment loans are typically used to finance purchases of cars, boats, appliances, furniture and other expensive items.

Secured loans use one of your assets, such as a car or boat, as collateral to guarantee that the lending institution will get the amount of the loan back even if you fail to make payments.

Because these loans are backed by collateral, they usually have lower interest rates. However, they are also very risky to you because you are in danger of losing whatever you put up as collateral, like your car.

Unsecured loans, also known as signature loans, do not require collateral and are generally offered only to borrowers with excellent credit histories. Unsecured loans typically have higher interest rates, which may range between 12 percent and 26 percent—sometimes even higher.

Fixed-rate loans maintain the same interest rate for the duration of the loan. The majority of consumer loans are fixed-rate loans. Usually lenders charge higher interest rates for fixed-rate loans than they do for variable-rate loans because lenders can lose money if market interest rates increase, leaving the loan rate lower than the current market interest rate.

Variable-rate loans have an interest rate that is adjusted at different intervals over the life of the loan. There is usually a maximum interest rate (or cap) that can be charged on the loan, as well as a maximum amount that the interest rate can increase each year. These interest rates may change monthly, semiannually, or annually. The interest rate is adjusted based on an index, such as the prime rate or the six-month Treasury bill, as well as on an interest-rate spread.

Lenders usually charge a lower interest rate up front for variable-rate loans because the lender will not lose money if the overall market interest rates increase.

Convertible loans are loans in which the interest-rate structure can change. For example, a convertible loan may start off having a variable interest rate and then switch to having a fixed interest rate at some predetermined time in the future; the opposite process may occur as well.

The Loan Contract

The **loan contract** is the most critical document of the loan process. It describes what the lender requires of your family once you are granted the loan. Whenever you borrow, you put your family's future into someone else's hands; therefore, you need to know what you are doing. Read the entire contract and make sure you fully understand the details of the loan before you sign the loan agreement. Remember that there is no pre-payment penalty for paying off the loan early.

Truth in Lending Act

The federal Consumer Credit Protection Act, or the **Truth in Lending Act**, requires that all lenders provide the consumer with certain information before they sign the credit contract. This information must be conspicuously displayed and contain two important pieces of information relative to the cost of the credit: the total *finance charge* expressed in dollars and the *annual percentage rate* of interest (APR). The Truth in Lending Act also states that lenders cannot require you to purchase credit life insurance from them. They can, however, require that you have life insurance to insure the payment of your loan in the event of your death.

Other Types of Loans

There are a number of special types of loans that are different from traditional consumer loans. We will cover mortgage loans and home equity loans in Chapter 7. Other common types of loans include student loans, automobile loans, payday loans, and family loans.

Student loans are often used to pay for higher education and have low, federally subsidized interest rates. Examples of federal student loans that are available to parents and students include federal-direct loans, plus-direct loans, Stafford loans, and Stafford-plus loans. One benefit of federal student loans is that some have specific advantages, such as subsidized interest payments and lower interest rates. Also, you can defer payment of federal-direct loans and Stafford loans until six months after you graduate or discontinue full-time enrollment. The disadvantages of these loans are that there is a limit to how much you can borrow and, like all debts, you must pay these loans back.

Automobile loans are secured by the automobile the loan is paying for. This type of loan usually has a term of two to six years. The advantage of an automobile loan is that it usually charges a lower interest rate than an unsecured loan. The disadvantage is that you must make interest payments, and since vehicles depreciate quickly, your family is often left with a vehicle that is worth less than what you

owe on the loan.

Payday loans are short-term loans of one or two weeks and are secured with a postdated check. The postdated check is held by the payday lender and cashed on the day specified. These loans charge very high interest rates—some payday loans charge more than 500 percent on an annual percentage rate basis (APR). Let's just repeat that: 500 percent interest!

Avoid payday loans like the plague.

Family loans are generally the least expensive loans. You should be very carefully in deciding to borrow from or loan to a family member. Many relationships suffer when such loans are made and then not paid back. If you choose to loan to or borrow from a family member, we suggest you write up a contract and have both parties sign a legal document.

To summarize, consumer loans are often unnecessary and unwise. When it comes to dealing with debt, remember Elder L. Tom Perry's counsel: "Avoid excessive debt. Necessary debt should be incurred only after careful, thoughtful prayer and after obtaining the best possible advice. We need the discipline to stay well within our ability to pay. Wisely we have been counseled to avoid debt as we would avoid the plague."[20] If we are to follow the counsel of prophets and apostles, then we should avoid the bondage of consumer debt.

Truth in Lending Act

A law which requires that all lenders provide the consumer with certain information before they sign the credit contract.

Student loans

Loans which are often used to pay for higher education and have federally subsidized interest rates.

 Avoid payday loans like the plague!

Automobile loans

Short-term loans that are secured by the automobile the loan is paying for.

Payday loans

Short-term loans of one or two weeks which are secured with a postdated check.

Family loans

Borrowing and lending between family members.

A Matter of Marshmallows

Our struggle with waiting to purchase what we want until we have the money is key to developing the virtue of patience, which affects our success in this life and the next. President Dieter F. Uchtdorf tells the following story:

> In the 1960s, a professor at Stanford University began a modest experiment testing the willpower of four-year-old children. He placed before them a large marshmallow and then told them they could eat it right away or, if they waited for fifteen minutes, they could have two marshmallows.
>
> He then left the children alone and watched what happened behind a two-way mirror. Some of the children ate the marshmallow immediately; some could wait only a few minutes before giving in to temptation. Only 30 percent were able to wait.
>
> It was a mildly interesting experiment, and the professor moved on to other areas of research, for, in his own words, "there are only so many things you can do with kids trying not to eat marshmallows." But as time went on, he kept track of the children and began to notice an interesting correlation: the children who could not wait struggled later in life and had more behavioral problems, while those who waited tended to be more positive and better motivated, have higher grades and incomes, and have healthier relationships.
>
> What started as a simple experiment with children and marshmallows became a landmark study suggesting that the ability to wait—to be patient—was a key character trait that might predict later success in life.[21]

Debt Elimination

Debt-elimination calendar

A debt-elimination strategy in which you plan out all debt repayments, paying all minimum payments but focusing mostly on one until it is paid off, then using the amount of money previously paid toward that debt to pay off the next most important debt.

Prophets have counseled us to minimize and eventually eliminate debt. President Joseph F. Smith advised, "Get out of debt and keep out of debt, and then you will be financially as well as spiritually free."[22] This section will teach you two debt elimination strategies. As you study these strategies, recognize that the Lord wants your family to be both financially and spiritually free. He will help you in your debt elimination process. Ponder these words of the Lord:

> And if men come unto me I will show unto them their weakness. I give unto men weakness that they may be humble; and my grace is sufficient for all men that humble themselves before me; for if they humble themselves before me, and have faith in me, then will I make weak things become strong unto them.[23]

What if your family is already in debt? Is there a process that can help you get out? Thankfully, there is. The following process is essential for debt-reduction:

1. Recognize and accept that you have a debt problem.

2. Stop incurring debt. Don't buy anything else on credit. Be especially careful about using home equity to pay down debts until you have your spending under control. In the words of Will Rogers, "If you find yourself in a hole, stop digging."[24]

3. Make a list of all your debts.

4. Look for many different ways of reducing debt, not just one. Examples might include consolidating balances to a lower interest rate credit card, having a yard sale to earn money to pay down debt, or using savings to reduce debt.

5. Organize a repayment or debt-reduction strategy, such as a **debt-elimination calendar**, and follow it.

Debt-Elimination Calendar: Most Expensive Debt First

In his article "One for the Money," Marvin J. Ashton discusses his debt-elimination strategy.[25] His logic is that you should organize your debts and pay off your most expensive ones first. This can refer to either the largest debt or the one with the highest interest rate.

He recommends that you set up a spreadsheet or ledger with a row for every month you will be making payments on your debts and a column for each creditor. (See *Table 4.2*.) You start by paying off the debt with the highest interest rate; this way, you are paying off your most expensive debt first, which will save you the most money. Once your most expensive debt is paid off, continue applying the same total amount of money to other lines of credit until all of your debts are paid off.

After you have paid off one debt, you must keep paying the same amount of money but use that additional money to pay off the next most important debt. Then, once you have paid off all your debts, you can continue paying yourself in a way that is consistent with your family goals.

Debt-Elimination Calendar: Smallest Debt First

Dave Ramsey, among others, recommends that you pay off your smallest debt first.[26] With this approach, you see success as debts are

Table 4.2 Example Debt-Elimination Calendar ($600/month allocated to debt repayment)

	Credit Card	Auto Loan	Student Loan	Total Payment
Interest Rate	18%	8%	5%	
Amount Owed	$2,000	$4,400	$3,600	$10,000
Minimum Payment	$20	$200	$100	$320
July	$300	$200	$100	$600
August	$300	$200	$100	$600
September	$300	$200	$100	$600
October	$300	$200	$100	$600
November	$300	$200	$100	$600
December	$300	$200	$100	$600
January	$200 (paid off)	$300	$100	$600
February		$500	$100	$600
March		$500	$100	$600
April		$500	$100	$600
May		$500	$100	$600
June		$500	$100	$600
July		$400 (paid off)	$200	$600
August			$600	$600
September			$600	$600
October			$600	$600
November			$400 (paid off)	$400
December				$600 (invested!)

eliminated, which gives you more motivation to continue repaying your debts.

Either of these two methods can be helpful in eliminating debt. Most of the time, the difference is not significant, and either method will accomplish the same objective. The key is to act now.

Summary

In this chapter we have learned that minimizing and eventually eliminating debt brings peace of mind and strengthens family relationships. We have learned that credit helps your family buy a modest home and, in some cases, finance an education and transportation. The key to borrowing for these needs is to make sure that you have sufficient available income to make the required payments without undue stress.

We also learned that it is important to build your credit score in order to qualify for and receive low interest rates on home mortgages, car loans, and automobile insurance. To improve your credit score, it is important that you pay all of your bills and make all of your loan payments on time. It is also useful to open up a number of credit lines, even if you do not use them.

Credit cards are a convenience and can help your credit score to grow. Because their interest rates are so high, you must pay off the balance on each credit card monthly before the grace period expires. For this reason, it is best to use no more than two or three credit cards at a time. If you find yourself with lots of credit card debt, perform plastic surgery. In other words, shred the cards and operate on a cash spending basis instead.

We learned that consumer loans should usually be avoided. It is much better to save and sacrifice until you have the money to purchase wants. For needs, it is better to have a loan that is secured with collateral.

If you do incur debt, use an effective debt-elimination strategy to release your family from this bondage. Be consistent and diligent in paying off debts.

As a final note, we heartily agree with Elder Robert D. Hales, who taught that "We must practice the principles of provident living: joyfully living within our means, being content with what we have, avoiding excessive debt, and diligently saving and preparing for rainy-day emergencies."[27] May you be blessed as you exercise patience to minimize and eventually eliminate your family's debt.

Other Resources

- www.annualcreditreport.com
- www.creditcards.com
- www.creditkarma.com
- www.mint.com
- www.myfico.com
- www.usdebtclock.org
- Saturday Night Live sketch: "Don't Buy Stuff You Cannot Afford"
- http://www.nbc.com/saturday-night-live/video/dont-buy-stuff/n12020

Notes

1. Robert D. Hales, "Becoming Provident Providers Temporally and Spiritually", (April 2009), https://www.lds.org/general-conference/2009/04/becoming-provident-providers-temporally-and-spiritually?lang=eng.
2. J. Reuben Clark, Jr., *Conference Report*, (Salt Lake City: The Church of Jesus Christ of Latter-day Saints, 1938), 102–109. https://archive.org/details/conferencereport1938a.
3. Ivan F. Beutler, Clinton G. Gudmunson, E.Jeffrey Hill, Craig L. Israelsen, and J. Kelly McCoy, "Linking Financial Strain to Marital Instability: Examining the Roles of Emotional Distress and Marital Interaction," *Journal of Family and Economic Issues* 28, no. 3 (2007): 357–76.
4. Sonya Britt, Jeffrey Dew, and Sandra Huston, "Examining the Relationship Between Financial Issues and Divorce," *Family Relations* 61, no.4 (October 2012): 615–28.
5. Marvin J. Ashton, "One for the money," (September 2007), https://www.lds.org/ensign/2007/09/one-for-the-money?lang=eng.
6. Bernard E. Poduska, *Till Debt Do Us Part: Balancing Finances, Feelings, and Family*. (Salt Lake City, UT: Deseret Book Company, 2000).
7. Dieter F. Uchtdorf, "Continue in Patience," (May 2010), https://www.lds.org/ensign/2010/05/continue-in-patience?lang=eng.
8. Julie A. Dockstader, "'That noble gift: love at home,'" *Church News: The Church of Jesus Christ of Latter-day Saints* (May 2001), http://www.ldschurchnewsarchive.com/articles/39860/That-noble-gift---love-at-home.html.
9. Gordon B. Hinckley, "'Thou Shalt Not Covet,'" (March 1990), https://www.lds.org/ensign/1990/03/thou-shalt-not-covet?lang=eng.
10. Ezra Taft Benson, "Prepare for the Days of Tribulation", (Oct. 1980), https://www.lds.org/ensign/1980/11/prepare-for-the-days-of-tribulation?lang=eng.
11. W. Eugene Hansen, "The Search for Happiness," (Oct. 1993), https://www.lds.org/general-conference/1993/10/the-search-for-happiness?lang=eng.
12. http://www.investopedia.com/terms/c/credit.asp.
13. http://www.usdebtclock.org/.
14. https://www.treasurydirect.gov/govt/reports/ir/ir_expense.htm.
15. Joseph B. Wirthlin, "Earthly Debts, Heavenly Debts," (May 2004), https://www.lds.org/ensign/2004/05/earthly-debts-heavenly-debts.p1?lang=eng.
16. L. Whitney Clayton, "Marriage: Watch and Learn," (May 2013), https://www.lds.org/ensign/2013/05/marriage-watch-and-learn?lang=eng.
17. http://www.moneycrashers.com/you-spend-more-money-when-you-use-a-credit-card/.
18. L. Tom Perry, "'If Ye Are Prepared Ye Shall Not Fear,'" (Oct. 1995), https://www.lds.org/ensign/1995/11/if-ye-are-prepared-ye-shall-not-fear?lang=eng.
19. http://www.businessdictionary.com/definition/consumer-loan.html.
20. L. Tom Perry, "'If Ye Are Prepared Ye Shall Not Fear,'" (Oct. 1995), https://www.lds.org/ensign/1995/11/if-ye-are-prepared-ye-shall-not-fear?lang=eng.
21. Dieter F. Uchtdorf, "Continue in Patience," (May 2010), https://www.lds.org/ensign/2010/05/continue-in-patience?lang=eng
22. Joseph F. Smith, *Conference Report,* (Oct. 1903), 5. https://archive.org/details/conferencereport1903sa.
23. Ether 12:27.
24. http://www.parks.ca.gov/?page_id=23998.
25. Marvin J. Ashton, "One for the money," (September 2007), https://www.lds.org/ensign/2007/09/one-for-the-money?lang=eng.
26. http://www.daveramsey.com/blog/get-out-of-debt-with-the-debt-snowball-plan/.
27. Robert D. Hales, "Becoming Provident Providers Temporally and Spiritually", (April 2009), https://www.lds.org/general-conference/2009/04/becoming-provident-providers-temporally-and-spiritually?lang=eng.

5 Tax Planning

Keeping More of the Income Your Family Makes

LEARN

- About different types of taxes and understand how they affect your family
- How to correctly calculate your family's federal income tax
- How to implement tax strategies to save your family money
- What resources can help you prepare and file your family's taxes

Let me confess to you the biggest financial mistake I have ever made. It is pertinent to this chapter because the reason for this mistake was that I did not understand the basics of the United States income tax system, and I did not keep up with changes to that system. It is my hope that this chapter will help you avoid mistakes like this.

Juanita and I began saving 10 percent of my income from IBM in a Traditional 401(k) early on in my career, investing it in a diversified, primarily stock-based mutual fund. I was delighted that my contributions reduced my income, which also reduced the amount of income tax I paid every year. Also, the tax on the gains in this account was delayed until retirement.

About twenty years ago, I did not pay attention when the Roth 401(k) was introduced. This would have allowed me to invest in a retirement account with after-tax dollars, keeping the principal and the earnings tax free forever.

Last year, I was so excited that I could start withdrawing money from my Traditional 401(k) without penalty. Imagine my disappointment when I withdrew my first $30,000 and found that I owed more than $10,000 in federal income taxes. And then I realized how foolish I had been. Had I invested my retirement in a Roth 401(k) instead of a Traditional 401(k), the $30,000 would have been tax-free. I was shocked to realize that, although I had only saved about 10 percent in taxes on my contributions, I would now have to pay about 30 percent on everything I withdrew.

We'll talk about this more in Chapter 8, but the bottom line is that because of the tax consequences of my decision to invest in a Traditional instead of a Roth 401(k), I will have hundreds of thousands of dollars less to spend in retirement.

All of this could have been avoided had I internalized the content of this chapter. I invite you to pay attention in this chapter about taxes!

Tax Freedom Day
The day of the year on which you have earned enough money to pay for all of your taxes for that year.

The Importance of Taxes

Benjamin Franklin wrote, "In this world nothing can be said to be certain, except death and taxes."[1] Given that taxes are certain, it is also certain that you must have at least a basic understanding of the tax structure in order to be a wise financial steward for your family. Paying unnecessary taxes reduces the amount of money you have for your family's necessary expenditures. Your objective should be to legally minimize the amount of money you pay in taxes in order to maximize resources you have left for your financial stewardship.

Informed tax planning is important because taxes are the largest single annual expense for most families. In fact, the average American spends more on taxes than on food, clothing, and medical care combined.[2] The day on which families stop earning money for the government and start earning money for themselves is known as **"Tax Freedom Day."** In 2015, that day fell on April 24, meaning that Americans needed to work 114 days to cover the costs of their federal, state, and local taxes. Tax Freedom Day has steadily moved forward since 2009, when it was April 8.[3]

The present federal income tax system in the United States was established in 1913 with the passage of the Sixteenth Amendment to the Constitution. This amendment gave Congress the power to impose an income tax. When this tax was first established, only about one percent of the population had to pay income taxes. Since that time, tax laws have changed dramatically. Currently, about 57 percent of the population pay income taxes.[4] Paying taxes has become one of the most complex procedures citizens must go through to fulfill their civic responsibilities.

Regarding taxes and the other laws of the land, the Lord has stated, "Let no man break the laws of the land, for he that keepeth the laws of God hath no need to break the laws of the land. Wherefore be subject to the powers that be, until he reigns whose right it is to reign and subdues all enemies under his feet."[5] He also wisely said, "Render therefore unto Caesar the things which are Caesar's; and unto God the things that are God's."[6]

Whether we like it or not, taxes are a fact of life. Taxes are also a critical part of any financial plan; it is important that you understand and plan for them so that you can achieve your family goals. We should all obey the laws of the land, including the laws that require us to pay taxes. However, we should learn to be wise stewards so that we pay all the taxes we legally owe—and not a penny more.

Income taxes are essential to pay for the services that the federal government provides.

These services include defense and international security assistance; Medicare, Medicaid, and CHIP; Social Security; transportation infrastructure; safety net programs; benefits for federal retirees and veterans; science and medical research; education; and interest on the debt.

The revenues government receives are less than the amount the government spends. When government engages in deficit spending it must choose to raise taxes, lower expenditures, or borrow more money. Typically, the answer has been to borrow more money, adding to the national debt. Since 1965 the government has run a deficit 45 out of 50 years. The only years of surplus were 1969 and 1998–2001.[7]

The primary way that the United States finances its debt is by selling treasury bills and bonds. These are purchased by individuals, companies, investment firms, even countries. You can purchase a treasury bill by going to www.treasurydirect.gov. As of April 2, 2016, the national debt in the United States was $19.2 trillion. Of that amount, $6.1 trillion is held by foreign countries.[8]

Types of Taxes

Before we learn more about how taxes work, let's learn about some of the most common types of taxes in the United States.

Taxes on Purchases

- **Sales taxes** are percentage taxes applied to the purchase price of taxable goods. Sales tax rates are set by state and local governments. There is no national sales tax.
- **Excise (or quantity) taxes** are levied against certain specific products or services (such as fuel, liquors, and cigarettes) on a per unit basis.

Taxes on Property

- **Property taxes** are levied against the assessed value of land and buildings. Property taxes have traditionally been used to support public schools.
- **Personal property taxes** are levied by states on certain personal assets such as vehicles, farm equipment, cattle, recreational vehicles, etc.

Taxes on Wealth

- **Estate (and gift) taxes** are collected by the federal government on the value of a person's estate upon their death if the estate is sufficiently large.
- Similarly, **inheritance taxes** on money and property received by heirs are collected by many states.

Sales taxes
A percentage tax applied to the purchase price of taxable goods.

Excise taxes
A tax levied against certain specific products or services (such as fuel, liquors, and cigarettes) on a per unit basis.

Property taxes
A tax levied against the assessed value of land and buildings.

Personal property taxes
A state and local tax against certain personal assets.

Estate taxes
A tax charged on the value of a person's estate upon his or her death if the estate is sufficiently large.

Inheritance taxes
A tax on money and property received by heirs.

TAXES ON EARNINGS

- **Social Security** and **income taxes** are levied against the earnings of workers.

Calculating Your Federal Income Tax

Almost every independent person with an income of more than $10,300 per year in the United States is required to file a federal income tax form. If your parents claim you as a dependent, you are required to file if you make more than $6,300 per year. However, you *can* file at any income level, and you *must* file if you want income tax withholdings to be refunded to you.

Since the federal income tax is so ubiquitous, we will spend some time explaining the basic parts of filing your return. It is important to note that in 2015 the income tax code is incredibly complex and contains 73,954 pages.[9] Just to read the code would require several decades of a 40-hour work week. That said, we will focus on the basics and help you learn how to calculate your family's federal income tax. For something so complicated, calculating your federal income tax is as easy as 1-2-3-4. It consists of finding four simple answers to four basic math problems:

```
  Gross Income
– Adjustments to Income
= Adjusted Gross Income (1)

– Deductions
– Personal Exemptions
= Taxable Income (2)

× Tax Rate(s)
= Tax Liability (3)

– Tax Credits
– Federal Taxes Already Withheld
= Tax Due or Tax Refund (4)
```

Let's go through these steps one by one.

Step 1:

Calculate Your Family's Adjusted Gross Income

To do this, you will subtract your adjustments to income from your gross income.

```
  Gross Income
– Adjustments to Income
= Adjusted Gross Income
```

To put it simply, gross income is all of your income. In other words, it is what you were paid during that tax year. If you are married and filing jointly, it is the combined income of you and your spouse. Now we will give you just enough specificity to highlight how complex this can actually be.

Gross income comprises income from all sources except that which is allowed to be specifically excluded or deferred by the IRS. It includes active income (wages, tips, salaries, commissions, and income from businesses in which you actively participate);[10]

Social Security taxes

A tax levied against the earnings of workers to fund the Social Security system.

Income taxes

A tax levied directly against the earnings of workers; this tax is one of the main sources of government funds.

passive income (earnings from a rental property, limited partnership, or other enterprise in which you are not actively involved);[11] and investment income (earnings from interest, dividends, and capital gains from securities). Gross income also includes alimony received, business income, distributions from taxable individual retirement accounts (such as Traditional IRAs and Traditional 401(k) plans), tax refunds from the previous year (but only if the excess was deducted in the previous year), royalties, farm income, unemployment compensations, taxable Social Security benefits, and any other income not specifically excluded by the IRS.

Occasionally, the IRS allows certain sources of income to be excluded from your gross income. These waived amounts are called exclusions to income. They include certain employer-provided fringe benefits, life insurance compensation received because of a death, scholarships or grants not in excess of college expenses, interest on US Series I or EE savings bonds (when the principal and interest from these bonds have been used for qualified educational expenses), municipal bond interest, inheritances (up to a specific amount), alimony paid, and some welfare benefits. In addition, gross income does not include distributions from Roth IRA or Roth 401(k) retirement accounts.

Once you know your gross income, subtract your adjustments to income. Common adjustments include contributions to Traditional IRAs and Traditional 401(k) plans, interest payments on student loans, and tuition and fees deductions. Other less common adjustments include contributions to flexible spending plans or health savings accounts (where money for medical expenses is paid before tax), and deductions for one-half of the self-employment tax. As your adjusted gross income increases beyond a specific amount, certain adjustments to your income are phased out or eliminated. Such adjustments affect those making a substantial income.

Your gross income minus these adjustments gives you your **Adjusted Gross Income**

Gross Income

Gross income includes the following:

- Active income
  - Wages
  - Tips
  - Salaries
  - Commissions
  - Income from businesses in which you actively participate
- Passive income
  - Earnings from a rental property
  - Earnings from a limited partnership
  - Earnings from enterprises in which you passively participate
- Alimony received
- Business income
- Distributions from taxable individual retirement accounts
- Tax refunds from the previous year (if the excess was deducted in the previous year)
- Royalties
- Farm income
- Unemployment compensations
- Taxable Social Security benefits
- Other income not specifically excluded by the IRS

Exclusions to income include the following:

- Employer-provided fringe benefits
- Life insurance compensation received because of a death
- Scholarships or grants not in excess of college expense
- Interest on US Series I or EE savings bonds (when the principal and interest from these bonds have been used for qualified educational expenses)
- Municipal bond interest, inheritances (up to a specific amount)
- Alimony paid
- Some welfare benefits
- Distributions from Roth IRA or Roth 401(k) retirement accounts

Adjustments to income include the following:

- Contributions to Traditional IRAs and Traditional 401(k) plans
- Interest payments on student loans, and tuition and fees deductions
- Contributions to flexible spending plans or health savings accounts (where money for medical expenses is paid before tax)
- Deductions for one-half of the self-employment tax

(**AGI**). You have now successfully completed Step 1. Way to go!

Step 2:

Calculate Your Family's Taxable Income

Once you know your family's AGI, the next step is to determine your deductions. **Deductions** are IRS-allowed reductions to your AGI that are used to reduce your taxable income. You must choose between two different ways to determine deductions. The first type of deduction is the **standard deduction**; this is determined by the government. The other type is the **itemized deduction**; you must calculate this yourself. It is important for you to understand what can and cannot be deducted because every deduction reduces the tax you must pay, allowing you to keep more money and achieve your family goals.

```
  Gross Income
- Adjustments to Income
= Adjusted Gross Income

- Deductions
- Personal Exemptions
= Taxable Income
```

The first method of calculating deductions is to let the government calculate them for you via the "standard deduction." Each year, the government determines this figure based on an estimate of what the average family would be able to deduct by itemizing. The standard deduction amount varies depending on your filing status: the amount will be different

Adjusted Gross Income (AGI)

The first step of calculating your federal income tax, determined by subtracting your adjustments to income from your gross income.

Deductions

IRS-allowed reductions to your adjusted gross income that are used to calculate taxable income.

Standard deduction

The dollar amount set by the government that any tax filer may use as a reduction to AGI; the amount differs depending on filing status.

Itemized deduction

The sum of the possible deductions from AGI that you qualify for.

Filing Status

1. Single: Generally, if you are unmarried, divorced, or legally separated, your filing status is single.
2. Married filing jointly: If you are married, you and your spouse may file a joint return. This is usually advantageous when one spouse makes much more than the other spouse.
3. Married filing separately: Married taxpayers may elect to file separate returns. This is usually advantageous when both marriage partners make significant incomes.
4. Head of household: If you are unmarried and paid more than half the cost of maintaining a home for you and a qualifying person during the year you are filing for, you may file as head of household.

depending on whether you are single, married filing jointly, married filing separately, or head of household. Your marital status on the last day of the year determines your status for the entire year.

Standard Deductions

Filing Status	Standard Deduction (2015)
Single	$6,300
Married filing jointly	$12,600
Married filing separately	$6,300
Head of household	$9,250

The second method for determining deductions is for the taxpayer to itemize all the deductions he or she can legally take. The government allows taxpayers to deduct certain expenses it deems important from a taxpayer's income. There are myriad possible deductions, but the five most common are home mortgage interest, charitable donations, state and local income taxes paid, real estate taxes paid, and medical and dental expenses.

Home mortgage interest. Because the government wants to encourage home ownership, you can deduct from your income what you pay in interest for any loan secured by your main home or a second home. This could include a primary mortgage, a second mortgage, a home equity loan, or a line of credit secured by your home. You will usually get a 1098 form from your lender to document the amount of interest you paid during the year.

Charitable donations. What you donate to qualified charitable or nonprofit organizations is tax deductible. The Church of Jesus Christ of Latter-day Saints qualifies, so everything you contribute in tithing or other offerings is fully deductible. You cannot deduct money if you got something of material value for the contribution. That means you cannot deduct money you paid in the "Other" category for things like girls' camp and Scout camp. The ward financial clerk will give you a receipt in January of all of your cash contributions, or you can get a receipt anytime at lds.org/donations. You can also deduct the fair market value of property donated to these organizations. This means you can deduct the fair market value of donations made to Deseret Industries. Be sure to ask for and fill out a receipt to indicate the donation and the fair market value of the donation.

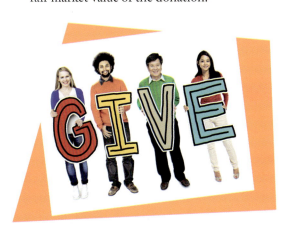

Income taxes paid. You may deduct any state and local income taxes that you paid during the tax year. The state or local government will provide you with a statement of the taxes paid. You may not deduct the federal income taxes that you paid, nor employment taxes such as Social Security and Medicare.

Real estate taxes paid. You may deduct real estate taxes on your home or any piece of property that you own. The taxes must be based on assessed valuation. For those with a mortgage, real estate taxes are often reported by the lender in the 1098 form that is provided to document interest expense.

Medical and dental expenses. The government allows deductions for medical and dental expenses that exceed 10 percent of your AGI. For example, if your AGI is $50,000, you can only deduct medical expenses that are more than $5,000 (50,000 × .10). Be sure to document your expenses with receipts.

Your challenge as a taxpayer is to determine whether your itemized deductions are greater than the government's standard deduction. If the total of your itemized deductions is less than the government's standard deduction, then it is to your advantage to take the standard deduction. Once you understand the tax system, you can utilize the deductions that minimize your tax payments and maximize the amount that is left over for your personal and family goals. We'll talk more about tax strategies later.

After you have subtracted your deductions to income (whether standard or itemized), subtract your personal exemptions. An exemption is a government-determined amount for each person who is supported by the income—you, your spouse, and any dependents. Dependents must be under nineteen for the full tax year (with the exception of students, who must be under twenty-four), and disabled persons. Children who file taxes themselves must not

Chapter 5: Tax Planning

Personal exemption
A specific amount of money that can be deducted from AGI for each qualifying person in the household.

Taxable income
The second step of calculating your federal income tax, determined by subtracting your deductions and exemptions from your AGI.

Tax liability
The third step of calculating your federal income tax, determined by multiplying your taxable income by government-set tax rate(s).

Marginal tax rate
The rate at which the next dollar earned is taxed.

Tax due/Tax refund
The final step of calculating your federal income tax, determined by subtracting tax credits from your tax liability.

Tax credits
Dollar-for-dollar reductions from your tax liability.

claim the personal exemption for themselves if they are to be claimed as dependents by their parents. A **personal exemption** is a specific amount of money that can be deducted for each qualifying person in the household. In 2015, the personal exemption was $4,000. That means that a couple with three children could subtract $20,000 ($4,000 × 5) from their AGI for personal exemptions.

Subtract your deductions and exemptions from your AGI. The resulting total is your **taxable income**. Congratulations! You have now completed step 2.

Step 3:
Calculate Your Family's Tax Liability

Once you have determined your taxable income, you can calculate your **tax liability**.

```
    Gross Income
  – Adjustments to Income
  = Adjusted Gross Income

  – Deductions
  – Personal Exemptions
  = Taxable Income

  × Tax Rate(s)
  = Tax Liability
```

This is done using the IRS tax tables for the current year. Find the table and the line that represents your taxable income for the year. Cross-reference this amount with your filing status to determine the rate(s) at which you will be taxed. The rate at which your next dollar earned would be taxed is called your **marginal tax rate**. Below is a simplified example of a tax table. Note how the percentage of income that is due in taxes increases as taxable income increases. This demonstrates that the federal income tax is a progressive tax.

EXAMPLE:

Harry and Sally have $121,000 of taxable income, and they are filing jointly. The first $18,450 is taxed at a rate of 10% ($18,450 × .1), the next $56,450 ($74,900 – $18,450) is taxed at 15% ($56,450 × .15), and the final $46,100 ($121,000 – $74,900) is taxed at 25% ($46,100 × .25). $1,845 + $8,467.50 + $11,525 = $21,837.50, so Harry and Sally have a tax liability of $21,837.50.

Most tax filers use tax preparation software (such as TurboTax, TaxACT, H&R Block, or Tax Slayer), which calculates the tax liability for you.

That was an easy step! Just one more step to go!

Step 4:
Calculate Tax Due or Tax Refund

After calculating your tax liability, you subtract tax credits and federal income tax withholdings to find your **tax due** or a possible **tax refund**. **Tax credits** are different from itemized deductions. Credits are more valuable because they are dollar-for-dollar reductions in your tax liability, whereas deductions only reduce taxable income. Credits are either refundable (paid to the taxpayer even if the amount of the credits exceeds the tax liability) or non-refundable. Refundable credits include reductions for earned income, taxes withheld on wages, and estimated income tax payments. Non-refundable credits include child tax, child and dependent care, elderly and disabled care, adoption, and education. Many of these credits are phased out for taxpayers in higher income brackets.

2015 Federal Income Tax Rates

Married Filing Jointly		Filing Single	
Taxable Income (Over x but less than y)	Tax Rate	Taxable Income (Over x but less than y)	Tax Rate
$0 / $18,450	10%	$0 / $9,225	10%
$18,450 / $74,900	15%	$9,225 / $37,450	15%
$74,900 / $151,200	25%	$37,450 / $90,750	25%

Calculating Your Federal Income Tax

```
    Gross Income
  − Adjustments to Income
  ─────────────────────────
  = Adjusted Gross Income

  − Deductions
  − Personal Exemptions
  ─────────────────────────
  = Taxable Income

  × Tax Rate(s)
  ─────────────────────────
  = Tax Liability

  − Tax Credits (including federal
    taxes already withheld)
  − Federal Taxes Already Withheld
  ─────────────────────────
  = Tax Due or Tax Refund
```

The Child Tax Credit is given for each qualifying child in a household. A qualifying child is one whom the taxpayer can claim as a dependent and who was younger than seventeen (sixteen years old or less) on the last day of the tax year. This credit is given in addition to the exemption claimed for the child, and it can even become a tax refund for low-income families. However, the Child Tax Credit begins to phase out after the taxpayer's income exceeds a specific amount. The amount phased out is based on the number of credits; it is not a percentage phase-out.

Education tax credits include the American Opportunity Tax Credit and the Lifetime Learning Credit. The American Opportunity Tax Credit gives parents or students a 100 percent tax credit for the first $2,000 paid and a 25 percent tax credit on the next $2,000 paid for the first four years of college. The result is a credit of up to $2,500 per year for the first four years of college.

Qualifying expenses include tuition and books (but not room and board) at an accredited vocational school, college, or university. After the fourth year of college, the Lifetime Learning Credit can be applied to offset 20 percent of the first $10,000 for tuition and related expenses for all eligible students in the family (up to $2,000).

Another important credit is the Adoption Credit, which allows for a credit of up to $13,400 for the qualifying cost of adopting a child under the age of eighteen.

Taxpayers may be eligible for additional credits if they are disabled, are older than sixty-five with a low income, pay taxes in other countries, or overpay Social Security taxes because they work more than one job.

Once you have calculated the total tax you owe, subtract the amount of federal income taxes you have already paid. The result will either be the amount of taxes you owe or the amount you will have refunded to you.

Wow, that was a lot of information, and calculating your family's federal income tax can certainly be a long process! But it's not the big, scary monster a lot of people think it is. Once you are familiar with the process, taxes aren't so bad after all!

Somebody said, "Money can't buy happiness," but his friend said, "Maybe not, but it does enable one to pick out the particular kind of misery that he enjoys the most." And someone has pointed out that if there is anyone who can't buy happiness with money it must be that he just doesn't know where to shop. We can build temples with money, we can send out missionaries with money, we can erect educational institutions,

operate hospitals, and pay our tithing with money. We can feed and clothe our families with money, and in many ways we can build up the kingdom of God with money.
—Sterling Sill [12]

Tax Strategies

Your goal related to taxes is to pay just what you legally must—no more and no less. There are several tax strategies that can help you reduce the amount of taxes you pay so that you have more money to support your family and invest in the future.

Remember your Roth every year!

In 1997, Senator William Roth from Delaware[13] sponsored tax legislation that you should take advantage of every year. Investing in a Roth 401(k) (set up by your employer) and/or a Roth IRA (that you set up) is perhaps the most important tax strategy to reduce your lifetime income tax burden. We will talk much more about these in Chapter 8. For now, know that earnings from a Roth 401(k) or Roth IRA are tax free forever! When you are older (like your Family Finance professor), that could mean saving 25 percent, 28 percent, or more in tax liability on your retirement withdrawals.

Itemize your deductions or don't—but get it right.

The government wants to encourage you to spend money in certain ways (e.g., contributing to education, your church, charities, political parties, etc.), so it offers itemized deductions for that purpose. However, the government also offers a standard deduction, even if you have no itemized deductions. When you file your taxes, you ought to claim the greater deduction, either the total of your itemized deductions or the standard deduction. Make sure you get it right. The government won't choose your method for you.

Itemize your deductions every other year.

One strategy of getting the maximum benefit from itemized deductions for your family is kind of tricky but totally legal. Make all of your contributions that count as itemized deductions every other year. Then claim the standard deduction in the other years. For example, during 2015 you pay tithing and interest on your house as normal. Then on December 31, 2015, you pay ahead the tithing and all of the interest on your house for 2016. You itemize in 2015, claiming double tithing and interest. Then in 2016 you pay no tithing and no interest and claim the standard deduction. If you are in the 25 percent marginal tax bracket, this will save you about $1,000 in taxes. Of course, you must have sufficient resources to pay your tithing and interest ahead one year, but it is an option to think about.

File for Earned Income Tax Credit (EITC) if you qualify.

The Earned Income Tax Credit (EITC) is very special to some because it may give you a tax credit that goes beyond bringing your tax liability to zero; it may actually pay you money. It is the government's way to get money into the hands of the working poor in order to better meet their basic financial needs. Many BYU students who marry and have children qualify for this credit, and sometimes it is quite lucrative. For example, a married couple with three children who made less than $17,530 per year would get $6,044 back from the government. That is amazing!

Claim your college-age emerging adult as a dependent.

Parents often have college-age children who are making enough money to file an income tax form in order to get the tax refund for the tax withholdings from their income. Often these emerging adults can qualify as dependents, even if they are away living at college. In these cases parents can legally claim the exemption for their college student and the student cannot. Because parents have a higher marginal tax rate and are paying more taxes than a college student, there are greater overall tax savings when parents claim the exemption. However, when parents claim the exemption, emerging adults are sometimes left with tax bills which they would not have had otherwise. One way to equitably resolve this issue is to have the parents claim the exemption (which is often worth about $1,000 in tax savings) and then reimburse their emerging adult what he or she would have gotten back from a tax refund (often a couple of hundred dollars or less).

Have a large family.

The government wants to encourage you to have children. In 2015, the tax exemption for each dependent child (under age nineteen, or students under twenty-four) was $4,000 and an additional $1,000 tax credit for each child (under age seventeen). Having a large family can dramatically decrease your tax liability. For example, I knew of a family that had fifteen children. Fourteen children were dependents and eight were under the age of seventeen. For this family, the exemptions for

the children alone would reduce their taxable income by $56,000. In addition, the family would offset $8,000 of tax liability because of the child tax credit (eight children under seventeen). By the time you add their own personal deduction and itemized deductions for their mortgage payment and tithing, this family would need to earn well over $120,000 before paying any federal income tax at all.

Time the births of your children.

Babies who take even one breath within a tax year (i.e., are born at 11:59:59 p.m. on December 31) count as a full $4,000 exemption and a full $1,000 tax credit. So, given a choice, give birth on December 31, not January 1.

Time your own death.

As long as you take even one breath in a tax year before you die, you count as an exemption for income tax purposes. For example, if you die at 12:00:01 a.m. on January 1 in 2016, your spouse will still be able to claim the married filing jointly exemption. So, if you are on your deathbed and are just trying to live until Christmas, hang on for another week and your spouse will have a tax advantage that could be worth about $1,000.

Pay your tithing or other contributions with appreciated stock.

Appreciated stock is *not* stock that you appreciate (although you will probably be very grateful for it in the future) . . . it *is* stock that has increased in value. As you will learn in Chapter 8, we don't generally suggest purchasing individual stocks. However, if you disregard our suggestion and *do* buy individual stock, it has a tax advantage if you donate the stock directly to the Church (e.g., pay your tithing to the Church). Here is how and why that works: if you were to sell the appreciated stock, you would have to pay long-term or short-term capital gains taxes on the stock when you filed your income tax. However, if you contribute the stock directly, you don't have to pay any taxes because you never sold the stock. One way to do this is to contribute your stock to the Church for tithing. To do so, you contact the Donations-in-Kind office at Church headquarters at 801–240–2554.[14] They will tell you how to do it. The ward is not involved in this kind of contribution. You simply claim the value of the stock on the day you donate it as a charitable deduction when you file your taxes.

Be generous and get tax deductions at the same time.

Let's say you want to use your resources to help some financially struggling ward members support two missionaries in the field. Instead of just giving them the money directly, ask if you could help support the missionaries. This help will be easier to accept, and, if contributed directly to the ward missionary fund, it will be wholly tax deductible.

We hope you will consider using these tax strategies to lower the amount of money you pay in taxes so that you can have more resources with which to bless your family and others.

Filing Your Taxes

Resources

Although it is important to understand how to calculate your family's taxes, there are many resources available to you that can make the process much more efficient. Most families are moving toward online filing instead of pen-and-paper filing. These resources can be a great help, but it is unwise to rely entirely on a third party when dealing with taxes. Mistakes may cause you to either pay more taxes than is necessary or not pay enough. If you pay less taxes than you are legally obligated to, your family may be audited by the IRS, in which case you have to pay penalties plus interest.

A few of the resources that make taxes easier include tax professionals, online tax software, BYU's VITA, and www.irs.gov.

Tax Professionals. While this is a more expensive option, there are obvious benefits to working with a real person who is an expert at taxes as opposed to working with software. Do your research to find a well-known, trusted professional in your area.

Online Tax Software. This is becoming a common way to get taxes done easily and cheaply. While some software is free, other software is available for purchase at a rate that is probably still cheaper than hiring a professional. TurboTax, TaxACT, H&R Block, IRS Free File, and TaxCut are some commonly used software.

BYU's VITA. This is a great option for those with an income of less than $53,000, and it's free. VITA allows you to schedule an appointment to meet with a BYU accounting student one-on-one. They are often very busy, though, so don't put it off until the last minute.

www.irs.gov. The IRS website is becoming more user-friendly. Often, you can find the answers to your tax questions by searching their website with keywords or by looking in the "Help & Resources" tab.

Again, if you decide to get outside help with your taxes, remember to take a critical look for yourself to make sure they are being done correctly. No one is as invested in your tax refund as you are. Be especially aware of any deductions or credits that they may have overlooked.

Tax Forms

Another thing to consider is which tax form(s) to use. If you use a tax software or another outside resource, they will use the correct form(s) for you. If you are filing yourself, it is important to be able to pick the right form(s).

Some of the most common forms include 1040EZ, 1040A, 1040, Schedule A Itemized Deductions, Schedule B Interest and Dividend Income, Schedule D Capital Gains and Losses, Publication 596 Earned Income Credit, and Publication 970 Tax Benefits for Education. Here is a little information about the most common tax forms:

1040EZ. This is the simplest form. If your taxable income is below $100,000, you are claiming no dependents, and you are claiming the standard deduction, this may be the form for you.

1040A. This is a little more complicated than 1040EZ but still for those with taxable income below $100,000. You must also be taking the standard deduction. If you have capital gain distributions, certain tax credits, or have made adjustments to income for IRA contributions or student loan interest, this form will be able to handle your more complicated taxes.

1040. This is the longest and most complex form, but cheer up! The longer the form, the more money you may potentially save. If you are fortunate enough to have an income above $100,000, you *must* use this form. This is also for those who are taking an itemized deduction or have certain adjustments to gross income or tax credits.

Schedule A Itemized Deductions. If you are itemizing your deductions, you must use a 1040 form and attach this form as a report of your deductions.

Schedule B Interest and Dividend Income. This may be used with both 1040A and 1040. If the income you've received on interest and dividends exceeds $1,500, you must list the sources separately on this schedule.

Schedule D Capital Gains and Losses. This is the government's way of promoting long-term stock investments. If you have sold a capital asset during the tax year such as stock, a house, a car, etc., you must report the gains and losses on this schedule. Long-term capital gains are taxed at lower rates than short-term gains, which are taxed at the rate of your income. Use this schedule with a 1040 form.

Publication 596 Earned Income Credit. If you have a low income and/or children, you may want to look into this tax credit. This credit is refundable, meaning that even if you don't have to pay any taxes, you could receive a check from the IRS. Simply attach this to the 1040 form.

Publication 970 Tax Benefits for Education. If you are itemizing your deductions and have paid tuition or other educational fees in the last year, you will want to take advantage of this deduction and attach this to the 1040.

More detailed explanations of these and all other tax forms can be found at www.irs.gov and other places online.

> *Attitude is an important part of the foundation upon which we build a productive life. In appraising our present attitude, we might ask: "Am I working to become my best self? Do I set worthy and attainable goals? Do I look toward the positive in life? Am I alert to ways that I can render more and better service? Am I doing more than is required of me?" Remember, a good attitude produces good results, a fair attitude fair results, a poor attitude poor results. We each shape our own life, and the shape of it is determined largely by our attitude.*
> —M. Russell Ballard [15]

Summary

In this chapter, we learned about different types of taxes. We delved into the federal income tax and how to calculate it. We presented tax strategies that may save your family money. Finally, we introduced various tax resources and tax forms. Death and taxes may be the only certain things in life, but at least one of them isn't so bad (we won't say which one).

Other Resources

- http://www.bankrate.com/taxes.aspx
- http://www.fairmark.com/
- http://www.irs.gov
- http://moneycentral.msn.com/tax/home.asp
- http://www.smartmoney.com/tax/

Notes

1. http://www.brainyquote.com/quotes/quotes/b/benjaminfr129817.html
2. Duncan, K. (2012, May 03). Americans paying more in taxes than for food, clothing, and shelter. *Tax Foundation*. Retrieved from http://taxfoundation.org/article/americans-paying-more-taxes-food-clothing-and-shelter
3. https://en.wikipedia.org/wiki/Tax_Freedom_Day
4. http://www.forbes.com/sites/beltway/2013/09/12/most-americans-do-indeed-pay-federal-taxes-including-the-poor/
5. D&C 58:21-22
6. Matthew 22:21
7. http://www.davemanuel.com/history-of-deficits-and-surpluses-in-the-united-states.php
8. http://www.usdebtclock.org/index.html
9. http://finance.townhall.com/columnists/politicalcalculations/2014/04/13/2014-how-many-pages-in-the-us-tax-code-n1823832
10. http://www.investopedia.com/terms/a/activeincome.asp
11. http://www.investopedia.com/terms/p/passiveincome.asp
12. Sterling W. Sill, "A Fortune to Share," (Oct. 1973), https://www.lds.org/general-conference/1973/10/a-fortune-to-share?lang=eng
13. https://en.wikipedia.org/wiki/Roth_IRA#History
14. http://tech.lds.org/forum/viewtopic.php?t=17263
15. M. Russell Ballard, "Providing for Our Needs," (April 1981), https://www.lds.org/general-conference/1981/04/providing-for-our-needs?lang=eng

Form **1040EZ**

Department of the Treasury—Internal Revenue Service

Income Tax Return for Single and Joint Filers With No Dependents (99) **2015**

OMB No. 1545-0074

Your first name and initial	Last name	**Your social security number**
If a joint return, spouse's first name and initial	Last name	**Spouse's social security number**
Home address (number and street). If you have a P.O. box, see instructions.	Apt. no.	▲ Make sure the SSN(s) above are correct.
City, town or post office, state, and ZIP code. If you have a foreign address, also complete spaces below (see instructions).		**Presidential Election Campaign** Check here if you, or your spouse if filing jointly, want $3 to go to this fund. Checking a box below will not change your tax or refund. ☐ You ☐ Spouse
Foreign country name	Foreign province/state/county	Foreign postal code

Income

Attach Form(s) W-2 here.

Enclose, but do not attach, any payment.

1	Wages, salaries, and tips. This should be shown in box 1 of your Form(s) W-2. Attach your Form(s) W-2.	1	
2	Taxable interest. If the total is over $1,500, you cannot use Form 1040EZ.	2	
3	Unemployment compensation and Alaska Permanent Fund dividends (see instructions).	3	
4	Add lines 1, 2, and 3. This is your **adjusted gross income.**	4	
5	If someone can claim you (or your spouse if a joint return) as a dependent, check the applicable box(es) below and enter the amount from the worksheet on back. ☐ **You** ☐ **Spouse** If no one can claim you (or your spouse if a joint return), enter $10,300 if **single;** $20,600 if **married filing jointly.** See back for explanation.	5	
6	Subtract line 5 from line 4. If line 5 is larger than line 4, enter -0-. This is your **taxable income.** ▶	6	

Payments, Credits, and Tax

7	Federal income tax withheld from Form(s) W-2 and 1099.	7	
8a	**Earned income credit (EIC)** (see instructions)	8a	
b	Nontaxable combat pay election. 8b		
9	Add lines 7 and 8a. These are your **total payments and credits.** ▶	9	
10	**Tax.** Use the amount on **line 6 above** to find your tax in the tax table in the instructions. Then, enter the tax from the table on this line.	10	
11	Health care: individual responsibility (see instructions) Full-year coverage ☐	11	
12	Add lines 10 and 11. This is your **total tax.**	12	

Refund

Have it directly deposited! See instructions and fill in 13b, 13c, and 13d, or Form 8888.

13a	If line 9 is larger than line 12, subtract line 12 from line 9. This is your **refund.** If Form 8888 is attached, check here ▶ ☐	13a	
▶ b	Routing number ▶ **c** Type: ☐ Checking ☐ Savings		
▶ d	Account number		

Amount You Owe

14	If line 12 is larger than line 9, subtract line 9 from line 12. This is the **amount you owe.** For details on how to pay, see instructions. ▶	14	

Third Party Designee

Do you want to allow another person to discuss this return with the IRS (see instructions)? ☐ **Yes.** Complete below. ☐ **No**

Designee's name ▶ Phone no. ▶ Personal identification number (PIN) ▶

Sign Here

Joint return? See instructions.

Keep a copy for your records.

Under penalties of perjury, I declare that I have examined this return and, to the best of my knowledge and belief, it is true, correct, and accurately lists all amounts and sources of income I received during the tax year. Declaration of preparer (other than the taxpayer) is based on all information of which the preparer has any knowledge.

Your signature	Date	Your occupation	Daytime phone number
Spouse's signature. If a joint return, **both** must sign.	Date	Spouse's occupation	If the IRS sent you an Identity Protection PIN, enter it here (see inst.)

Paid Preparer Use Only

Print/Type preparer's name	Preparer's signature	Date	Check ☐ if self-employed	PTIN
Firm's name ▶		Firm's EIN ▶		
Firm's address ▶		Phone no.		

For Disclosure, Privacy Act, and Paperwork Reduction Act Notice, see instructions. Cat. No. 11329W Form **1040EZ** (2015)

Figure 5.1 An example of a 1040 EZ form.

6

Risk Management and Insurance

Protecting Your Family's Financial Health

LEARN

- The importance of insuring your family against catastrophic financial loss

- About different types of insurance and insurance policies

- To make informed decisions on which insurance policies are best for your family's situation

Scenario 1: A few months after my wife passed away, I was visiting her grave in the Orem City Cemetery. Just north, I noticed a gray-haired man angrily weeping. I had seen him there several times before and this time I felt impressed to visit with him. When I approached and started a conversation, he said he was there to chastise his son-in-law who had died and left his daughter a widow with four small children. However, the reason for the tongue-lashing was not his son-in-law's death; it was his lack of life insurance. A few months earlier, money had been tight in the family so the son-in-law had canceled their term life insurance policy. Now the man's daughter was a grieving widow with four kids, no income, no assets, and no job.

Moral of the story: If you have anyone dependent on your income, you have an ethical responsibility to have sufficient life insurance.

Scenario 2: My brother-in-law and his wife took a vacation to Hawaii and left their younger children in the care of their adult daughter. Late one night, the daughter was horrified to see smoke billowing out of the vents in the living room. She hurriedly got all of the children out of the house, and just a few minutes later, the whole house was engulfed in flames. Within an hour, most of the structure had burned to the ground. The house was completely destroyed. I talked with the family a few days later. Of course they were sorry to have lost their home—but they had good homeown-

ers insurance, and they were excited to rebuild a brand new home. They saw in the event a silver lining whereby they could design a new home as an improvement of their old home.

Moral of the story: When you have adequate insurance, a so-called "disaster" can become a family opportunity.

Why Have Insurance?

Life is full of unexpected challenges, and some of them can be financially devastating. The purpose of this chapter is to help you protect your family from financial tragedies through prudent insurance coverage. When catastrophes occur—and they surely will—you can rest assured that you and your family are financially protected if you have adequate insurance.

Prudent financial planning helps make life less stressful for our families. When financial stress is minimal, there is less conflict in your home and your family is happier. However, unpredictable events (accident, injury, illness, fire, theft, legal action, etc.) may occur at any time and have potentially devastating financial consequences. Insurance protects your family's financial assets in the case of these unanticipated events, thereby reducing the stress and strain that your family may experience. Prudent risk management through adequate insurance will bless your family in times of trial. Even if none of these catastrophes affect you, you will have peace of mind that your family is financially protected. You will sleep better at night!

Insurance is "a contract (policy) in which an individual or entity receives financial protection or reimbursement against losses from an insurance company. The company pools clients' risks to make payments more affordable for the insured."[1] Every family faces the risk of significant financial loss every day; your house could burn down, your car could be totaled, your daughter could get leukemia, or your spouse could die. By pooling risk through an insurance policy, you can protect your family at an affordable cost. For example, according to rough extrapolations[2] from data provided by the United States Fire Administration,[3] the chances of a house fire in any given year are about 1 in 200. Let's say the average loss is $100,000. If 200 people pay $550 a year, there will be enough money to cover the one house fire as well as to pay the insurance company overhead. In other words, for a manageable cost ($550), you and a pool

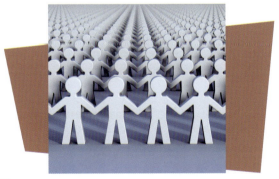

of other families are able to protect themselves from the 1 in 200 chance of losing $100,000.

Acquiring insurance is an important step toward becoming financially self-reliant, and it is key to taking care of the family that God has placed in your stewardship. Elder Marvin J. Ashton offered the following counsel on insurance: "It is most important to have suffi-

Insurance

A contract in which an individual receives financial protection or reimbursement against losses from an insurance company.

cient medical, automobile, and homeowner's [sic] insurance and an adequate life insurance program. Costs associated with illness, accident, and death may be so large that uninsured families can be financially burdened for many years."[4]

> *It is most important to have sufficient medical, automobile, and homeowner's insurance and an adequate life insurance program. Costs associated with illness, accident, and death may be so large that uninsured families can be financially burdened for many years."*
> —Marvin J. Ashton[5]

Managing Risk

If you purchase too much insurance or the wrong kind of insurance, you are wasting money. If you purchase too little insurance, you are exposed to unnecessary risk. Understanding risk is an important part in determining the right level of insurance you should have. You can manage risk in four ways: you can avoid it, reduce it, assume it, or transfer it. Let's talk about each of these as they relate to the risk management table. (See Table 6.1.)

Table 6.1 Risk Management

	Low Frequency	High Frequency
Low Severity	Assume (losing your wallet)	Reduce (common cold)
High Severity	Transfer (home fire)	Avoid (lung cancer caused by smoking)

You can avoid some risks by choosing not to participate in activities where you will likely be hurt, such as bull riding, bungee jumping, and playing in the National Football League. Similarly, you can choose to avoid the risks associated with smoking and drinking by simply not smoking or drinking. Insuring against high-severity, high-frequency risk activities is expensive (e.g., life insurance rates for smokers), so the cost-effective solution is to avoid them altogether.

You can reduce some risks. For example, regular exercise, adequate sleep, and good nutrition can reduce the need for medical care. You can reduce the risk of damage to your home by purchasing a fire extinguisher. You can reduce the chance of injury or death in a car accident by wearing your seat belt. The best course is to reduce risk wherever possible.

You can assume (or retain) some types of risk through self-insurance, setting aside some funds to cover potential losses. With self-insurance, you pay no premiums, but you bear all of the risk yourself. For example, I decided not to purchase collision and comprehensive insurance on my 2004 Camry because it was getting old. It saved me quite a bit on insurance premiums. However, when my son wrecked the car, I lost potential insurance compensation because I was self-insured.

You can transfer risk to others by purchasing insurance, thus transferring financial responsibility for a specific low-frequency, high-cost risk from yourself to an insurance company. This is why you should get some form of life insurance, homeowners insurance, health insurance, disability insurance, and automobile insurance.

As with everything in life, moderation is important. You should maintain a reasonable relationship between the cost and the benefit of insurance. Not planning for high-severity,

Sidebar Definitions

Premium
A specified amount paid regularly (usually monthly or annually) to an insurance company in exchange for coverage.

Deductible
A specified amount that you must pay to cover an expense that could qualify for your insurance coverage before your insurance begins paying for eligible expenses.

Life insurance
Insurance against the financial loss resulting from the death of the insured.

Beneficiary
The recipient of life insurance who benefits in the event of the death of the insured.

Cash value
The total account value that is available to the life insurance policy owner while he or she is alive.

Face value
The basic benefit the life insurance company will pay the beneficiaries upon the death of the insured.

Policy owner
The individual or business that pays for and owns the insurance policy.

---

low-frequency risks is foolish, but so is going into excessive debt to pay insurance premiums.

There are a few terms that you should be familiar with before we delve further into insurance. First, you pay the insurance company a **premium** on a regular basis (e.g., monthly, quarterly, annually) in return for covering certain losses. The other main payment associated with insurance is called a **deductible**. The deductible is the specified amount that you must pay out-of-pocket before the insurance company begins to compensate you. For example, if you are in an accident and have $2,000 in repairs and a $500 deductible, you must pay the first $500, and then the insurance company will pay the remaining $1,500. Once the deductible is met in a calendar year, the insurance company will pay for any additional eligible costs incurred during the rest of that year. Typically, if an insurance policy has higher deductibles, it will have lower premiums. If it has lower deductibles, it will have higher premiums.

Consider this wise counsel from President Gordon B. Hinckley:

> "I do not predict any impending disaster. I hope that there will not be one. But prudence should govern our lives. Everyone who owns a home recognizes the need for fire insurance. We hope and pray that there will never be a fire. Nevertheless, we pay for insurance to cover such a catastrophe, should it occur. We ought to do the same with reference to family welfare."[6]

Now let's learn more about each of the main types of insurance: life, health, homeowners/renters, and automobile.

Life Insurance

The purpose of **life insurance** is to reimburse the financial loss resulting from the death of the insured. Life insurance is not for you (the insured); its benefits are for survivors. It replaces your earnings if you (the earner) die. If you have someone who is dependent upon your income or labor, you have a moral responsibility to have some form of life insurance. If there are children in the home this is true for both spouses even if only one had paid employment. A stay-at-home spouse is providing valuable labor in the home that would need to be replaced economically (e.g., hiring a nanny or housekeeper).

You should understand the following important terms as you learn about life insurance:

Beneficiary: The recipient of benefits in the event of the death of the insured

Cash value: The total account value that is available to the policy owner while he or she is alive

Face value: The basic benefit the insurance company is to pay the beneficiaries; the face value is due upon the death of the insured

Policy owner: The individual or business that pays for and owns the insurance policy

Four Questions Regarding Life Insurance

The purchase of life insurance involves four questions.

1. Do I need life insurance?
2. How much life insurance should I purchase?
3. What kind of life insurance should I buy?
4. How should the life insurance death benefit be received?

Question #1: Do I need life insurance?

If your death will not cause financial loss to anyone, you do not need life insurance. However, if you provide for one or more people who depend on your income or labor, you have a moral obligation to have sufficient life insurance to take care of their needs in case of your death. Children are the most obvious financial dependents. But remember, dependents might also include parents or siblings. Life insurance also benefits your family if you have a lot of debt, expensive funeral plans, etc. Again, both husband and wife should have life insurance when there are dependents involved.

Generally, as people get older, they are more financially able to be self-insured. High net worth as well as investments and savings may reduce the need for life insurance because your dependents would have enough to live on in the case of your death. Keep this in mind as your financial situation changes throughout your life.

Question #2: How much life insurance do I need?

Simply put, you need enough insurance to replace your lost earnings and labor. Four common methods used to determine the needed amount of life insurance are multiple of income, desired income, human life value, and needs analysis. These are explained in detail in the *Fundamentals of Family Finance Workbook*.

Question #3: Which kind of life insurance should I buy?

All life insurance companies use mortality tables[7] to determine life insurance premiums. Premiums that insure your life always increase with age because the older you get, the more likely you are to die.

Though other types of life insurance exist, in this book we will discuss the two major types—term and whole life insurance.

With **term life insurance**, the face value of the policy is paid to the beneficiaries if the policyholder dies while the policy is in force. There is no cash value building up within the insurance policy. As the policyholder gets older, the premium increases. Term insurance usually cannot be purchased beyond ages between 65 and 75 (depending on the company). While you are young, premiums for term life insurance are much less expensive than premiums for whole life insurance. It pays to shop around to find the best rates for term life insurance. One site that does a good job of this is www.term4sale.com.

With **whole life insurance**, the premiums are divided between death protection and investment. The investment portion is put into an account that earns tax-deferred interest, dividends, or investment gains. This type of insurance is intended to provide the policyholder benefits over a lifetime. If you have the self-motivation to manage your own investments, then you are usually better off purchasing term insurance and investing in a broad, primarily stock-based mutual fund because you will likely yield a higher rate of return. However, if you are the kind of person who spends your paycheck every month and never gets

Term life insurance
A policy in which the face value is paid to the beneficiaries when the insured dies.

Whole life insurance
A policy in which the premiums are divided between death protection and safe, relatively low return investments.

Table 6.2: Term and Whole Life Insurance (Pros and Cons)

	Pros	Cons
Term	Inexpensive (at young age) Easy to understand Low commissions	Premiums increase as the insured ages No cash value Can't be purchased after a certain age (65–75, depending on the company)
Whole	Builds cash value Cash value is tax-deferred Premium stays level	Expensive Low rate of returns compared to diversified stock investments Complex Can be misleading

around to investing, it is better to have whole life insurance. The required monthly payment will force you to be an investor.

Question #4: How should life insurance proceeds be received?

When an insured person dies, the named beneficiary is entitled to a tax-free cash death benefit. There are several options for how to receive the face value.

Lump Sum

One option is for the entire death benefit to be paid to the beneficiary in one lump sum. The life insurance benefit received by beneficiaries upon the policyholder's death is not taxable as income. The beneficiary then must decide how to invest the proceeds.

Interest Payment

There is also the interest payment option in which the face value is left with the insurance company to be invested. The interest from the investment is paid to the beneficiary over a stated period of years, at the end of which the face value is paid to the beneficiary. The portion of the payments received by beneficiary that corresponds to the interest will be taxable as regular income.

Installment/Annuity

Instead of receiving a lump sum from the insurance company, you may receive the money over a period of time, generally monthly, with an installment (or annuity) option. You can choose an amount (PMT) to be received each month and the insurance company will tell you how long the annuity will last (N) given their assumed interest rate (I). Alternatively, you can choose a period of time (N) that you would like the annuity to last and the insurance company tells you how much money you will receive each month (PMT) given their assumed interest rate (I). In many cases, the death benefit becomes a person's living allowance. A portion of it will be taxable as interest income.

Life Annuity

With a life annuity, you (the beneficiary) are guaranteed to receive a monthly annuity payment for as long as you live. If you are willing to receive somewhat less each month, the annuity will last for a specified length of time, say ten years, regardless of when you die. If, say, you die in seven years, your beneficiaries (secondary beneficiaries) will receive the annuity payment for three years. For example: Husband dies first. Wife decides to receive a life annuity with a twenty-year guaranteed period. Wife dies in eight years. Her beneficiaries (two children) split the annuity for the next twelve years.

Summary

Adequate life insurance is an ethical responsibility if there is anyone who depends on your income or labor. Both husband and wife should have life insurance. If you are the kind of person who is a diligent and wise investor, it will be more financially rewarding to buy term life insurance and do the investments yourself. If you are not the kind of person who is a diligent and wise investor, you should probably invest in whole life insurance which will provide a forced investment plan while insuring your life.

Health and Disability Insurance

"Nothing seems so certain as the unexpected in our lives. With rising medical costs, health insurance is the only way most families can meet serious accident, illness, or maternity costs, particularly those for premature births.... Every family should make provision for proper health and life insurance."
—N. Eldon Tanner[8]

Health and disability insurance is a necessary part of any financial plan. There are two kinds of financial loss that are associated with health problems: the cost of medical care and the loss of income. The risk of financial loss associated with medical care is dealt with by purchasing health or medical insurance. The risk of financial loss associated with loss of income (due to injury or illness) is dealt with by purchasing disability income insurance.

In the United States, health insurance has traditionally been provided by employers in group plans. In this situation, employers pay most of the health insurance premiums and employees pay a smaller amount. However, in 2013 only 48 percent of the population was covered by employer-sponsored healthcare; 6 percent were covered by other private programs (generally very expensive); 33 percent were covered by public programs such as Medicaid and Medicare; and 13 percent were uninsured.[9] Many of the uninsured were working without employee-sponsored care and could not afford private coverage. In order to address this need and other perceived shortcomings in the health insurance domain, the Patient Protection and Affordable Care Act (PPACA) was passed and signed into law in 2010. This is also known as the Affordable Care Act (ACA) or simply Obamacare.

The Affordable Care Act (ACA)

The Affordable Care Act (ACA) requires nearly everyone in the United States to have qualifying health insurance or to pay a penalty. The penalty for not having qualifying health insurance in 2016 is the *higher* of 2.5 percent of your household income or $695 for each adult in the family and $347.50 per child under 18. The maximum penalty per family for this method is $2,085.[10] This encourages young, healthy people to pay for insurance in order to subsidize other groups, such as the elderly.

Some are exempt from paying the penalty for not having health insurance.[11] You may qualify if:

1. The lowest-priced coverage available to you would cost more than 8.05 percent of your household income

2. You do not file a tax return because your income is too low

3. You are uninsured for less than 3 months of the year

4. You are a member of a recognized religious sect with religious objections

Health insurance
Insurance for expenses relating to health and medical procedures.

Disability insurance
Insurance that provides payments to insured individuals in the event that regular income is interrupted by illness or an accident.

to insurance (e.g., Amish ... but not Mormons), including Social Security and Medicare

5. You're incarcerated
6. You're not lawfully present in the US

Some college health plans, including BYU's Health Plan, do not meet the qualifying standards of the Affordable Care Act. Students enrolled in the BYU Health Plan will have to pay a penalty unless they qualify for an exemption (see above, e.g., income is too low to file).

Popular benefits of the Affordable Care Act include: young adults can stay on their parents' health insurance until the age of 26 (which is a great boon to BYU students who want to start a family); if anyone gets really sick, insurance companies cannot terminate coverage nor limit the amount of coverage; wellness and pregnancy exams are now free to the patient; and health insurance companies are required to use at least 80 percent of premiums on providing actual medical services.[12]

For those without other sources of insurance, the ACA provides for state insurance exchanges where insurance companies can compete for your business. These plans are grouped into three categories:

1. Bronze – least expensive premiums (high deductibles, catastrophic protection)
2. Silver – moderately expensive premiums (moderate deductibles)
3. Gold – expensive premiums (low deductibles and greatest choice in service)
4. Platinum – most expensive premiums

Generally, if you use healthcare services less than average, it would be a wise financial decision to choose a Bronze plan. If you use healthcare services more than average, it will generally be a wise financial decision to choose a Silver, Gold, or Platinum plan.

For more information on the ACA, visit https://www.healthcare.gov/ and http://kff.org/health-reform/.

Health Insurance Terms

We've already learned about premiums. Here are a few more terms that will help you understand health insurance.

Remember the **deductible** is the amount the insured must pay before the insurance company pays anything. This payment acts

as a deterrent to unnecessary medical care. The deductible usually renews annually and is based on the calendar year. For this reason it is financially advantageous to group medical procedures in the same calendar year if possible.

Co-insurance (or **co-payment**) is the portion of expenses beyond the deductible that the insured person pays—up to an annual maximum as stated in the policy.

Most health insurance policies have a **maximum annual co-payment.** Generally, after the deductible is met, the insured will pay a percentage of the medical expenses up to a maximum amount. For example, suppose you have insurance with a co-payment of 20 percent of eligible expenses to a maximum co-payment of $3000. If you had surgery and hospitalization that totaled $50,000, you would have a co-payment of $3000 towards

---

Deductible

A specified amount that you must pay to cover an expense that could qualify for your insurance coverage before your insurance begins paying for eligible expenses.

Co-insurance/ Co-payment

The portion of expenses beyond the deductible that the insured person pays, up to an annual maximum.

Maximum annual co-payment

The most you can pay towards co-insurance in any given year.

the 20 percent of the first $15,000 of expenses. The insurance company would pay the remaining $35,000 of expenses at 100 percent. Altogether, you would pay $3000 and the insurance company would pay $47,000.

Maximum annual out-of-pocket cost is the most you can pay for health care costs in any calendar year. It equals the insurance premium + annual deductible + maximum co-payment. This figure is, in essence, the worst-case scenario in terms of total annual cost for health care. This is also renewed on an annual basis and can be used strategically. For example, my daughter came home from her mission in October and needed elective hip surgery. We scheduled that surgery for December because we had already met our deductible and our out-of-pocket maximum for the year. Because we scheduled it before the end of the year the surgery did not cost us anything out-of-pocket. However, had we waited until January it would have cost $500 deductible plus our $4000 maximum co-payment.

If you have more than one insurer, they will "coordinate" payments to hospitals, doctors, etc. so as to avoid double paying. This is called **coordination of benefits**.

If you forget to pay your insurance premium, you are generally allowed a **grace period** before your insurance is canceled.

Types of Medical Insurance

There are various types of health insurance, but there are three types beyond your normal health insurance that you should be familiar with and should possibly consider purchasing. These are health savings accounts (HSA), disability insurance, and long-term care (LTC) insurance.

A **health savings account (HSA)** is an account created by an employer on behalf of an employee to save money toward medical expenses. Money in the account can be used to help pay co-payments, deductibles, and other qualified medical expenses. Typically, HSA plans have larger deductibles and co-payments, as the HSA philosophy is to encour-

age the insured to reduce health care costs by engaging in health promoting behaviors, reducing or eliminating behaviors that present health risks, and comparison shopping for medical services.

The benefits of having such an account include tax deductions (as an adjustment to income), portability (changing jobs does not mean that you lose your account), insurance benefits (reduced rates because of higher deductibles), and savings capability (earnings are tax-deferred). After age 65, money may be withdrawn from a health savings account for any reason without consequence. As such, the residual balance in an HSA account may complement retirement savings.

Disability insurance provides payments (between 50 and 80 percent of after-tax income) to insured individuals in the event that regular income is interrupted by illness or an accident. Anyone who depends on earned income should look into disability coverage. The risk of disability is even higher than the risk of premature death.

Long-term care (LTC) insurance covers the costs of nursing home facilities and long-term home health care. This type of insurance provides a daily dollar benefit—for example,

Maximum annual out-of-pocket cost

The most you can pay towards medical care in any given year (insurance premium + annual deductible + maximum co-payment).

Coordination of benefits

Multiple insurers coordinating insurance claims medical payments so as to avoid double paying.

Grace period

The period of time between the payment due date and the cancelation of your insurance.

Health savings account (HSA)

An account that is created by an employer on behalf of an employee to save money toward medical expenses.

Disability insurance

Insurance that provides payments to insured individuals in the event that regular income is interrupted by illness or an accident.

Long-term care (LTC) insurance

Insurance that covers the costs of nursing home facilities and long-term home health care.

$100 per day for the cost of long-term care. It may help families with a history of long-term diseases or disability to plan for the future. Two disadvantages of this type of insurance are the expense and the many exceptions and conditions for coverage.

Homeowners and Renters Insurance

Home ownership may be the most expensive investment you ever make. It is essential for your financial security that you protect real estate investment with an insurance policy that provides adequate protection for the home, its contents, and the liability that comes hand-in-hand with property ownership.

> *"The Church cannot be expected to provide for every one of its millions of members in case of public or personal disaster. It is therefore necessary that each home and family do what they can to assume the responsibility for their own hour of need."*
> —James E. Faust[13]

Homeowners insurance is insurance that covers a personal residence combined with other personal protections for the owner(s). Most homeowners' policies contain three types of coverage:

Homeowners insurance
Insurance that covers a personal residence combined with other personal protections for the owner(s).

Exclusions
Specific conditions or items that are not covered by the standard insurance policy.

1. Structure: cost of rebuilding or repairing the home
2. Contents: cost of replacing personal property that is damaged, destroyed, or stolen
3. Liability: cost to fulfill responsibility for injury to other people on your property or damage caused by family members to others' property

Let's now look at each of these types of coverage separately.

Structure

This portion of your homeowner's policy provides protection for losses that might occur to your house and to other structures attached to your home as a result of specific risks. Some risks that are usually covered include fire or lightning, windstorm or hail, explosion, riot, damage caused by aircraft or vehicles, smoke, vandalism, theft, breakage of glass, or volcanic

eruption. Other perils which are often covered include falling objects; weight of ice, snow, or sleet; collapse of building; leakage or overflow of water or steam from plumbing, heating, or air conditioning systems; cracking, burning, or bulging of a steam or hot water heating system or of appliances for heating water; freezing of plumbing, heating, or air conditioning systems or domestic appliances; and sudden and accidental injury from artificially generated currents to electrical appliances, devices, fixtures, and wiring. Most policies also enumerate **exclusions**, which are not covered by the

policy. Some common exclusions are floods, earthquakes, wars, nuclear accidents, and others which may be specified in an individual policy. To cover these exclusions you may have to get additional specialized insurance.

It is very important to have sufficient insurance to rebuild or repair your home. When you buy a home, your mortgage company or bank will require you to have adequate insurance to pay off the loan on the house. However, homes often increase in value so it is important that you evaluate your coverage and upgrade it as property values and construction costs increase.

Contents

This portion of the policy covers the replacement value of all of the contents within the home that are damaged, destroyed, or stolen because of a covered risk or peril. Typical coverage for the contents of the home range from 50 percent to 70 percent of the insured value of the structure to the home. For example, if you have $300,000 of coverage on the structure of the home you would want $150,000 to $210,000 on the contents of the home. This portion of insurance also frequently has coverage limits for jewelry, computers, and musical instruments. To cover these items above the limits, you may need to purchase an endorsement. One nice characteristic of the insurance on contents is that it also covers your possessions outside of your home. For example, if someone stole your luggage while on a trip to Hawaii, you could claim the loss on your insurance.

As part of your insurance program you should have a complete inventory of all of your belongings. In order to compensate you in the case of a disaster, the insurance will need to have reasonable proof of ownership. One easy way to do that is to take detailed pictures of each room in the house. We recommend keeping all receipts for major purchases (TVs, computers, jewelry, cell phones, washer, dryer, refrigerator, lawn mower, suits, wedding dress, etc.). Since you do not want your receipts to burn in a house fire, it would be a good idea to scan them and keep them in the Cloud.

Liability

This covers the cost of damage to others that occur during accidents on your property. For example, if a neighbor slips on your icy walk and breaks his wrist, you are liable to pay for that injury. This portion of the homeowners insurance also covers damage that you or family members cause to the property of others. For example, my brother was attempting to jump over the hood of a neighbor's sports car on his skateboard. He didn't quite make it and made quite a dent in the hood that cost quite a bit to repair. My parents' homeowners insurance covered it after the deductible was paid. Another example: if your daughter kicked a soccer ball through your neighbor's $1000 plate glass window, your homeowners policy would cover it, after the deductible was satisfied.

Renters Insurance

Renters insurance is often overlooked by BYU students. This policy offers coverage for personal property as well as liability coverage. If you have items in your apartment or house that are worth a lot of money (e.g., electronic equipment), consider purchasing insurance. When combined with your auto insurance, renters insurance can be very inexpensive. If your possessions are not worth very much and would be somewhat easy to replace (in comparison to the cost of insurance) then you may not want to have the expense of purchasing renters insurance.

Summary

Homeowners insurance is essential for the financial security of those who own homes. It is important to have enough insurance for the structure to be completely rebuilt or to repair your home if it is destroyed or damaged. Because the cost of home construction varies over the years, make sure you update your coverage regularly. Also confirm that personal property insurance covers the replacement cost, not the depreciated market value of the asset. Finally, if you are renting and have any significant possessions, be sure to invest in renters insurance.

Automobile Insurance

"There are many very good people who keep most of the Lord's commandments with respect to the virtuous side of life, but who overlook His commandments in temporal things. They do not heed His warning to prepare for a possible future emergency, apparently feeling that in the midst of all this trouble 'it won't happen to us.' It is not always the other fellow's problem. It is our problem also whenever there is economic trouble afloat."
—Mark E. Peterson[14]

Automobile insurance
Insurance against damage to your vehicle, damage to another vehicles, bodily injury, or damage to property resulting from an accident involving a vehicle.

Liability coverage
Auto insurance that pays for losses related to bodily injury, property damage, lawsuits, and defense costs.

There are 30 million automobile accidents in the United States annually, which equals about one accident for every five licensed drivers. These accidents result in over $100 billion in economic losses, two million injuries, and 40,000 deaths.[15] Because of the frequency of accidents and the magnitude of the losses involved, everyone who owns a car that drives on public roads is required to have some automobile insurance or proof of financial responsibility.

Types of Coverage

There are six basic types of automobile coverage: liability, medical payments, uninsured/underinsured motorist, comprehensive, collision, and no-fault (or Personal Injury Protection – PIP).

Liability coverage is legally required in every state except New Hampshire.[16] It pays for losses related to bodily injury, property damage, lawsuits, and defense costs. Bodily injury refers to expenses related to deaths or injuries resulting from an accident. Property damage refers to costs for damage to the car or cars involved in an accident as well as damages to other property (such as lamp posts or fire hydrants). Lawsuit coverage refers to losses related to any lawsuit resulting from an accident. In addition to the maximum amount of expenses your policy covers for a lawsuit, your policy may also cover your defense costs if the case goes to trial.

Liability coverage is generally expressed with three numbers that reflect the maximum amount the insurance company will pay for each of the specific types of liability for each accident. For example, if you have a 100/300/50 liability insurance policy, it means your limits are $100,000 per person for bodily injury liability coverage, $300,000 per accident for bodily injury liability coverage, and $50,000 per accident for property damage coverage. These dollar amounts are the maximum amounts your insurance company will pay per person or per accident. Should the cost of the accident exceed these limits, you will be responsible for paying the difference. We recommend limits of at least $100,000 per person and $300,000 per accident with at least $50,000 for property damage.

Medical payment coverage pays for accident-related medical costs and funeral expenses incurred by you or your family members within three years of an accident. It also covers you (the insured) while walking, even though you are not in a vehicle. We recommend a minimum medical payment coverage of $50,000.

Uninsured (or underinsured) motorist coverage is legally required in many states. It covers your costs if you are injured by an uninsured motorist or if you are injured in a hit-and-run accident. It also covers your costs if the other driver's insurance is insufficient to pay for your expenses (in other words, if the other driver is underinsured). The other driver must be at fault for you to collect on this coverage. We recommend that you keep your uninsured/underinsured insurance coverage the same as your liability coverage.

Collision coverage pays for damage to your car resulting from any collision with another vehicle or non-living object regardless of whose fault it might be. For example, it covers a two-vehicle impact accident, backing into your brick mail box, hitting the side of

your garage, or colliding with a cement pillar in a parking garage. If another driver is at fault and has liability insurance, your insurance company would fix your car but would get reimbursed for their expenses from the other driver's liability insurance.

Comprehensive coverage is also called OTC (other than collision) coverage. It covers damage to your vehicle that happens because of anything other than a collision. Your comprehensive coverage would cover damage to your car caused by a hailstorm, an earthquake, a lightning strike, a rock in the windshield, or a UFO. This coverage protects you if your car is stolen or vandalized. Surprisingly, it is this comprehensive coverage that pays for damages to your vehicle when you hit a deer, moose, rabbit, dog, giraffe, or other animal. When you get free rock chip repair on your windshield, it is your comprehensive insurance that pays the bill.

No-fault insurance is also called Personal Injury Protection or PIP. It was established as a way to reduce litigation costs. It provides those injured in an accident with direct payment from the company with which they are insured. This eliminates the need for accident victims to establish another's liability, or fault, through a civil lawsuit. As of 2014, twelve states (Florida, Hawaii, Kansas, Kentucky, Massachusetts, Michigan, Minnesota, New Jersey, New York, North Dakota, Pennsylvania, and Utah) and the District of Columbia have no-fault auto insurance laws that in some way restrict the right of parties to file legal suits.

Saving Money on Auto Insurance

Because there are several different possible automobile insurance coverage plans, it is important for you to be able to choose the coverage that best meets your family's needs. Are all the coverages necessary? For a new car, the answer is most likely yes. For an older car (perhaps more than ten years old), it may be prudent to either raise the deductible on collision and comprehensive or drop the coverage altogether. Raising the deductible reduces the size of your premium but increases your out-of-pocket cost in the event of an accident.

Medical payment coverage
Auto insurance that pays for accident-related medical costs and funeral expenses incurred by you or your family members within three years of an accident.

Collision coverage
Auto insurance that pays for damage to your car when it is involved in an accident, regardless of who is at fault.

Comprehensive coverage
Auto insurance that protects from risks other than vehicle collision.

Uninsured/Underinsured motorist coverage
Auto insurance that covers your costs if you are injured in a hit-and-run accident, or injured by an uninsured motorist or a motorist whose insurance is insufficient to pay for your expenses.

Reducing Your Auto Insurance Premium

There are things you can do to lower the cost of automobile insurance for your family. Companies may differ in what premium discounts they offer, but the following are some common discounts:

- Completing a driver training program
- Maintaining a certain GPA level
- Maintaining a great credit score
- Participating in a carpool
- Driving fewer than a certain number of miles per year
- Insuring two or more vehicles with the same company
- Establishing a safe driving record

On the other hand, premium rates may rise due to the following:

- Age (teenagers are expensive)
- Sex (males are more expensive than females)
- Marital status (it's good to be married!)
- Where you live (New York City costs more than Nephi, Utah)
- What the vehicle is primarily used for (higher rates for heavier usage)
- Accidents or tickets (if you do get a ticket, go to traffic school to get them off your record)
- Type of vehicle (a Ferrari costs more than a Toyota Camry)

Basically, don't be a nineteen-year-old, single male in New York City driving a Ferrari!

Here are some additional tips for keeping your automobile insurance costs down:

- Shop comparatively – look online at www.netquote.com or www.carinsurance.com
- Consider only high-quality insurance companies
- Make use of all available discounts
- Buy vehicles that are inexpensive to insure
- Drive defensively
- Be cautious of allowing others to drive your car
- Improve your credit score
- Review your insurance coverage on a regular basis

> *"It is the opinion of many that more difficult times lie ahead. We are deeply concerned about the welfare of our people and recognize the potential privation and suffering that will exist if each person and family does not accept the word of the Lord when he says, 'Prepare every needful thing' (D&C 88:119), and 'It must needs be done in mine own way' (D&C 104:16)."*
> —Victor L. Brown[17]

Summary

Insurance allows you to protect you and your family against catastrophic loss. Now that you have completed this chapter, it is our hope that you are more familiar with key aspects of insurance (managing risk, premiums and deductibles, etc.) and with different types of insurance policies. Having this basic understanding will help you make informed decisions about which policies are best for your family's financial situation. Obtaining the insurance that is best for you and your family will bring an added dimension of security, peace, and joy to your home.

Other Resources

- https://www.healthcare.gov/
- http://www.ehealthinsurance.com
- http://kff.org/health-reform/
- http://www.carinsurance.com/
- http://www.netquote.com/
- http://www.term4sale.com/

Notes

1. "Insurance Definition," *Investopedia,* http://www.investopedia.com/terms/i/insurance.asp.
2. "How Common Are House Fires? | Free By 50," http://www.freeby50.com/2012/04/how-common-are-house-fires.html.
3. *U.S. Fire Administration*, http://www.usfa.fema.gov/data/.
4. Marvin J. Ashton, "Guide to Family Finance," *Liahona* (April 2000) https://www.lds.org/liahona/2000/04/guide-to-family-finance?lang=eng.
5. Marvin J. Ashton, "Guide to Family Finance," *Liahona* (April 2000) https://www.lds.org/liahona/2000/04/guide-to-family-finance?lang=eng.
6. Gordon B. Hinckley, "To Men of the Priesthood," (Oct 2002), https://www.lds.org/general-conference/2002/10/to-men-of-the-priesthood?lang=eng.
7. "Actuarial Life Table," https://www.ssa.gov/oact/STATS/table4c6.html.
8. N. E. Tanner, "Constancy Amid Change," (Oct 2009), https://www.lds.org/ensign/1979/11/constancy-amid-change?lang=eng
9. "Health Insurance Coverage of the Total Population," http://kff.org/other/state-indicator/total-population/.
10. "Individual Mandate Penalty You Pay If You Don't Have Health Insurance Coverage," *HealthCare.gov,* https://www.healthcare.gov/fees/fee-for-not-being-covered/
11. "Exemptions from the Fee for Not Having Coverage," *HealthCare.gov,* https://www.healthcare.gov/health-coverage-exemptions/exemptions-from-the-fee/
12. http://obamacarefacts.com/benefitsofobamacare/
13. James E. Faust, "The Responsibility for Welfare Rests with Me and My Family," (April 1986), https://www.lds.org/general-conference/1986/04/the-responsibility-for-welfare-rests-with-me-and-my-family?lang=eng.
14. Mark E. Petersen, "Blessings in Self-Reliance," (April 1981), https://www.lds.org/ensign/1981/05/blessings-in-self-reliance?lang=eng.
15. "General Statistics," *Insurance Institute for Highway Safety Highway Loss Data Institute,* http://www.iihs.org/iihs/topics/t/general-statistics/fatalityfacts/state-by-state-overview
16. "Car Insurance Requirements by State," http://www.cars.com/go/advice/Story.jsp?section=ins&subject=ins_req&story=state-insurance-requirements
17. Victor L. Brown, "Prepare Every Needful Thing," (Oct 1980), https://www.lds.org/general-conference/1980/10/prepare-every-needful-thing?lang=eng

7

Understanding and Financing Major Family Purchases: Buying a Car

LEARN

- To buy a car that fits the needs and financial situation of your family

- That buying and financing a car that is too expensive for your budget can be a heavy burden on your financial health and family goals

"Sweetheart, we need a four-wheel-drive truck."

She asked, "Why do you think we need a new truck?"

He answered her question with what he believed was the perfect response: "What if we needed milk for our children in a terrible storm, and the only way I could get to the grocery store was in a pickup?"

His wife replied with a smile, "If we buy a new truck, we will not have money for milk—so why worry about getting to the store in an emergency!"

—Elder David A. Bednar's anecdote in "Bear Up Their Burdens with Ease"[1]

All families have transportation needs: you have to travel to work; you have to travel to school; you have to travel to Church; you have to travel on vacations. The choices you make to meet those transportation needs will make a big difference in your financial situation and determine whether or not you are a wise financial steward.

I made several mistakes the first time I bought a car. In 1979, Juanita and I were expecting our second child and we needed more reliable transportation than the 1960 Chevrolet Malibu station wagon that we owned at the time. In purchasing this vehicle, we made numerous mistakes but we did do one thing right: we avoided debt by "paying our car payment in advance to ourselves" each month. We saved $7,500 so that we could pay cash for the car. But then the mistakes came!

My first mistake was not bringing Juanita with me to the car lot. I went alone and was totally captivated by the first car I saw: a sporty-looking two-door Chevrolet Monza with only 7,000 miles on it. Had Juanita been with me, she would have helped me understand how difficult it would be to put a car seat in the back of that vehicle.

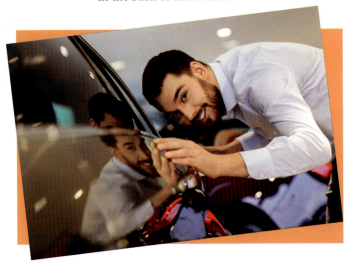

Then I drove the car. Wow! It had powerful engine pick up and was fun to drive. I wanted that car. I noticed the sticker price in the window was $7,500. Divine intervention! I had found my car! Not! My second mistake was failing to test drive other cars in that car lot and failing to investigate options in other car lots. I was in too much of a hurry. I excitedly told the sales person what a blessing it was that the asking price was exactly what we had saved. He said with a grin, "Then you can drive it home today!" I went into the sales office, signed the sales contract, and gave him a check.

Here I made the next two mistakes. First, I didn't check the bluebook value of the car. In my defense, in those days you had to go to the library and look up the bluebook value with a big blue book that was in the reference section. Still, I didn't do it! I later found out that the car I bought for $7,500 had cost $7,000 new, the year before! I felt so dumb. My second mistake was that I didn't go home to talk and pray about the decision with Juanita. You should never make a major financial decision without getting a good meal, talking about it with your spouse, making a joint decision, praying about it, sleeping on it, and praying again in the morning.

The next and, thankfully, last mistake was that I hadn't included taxes, licensing, and registration in the amount I had saved. I paid cash for the car, but things were tight for several months in our budget because I had neglected to account for the total cost of that car.

I hope you learn from my mistakes—which probably cost us about $2,000 and some family stress. I do need to tell the rest of the story to show that I am not entirely a dork. Juanita and I drove that car for 120,000 miles in six years. I changed the oil religiously every 3,000 miles. I performed all of the scheduled maintenance. We never had a single mechanical problem. Even though I had been foolish on the front end, I was wise on the back end and our 1979 Chevrolet Monza ended up as a good investment.

Buying a Car

This chapter will address principles of effective car ownership, ways to finance a car, the decision to buy new or used, and the purchasing process.

Principles of Effective Car Ownership

Here are three principles of effective car ownership.

1. **Understand why you are buying a car.** Ideally, your purpose should be to provide safe, dependable transportation in a cost-effective manner. Your purpose should not be based in vanity. Realize that a car is a tool to achieve your other

goals, not necessarily a goal in and of itself. With this in mind, not every person in every circumstance needs a car. For example, it may be more cost effective for a BYU student to avoid the cost of car ownership and use the BYU Car Sharing program to rent vehicles from Enterprise-Rent-a-Car at $5 to $10 an hour when needed for special occasions.[2]

2. **Understand the total cost of owning the car.** This includes depreciation of the value of the car (which is most significant when you buy a new car), taxes, licensing, fees, insurance premiums, financing charges, fuel costs, scheduled maintenance, and repairs. After determining the total cost of car ownership, you should also consider the opportunity cost— the potentially greater value of other things you could have purchased with the money you spent on the car. The website www.edmunds.com/tco.html provides an easy tool to calculate the total five-year cost of owning most new and used cars.

3. **Be a wise steward over your resources: take care of your car.** This means that you do the necessary repairs when needed and perform the maintenance on schedule to ensure that the car will last for many years. The most important thing you can do to maintain your car is to change your oil on time, every time. While skipping a scheduled maintenance may save you money short-term, in the long run it may result in higher maintenance and repair costs. It can also be dangerous.

Total Cost to Own a Car

On their website, www.edmunds.com/tco.html, Edmunds enables you to project the total typical cost of owning a particular car for five years. Whether or not you use the Edmunds website, their methodology is helpful to illustrate all of the different costs that quickly add up when you own a car. Edmunds uses the following seven factors:

- Depreciation: how much value the car loses each year
- Interest on financing: the amount of interest paid over five years
- Taxes and fees: the total of all sales tax, fees, and registry costs each year
- Insurance premiums: the average cost of insuring the car
- Fuel: how much you have to pay for the type of fuel that the car requires: regular gasoline, premium gasoline, or diesel fuel
- Maintenance: the total cost of performing all the scheduled maintenance found in the vehicle's owner's manual
- Repairs: the projected cost of fixing common mechanical problems for this vehicle

If you view a car as a tool to help you achieve other more important goals, you will make better decisions when purchasing your car.

How to Finance a Car

Cash (least expensive). Buying a car with cash is the least expensive purchasing option, if you can afford it, because you pay no interest and avoid debt. The easiest way to do this is to "pay your car payment to yourself each month." If there is no pressure to purchase a car by a specific date, you can invest this money in stock-based mutual funds and, on average, earn a good return. However, with stocks there is always a risk that you will lose money in a down market for a few years. If you must have the car you are saving for by a particular date, it is best to save the money in the bank. For some emerging adults, saving enough ahead of time may be implausible. It may be necessary to get a loan.

Depreciate

To lose value over time.

Lease

Long-term renting with a number of conditions.

Loan (next best). If you decide to take out a loan to buy a car, the first principle is to make as large of a down payment as you can reasonably afford. This will reduce the amount of money you spend on interest. Next, remember that banks and credit unions will charge different interest rates than the dealer will charge. Financing provided through the dealership is usually the most expensive type of financing, so compare interest rates on auto loans from multiple institutions before you purchase a car. When comparing different loans, look at the term of the loan, the interest rate, and the fees. Your credit score will have a major impact on the interest rate you will pay on your auto loan, so keep your credit score high. Also, realize that nearly all costs are negotiable.

Lease ("lease"st best). Leasing (or long-term renting) has become a popular way to acquire a new vehicle. About 25 percent of all new vehicles are leased rather than purchased outright.[3] In fact, you may have noticed that an increasing number of car ads give prices in terms of leasing rather than buying. Carefully compare the cost of buying (including the interest associated with a loan) and leasing over time. See www.consumerreports.org/cro/2012/12/buying-vs-leasing-basics/index.htm[4] for a great comparison of buying versus leasing. One of the biggest drawbacks to leasing is that you do not actually own the car and therefore do not have full freedom with it (when you can sell, how many miles you drive, customization, etc.). Most leases have a mileage cap, beyond which you may have to pay $0.20 or $0.25 per mile. This can be very expensive if you unexpectedly need to drive more often. Also, your leasing rate, like the interest you'd pay when buying a car, will be affected by your credit score. In summary, you generally come out money ahead if you buy rather than lease.

Buying New vs. Buying Used

A car loses some of its value the second you drive it off the lot, sometimes thousands of dollars! It is generally most economical to buy a car that is two to three years old because, by that point, it has already **depreciated** significantly but still has most of its useful life ahead. (See Table 7.1 for a typical depreciation schedule.) If you choose to buy a used car, you must be cautious as you evaluate the potential options. The nice thing about a brand new car is that you know it should be in perfect condition; you never quite know what you're getting into when you purchase a used car. Table 7.1 demonstrates that the depreciation of a new car is most rapid during the first two years of ownership. It is therefore generally most cost effective to buy a two- or three-year old car with low mileage.

Here are four bits of advice for buying a used car.

1. **Contact the seller:** Create a list of questions before calling the seller, then use those questions to decide whether or not you want to see the car. Ask for the price, because it may have been lowered since the date of the advertisement. Ask about the mileage, the number of previous owners, and how often the oil has been changed. Before you buy, ask to see receipts for oil changes and other major services. Also check carfax.com.

Table 7.1 Sample Depreciation Schedule of a Typical Vehicle

Period Percentage	Depreciation Value	Residual	Loss in Most Recent Period
12 Months	25%	75%	25%
24 Months	40%	60%	15%
36 Months	50%	50%	10%
48 Months	58%	42%	8%
60 Months	64%	36%	6%
72 Months	69%	31%	5%

2. **Verify the vehicle history:** Ask for and verify information about previous owners. On www.carfax.com, you can determine the following information: number of previous owners, where each owner purchased the car, accident history, repair history, and maintenance history. To obtain this information, you must input the vehicle's VIN number on the site and pay a fee. CARFAX will then give you a detailed vehicle history, including mileage listed on the odometer and a title check to ensure that the vehicle was not stolen. Check out the vehicle history of every potential purchase.

3. **Determine a fair price:** Know the blue book price (kbb.com) for the car you are calling about. The high blue book price is what you would likely pay for the car on a lot. The low blue book price is what you would expect to pay from a private party. If possible, come to an agreement with the seller on the quality of the vehicle (fair, good, or excellent) before you see the car. Coming to this agreement will allow you to determine a fair price beforehand.

4. **Inspect the vehicle carefully:** When you see the car, note your first impressions. Does the car appear to be well cared for? Have a mechanic do a thorough inspection of the car before laying any money down. This could save you from some nasty surprises after it is too late to change your mind.

The Purchasing Process

First, decide upon your financing plan before you go looking for a car. Know your family's financial goals, what kind of car would help you achieve those goals, and how much of your budget you would like to put towards car payments. Do not be swayed from your budget by the emotion you feel when you find a car you really want!

Second, it is critical that you comparison shop. You should compare prices, features, and quality to find out exactly what you want. Be informed. Go to car dealerships and look around online.[5] As you look at different cars, determine what is available in your price range and budget. Once you've narrowed the choices, test drive the exact vehicles you are considering. Do not buy any car without test driving it first. When making your final decision, it is critical that you remember to make your car fit your budget. Don't make your budget fit your car.

Once you have found the car you want to buy, negotiate a deal. Know the fair market value of the car and decide how much you can spend beforehand, then negotiate politely. Only enter into negotiations with a salesperson who makes you feel comfortable and who can make a deal. If you plan to pay in cash, let the seller know. Cash can do wonders for an agreement. If you think the price is too high, make a persuasive case to support your argument. For example, you could point out that the vehicle needs some work, that the body or paint doesn't justify the price, or that you have seen lower prices elsewhere. If you want to test the price, you can explain that the car isn't exactly what you're looking for, but at a lower price you might be interested. You can also let the seller know that the car is worth the price but you can only afford a lower price because of budgetary constraints. Make an opening offer that is low but in the ballpark of the seller's asking price—do not be unrealistic.

Don't be afraid to walk away if you're not getting anywhere; you don't have to buy the car. Leave if you get tired, hungry, or angry, or if you feel pressured. Don't be hurried into a decision. Don't be distracted by pitches for related items. Expect the salesman to try to improve the deal before you reach a final price. If the seller cannot meet your price (that you predetermined you could afford), walk way.

Avoid buying a car under pressure like the plague.

Finally, once you have made your purchase, read the owner's manual carefully and follow the suggested maintenance schedule. One of the best things you can do for your car is to change the oil every 3,000 miles. Don't ignore warning signals when your car doesn't work as it should. When a light illuminates on the dashboard, find out what it means and take care of it. When problems arise, get them fixed. Find a good garage with well-trained and experienced mechanics and let them take good care of your vehicle. Then enjoy the ride!

Avoid buying a car under pressure like the plague!

My Friend's Mistake

By Dr. E. Jeffrey Hill

A close friend of mine made a big mistake when he bought a sweet-looking truck from a car lot. He saw the truck and fell in love with it. The salesperson talked it up. The price was $12,900—about $1,000 under the blue book value. This was a bigtime deal. Then the salesperson said he'd lower the price by another $1,500 if my friend would buy today and take the responsibility of getting it inspected and licensed. My friend bought the truck on the spot. When I saw the beautiful truck, I asked my friend if he had run the CARFAX Report on it. He had not, and when we ran it, we were amazed to see that this truck had been sold and re-sold six times in five different states, including Hawaii. It did not pass the safety inspection because of electrical problems (which had always been with this truck). My friend tried to take the truck back, but the dealership wouldn't take it. To make a long story short, $6,000 and three major repairs later, my friend had a great truck. His total price: $17,400 . . . only $3,500 ABOVE the blue book value. Take it from my friend: when you buy a used car, get the CARFAX Report and have it checked out by a mechanic first!

Summary

In this chapter, we learned principles of effective car ownership. We learned about different financing options, and we discussed buying new versus buying used. We learned what to do before, during, and after purchasing your car. We learned that the most cost-effective way to purchase a car is to pay cash for a two- to three-year-old vehicle with low mileage and no mechanical problems.

Wisely handling the automobile purchase decision will contribute significantly to your wise financial stewardship. We hope that the important financial decision of buying a car now seems less intimidating and more exciting!

Other Resources

- www.carfax.com
- www.cargurus.com
- www.consumerreports.org/cro/2012/12/buying-vs-leasing-basics/index.htm
- www.edmunds.com
- www.kbb.com

Notes

1. David A. Bednar, "Bear Up Their Burdens with Ease," (April 2014), https://www.lds.org/general-conference/2014/04/bear-up-their-burdens-with-ease?lang=eng.
2. http://sustainability.byu.edu/car-sharing-program/
3. http://www.edmunds.com/about/press/leasing-is-shifting-the-new-car-market-but-it-isnt-the-best-choice-for-everyone-says-edmundscom.html
4. www.consumerreports.org/cro/2012/12/buying-vs-leasing-basics/index.htm
5. www.ksl.com; www.craigslist.com; www.cargurus.com ; www.carmax.com; www.edmunds.com ; are a few online sites.

How to Buy a Car

Before you make an offer

1. Develop an excellent credit score
2. Find cars you might want on websites such as www.cars.com or www.autotrader.com
3. Ask sellers several questions to determine the condition of each car
4. Run the CARFAX Reports at www.carfax.com
5. Determine five-year costs to own at www.edmunds.com
6. Determine fair prices at www.kbb.com
7. Decide which car to make an offer on

Making an offer and buying the car

1. Make a reasonable offer slightly below the fair price
2. Negotiate and agree to a price with seller
3. Take the car to a mechanic for a thorough inspection (if needed)
4. Obtain financing if needed (shop around, credit unions are often best)
5. Read and then sign the sales contract (no grace period)
6. Pay for the car, get the title, and drive away

Immediately after you buy the car

1. Add the car to your insurance policy
2. Go to the DMV
    - Pay license
    - Pay registration
    - Pay sales tax
3. Enjoy your car!

8

Understanding and Financing Major Family Purchases: Buying a Home

LEARN

- To buy a home that fits the needs and financial situation of your family
- About different types of mortgage loans
- That buying a house that is too expensive can be a heavy burden on your financial health and family goals

There is nothing to compare with a young couple's feelings when they step across the threshold into the entryway of their first home. Generally, there have been a few years of financial challenges and sacrifice to save for the down payment. The young family has probably been living in a small apartment and coping with neighbors on either side of them, and often above and below them as well. Now the time has arrived to enter their own home. It seems so expansive. The yard looks beautiful. They are excited to start mowing their own lawn and planting flowers in their own yard.

> *"Be it ever so humble, there's no place like home."* — John Howard Payne[1]

If this couple has planned wisely and purchased a modest home within their means, it is likely this place of abode "can be a heaven on earth."[3] However, if the couple has purchased an extravagant home beyond their means, this place may precipitate

financial ruin and family conflict, becoming a veritable hell on earth. In this chapter, we want to provide financial information so that when the time comes for you to purchase a home, you will choose heaven, not hell.

As with all material possessions, it is important to have a stewardship perspective towards your family and home(s). God gives us everything, and we are simply His stewards. Keeping this in mind will help your family be humble, make wise financial choices, and strive towards achieving your family goals. It will also help you to avoid making foolish decisions grounded in pride and appearances.

President Gordon B. Hinckley shared some lessons he learned about buying a home:

> When I was a young man, my father counseled me to build a modest home, sufficient for the needs of my family, and make it beautiful and attractive and pleasant and secure. He counseled me to pay off the mortgage as quickly as I could so that, come what may, there would be a roof over the heads of my wife and children. I was reared on that kind of doctrine.[4]

"A house is a hole in the middle of land that you pour money into." — Bryan Sudweeks[5]

Buying a home is not easy, and this purchase will likely be among the largest financial commitments you will ever make. You should not rush your decisions in these weighty matters. If you use wisdom and judgment in trying to decide what you need, what you want, and what you can afford, and if you will listen to and obey the promptings of the Holy Ghost, you will make wise decisions regarding your transportation and housing needs.

Buying a Home

Buying a home could be the biggest financial decision your family will ever make—so be wise. Everyone needs a roof over his or her head; the key is to be financially prudent.

There are many risks associated with purchasing a home. There are financial risks if you purchase too expensive a home, particularly if the housing market goes down. In fact, I believe the biggest financial mistake that young couples right out of BYU make is to purchase a home that is too big, costs too much, and has too large a payment. When a couple does that, other financial goals cannot be realized because of the large house payment. The couple becomes cash starved and unable to save. There is the added temptation if the value of the home goes up to get home equity loans to furnish and maintain the home. In this case, marriages and families may suffer from the added strain.

There are also skills risks if you purchase a "fixer-upper" at a low price, but you do not have the skills to maintain, repair, and/or remodel that home. And there is always the risk of buying a home in an iffy neighborhood and becoming stuck there for many years.

At the same time, there are many benefits of purchasing the right home in the right

Table 7.1 Advantages and Disadvantages of Housing Options

Housing Option	Advantages	Disadvantages
Renting	Easy and inexpensive to move No costs for repairs or maintenance Lower financial commitments One rent bill	Lack of stability (you may have to move at the end of the rental period) Lack of pride associated with ownership No modifications or renovations can be made Possibility for monthly payment to increase Restrictions on where you can rent because of zoning No tax benefits No potential for your property appreciating Less privacy
Buying	Pride associated with ownership Permanence and security You can make modifications Unchanging monthly payment You can own the house using borrowed money Interest payments on a home are tax deductible You can borrow against the equity of your home	Low mobility—houses are not liquid Significant upfront costs (down payment, closing costs) Costs more to own and operate (repairs, utilities, landscaping, etc.) The home's value could decrease Large financial commitment
Building	All advantages of buying plus the following: Customization—exactly how you want it Sometimes cheaper than buying New appliances—few repairs in the first years Location of your choice	All disadvantages of buying plus the following: Difficult to interpret building plans Often exceeds original budget Often has delays Construction loan interest and renting costs during the building process High stress
Renovating	All the advantages of buying plus the following: Faster than building Some customization Cheaper—especially if you can do some of the work Can often stay in your home during the renovation	All of the disadvantages of buying plus the following: Could be more expensive than building Often over budget Frequent delays Additional unexpected expenses (yard, fencing, etc.) Construction loan interest and renting costs during the building process May encounter additional problems that were not noted before High stress

neighborhood. A home can be a great financial investment. For example, my dad purchased a home overlooking Monterey Bay fifty years ago. In that time the home value increased 4000%!

President Gordon B. Hinckley gave excellent home-buying counsel: "I recognize that it may be necessary to borrow to get a home, of course. But let us buy a home that we can afford and thus ease the payments which will constantly hang over our heads without mercy or respite for as long as 30 years. . . . *I urge you to be modest in your expenditures; discipline yourselves in your purchases to avoid debt to the extent possible. Pay off debt as quickly as you can.* . . . That's all I have to say about it, but I wish to say it with all the emphasis of which I am capable."[5]

Please consider this chapter carefully so that you purchase the right home, at the right price, in the right neighborhood to bless your family.

Housing Options

Every family needs a roof over its head, but there are many options to meet that goal.

Will you rent, buy, build, or remodel? Each option has various advantages and disadvantages that are important to think about when considering your family's needs.

A key factor in the decision between renting and buying, building or renovating is the length of time you expect to be in the home. If you expect to be in a location for less than two years it is almost always wise financially to rent instead of buying. If you expect to be in a location for more than five years it is almost always wise financially to buy instead of rent. If you expect to be in a location two to five years, either one could be optimal depending on the housing market. The exception to this might be the ability to purchase a home at low cost (usually a "fixer-upper") and then add considerable value (especially if you do a lot of the work yourself).

Cost of Housing

Your monthly mortgage payment will typically be between 20 to 35 percent of your household budget. However, the difference in the cost of housing is largely based on where you live. For example, the median income for both Kokomo, IN and Los Angeles, CA is similar, but the median home price is $88,000 in Kokomo and $300,000 in Los Angeles! See Table 7.2 for the cost of housing in various regions from 1990 to 2010.

How Much House You Can Afford

In order to figure out how much you can afford to spend on a home purchase, it is critical that you know your affordability ratios, or how much debt the bank thinks you can handle.

There are two main ratios: the housing-expense ratio (or front-end ratio) and the debt-obligations ratio (or back-end ratio). Your front-end ratio is your monthly payment of principal, interest, property taxes, and insurance (PITI) divided by your monthly gross income. Banks have determined that if this ratio is 28 percent or less, there is a much greater chance that you will be able to pay back your loan. The back-end ratio is your monthly payment of principal, interest, property taxes, and insurance (PITI) plus any other long-term debt (including any debt older than twelve months, e.g., car payments, student loans, alimony payments, etc.), all divided by your monthly gross income. Banks have determined that if this ratio is 36 percent or less, it is an indicator that you have much more flexibility in your finances and are more likely to pay back your loan.

One of the worst financial mistakes you can make as a young couple is to buy a home that is too expensive. When you go to the

Table 7.2 Cost of Housing in the United States and by Region from 1990 to 2010					
Year	U.S.	Northeast	Midwest	South	West
1990	$92,000	$126,400	$75,300	$85,100	$129,600
1995	$110,500	$126,700	$94,800	$97,700	$141,000
2000	$139,100	$139,500	$123,600	$128,200	$183,400
2005	$219,000	$281,600	$168,300	$181,100	$340,300
2010	$172,900	$243,500	$141,600	$150,100	$214,800
Percentage Change from 1990 to 2010	88%	93%	88%	76%	66%

bank to apply for a mortgage loan, they will ask you to declare all your debts. LDS couples should count their 10 percent tithe as a long-term debt. If, as an LDS couple, you and your spouse don't declare tithing as a debt, you may be given a loan that you will not be able to pay back. This can cause immense stress and strain in your finances and relationships. Being house-rich and cash-poor occurs when your debt ratios go above the recommended limits and you are stretched to be able to make your mortgage payment. You can avoid this by calculating beforehand which mortgages you can afford (taking tithing into account) and buying a house accordingly.

Avoid being house-rich and cash-poor like the plague.

Owning a home free of debt is an important goal of provident living, although it may not be a realistic possibility for some. A mortgage on a home leaves a family unprotected against severe financial storms. Homes that are free and clear of mortgages and liens cannot be foreclosed on. When there are good financial times, it is the most opportune time to retire our debts and pay installments in advance. It is a truth that "the borrower is servant to the lender.
—James E. Faust[6]

Steps to Buying a Home

The most important things to remember as you engage in the process of buying a home are to take your time, do your homework, and avoid rushing into anything. Neglecting to do these things could easily leave you and your family stuck with a home that is above your financial capacity or below your desires and expectations. In this instance, the scripture "in your patience possess ye your souls,"[7] might be modified to read, "In your patience possess ye your ideal home!"

We have outlined nine steps to buying a home.

Before beginning to make offers on homes, complete the following three steps:

1. Carefully examine your monthly budget to determine how much you can afford to spend on housing.

2. Go to a lender (bank, credit union, etc.) and pre-qualify for a loan. In this process,

Avoid being house-rich and cash-poor like the plague!

the lender will help you determine the mortgages that are in your price range. Remember to count tithing (equivalent to 10 percent of your income) as a long-term debt.

3. Determine what you are looking for. How big do you want your home and yard to be? How many bedrooms and bathrooms would you like to have? What neighborhood would you like to live in? How near would you like to be (commute time) to work, school, church, or grocery stores?

Once you have determined the above factors, you are ready to go house hunting!

4. Get others to help you in the process of buying a home. Remember, you can't (and shouldn't) do everything by yourself. Get a good realtor who knows the

Home Buying Lessons I Learned in Atlanta

By Dr. E. Jeffrey Hill

I learned the hard way that buying the right home in the right neighborhood at the right price takes time. It cannot be rushed.

In ancient times, just after writing was invented, I got a great promotion at IBM with a 30 percent raise that required us to relocate to Atlanta, Georgia. IBM flew Juanita and me out for a week of house hunting. We made a goal to be prayerful and diligent, and to make a home-buying decision by the end of the week. It was a mistake to give ourselves this hard deadline.

On Monday, we looked at many houses for sale by owner to try to avoid the real estate commission and perhaps find a better deal. Most of these houses were not appealing, but we found one that we liked quite a bit. It had a large, open floor plan with four large bedrooms. The lot was a flat half acre with lots of play area, and it was located about four miles from my new office. The cost was $75,000.

The rest of the week, we went out with a very pleasant real estate agent. She carefully asked us questions to find out what we were looking for. By Thursday, we had looked at several dozen homes, but only one home was as nice as the first "by owner" home that we liked so much. This second home had all of the same features as the first, except the price was $89,500, and it was seven miles from my new office instead of four.

We decided to look at each of these homes again on Friday and then make a final decision that evening in order to meet our goal of purchasing our home before flying out on Saturday. On Thursday evening and all day Friday, we called the first "by owner" home, but no one answered. (This was LONG before cell phones.) We left several messages. On Friday evening, to meet our goal, we made an offer of $87,000 on the second home. Immediately, the owners made a counter offer of $89,000 and said it was their final offer. We didn't want to risk losing the home, so we accepted the offer.

The owners of the first "by owner" home called us back on Monday and were ready to sell us the home at a cost even below $75,000. However, we felt committed to the second home since we had signed a contract and put down $1,000 in earnest money.

This whole scenario was full of poor choices. The biggest poor choice was that we rushed the decision. Let me weep a bit as I tell you some of the consequences of that poor decision. First, we paid about $15,000 too much for the home. We later found out that that was the highest amount anyone had ever paid for a house in that subdivision. Second, the home we purchased was three miles further from my office, but I later found that with the horrendous traffic, these three miles added fifteen minutes each way to my commute. Third, the ward of the home we purchased was full of transplanted Utah executives. There were about sixty former bishops in the ward, and we did not get as great an opportunity to serve in that ward as we would have had in the other. This was a disappointment. Finally, we recognized that we had made a mistake just a few days after we signed the papers. It would have been better to get out of our contract, forfeit the earnest money, and then purchase the first home.

The moral of this story is to take your time when you purchase a home. Never rush into it. And if you make a poor choice, it is better to get out of the contract (perhaps forfeiting the earnest money) than to continue on.

neighborhood. Get a good appraiser who can help you make sure you don't pay too much for a house. Get a good lawyer who can help you fill out the correct forms. Most importantly, get a good home inspector. The last thing you want to do is buy someone else's problems.

5. Look at many different homes. There are websites that have excellent home search capabilities, such as zillow.com. Friends and relatives might also be able to refer you to people who are selling.

6. Determine down payment and up-front costs. Before you buy, remember that the down payment on a loan may be from 3 to 20 percent of the cost of the home, and the closing costs may be an additional 2 to 5 percent. Be aware that these costs are significant; given that these costs are paid up front, they must be planned for before you purchase the house. Also be advised that the golden down payment is 20 percent—at that point you avoid private mortgage insurance (PMI) and save on your monthly payment.

In home buying, there is something called "points." One **point** is equal to one percent of the loan value (two points on a $200,000 loan would be $2,000). Points are paid at closing by the borrower to the lender in order to reduce the interest rate on the loan. For example, the interest on a $200,000 loan might be 4.5% without points, 4.1% with one point, and 3.7% with two points. You are generally wise to pay for points for a lower interest rate when you plan to have the mortgage long enough to recover the expense.

Other up-front costs include title insurance, attorney fees, property survey fees, recording fees, lender's origination fees, appraisals, credit reports, termite/mold inspections, escrow payments, and the home inspection report.

7. Once you have found a house you are interested in, contact the seller of the home, either directly or through the realtor, and make a written offer of purchase price with a statement of your intent to make an earnest money deposit.

8. The seller may reject your offer and counteroffer with a higher price. Negotiating the price of a home is a process that may take two or three iterations. One common strategy is for the buyer and seller to meet halfway between the asking price and the first counter-offer.

9. Once the contract has been agreed upon, both parties (buyer and seller) sign it. You now make an earnest money deposit, which is an amount held in escrow to be given to the seller if you back out of the contract. This is why it is very important to be sure about your decision before purchasing the home. If you stay with your purchase and don't back out of the contract, the earnest money is applied toward the purchase price.

Point

Equal to one percent of the mortgage loan value, points are paid to the lender in exchange for a lower interest rate.

Mortgage Financing

Most of us do not have enough money at one time to pay cash for a house, so we must borrow money. A **mortgage** is a loan from a lending institution (bank, credit union, etc.) in which the home or property serves as the loan collateral. Your credit score (and that of your spouse) will affect the interest rate of your mortgage.

At the end of 2015, the amount of residential mortgage debt in the United States was more than $13.8 trillion.[8] Assuming a United States population of about 322 million people, this equates to about $42,860 of mortgage debt *per capita* (i.e. for every man, woman, and child). Although mortgage debt is often necessary, too many people do not get out of debt as quickly as they could. Do not drag out your loan for longer than is necessary. For example, your family may consider a fifteen-year mortgage instead of a thirty-year mortgage (see Table 7.3).

Amortization

The amount and frequency of equal payments that will gradually repay a loan (including principal and interest) over the length of the loan.

Mortgage

A loan in which the home serves as loan collateral.

Table 7.3 Fifteen-Year vs. Thirty-Year Mortgage

15-Year	30-Year
Higher monthly payments	Lower monthly payments
Lower interest rate	Higher interest rate
Lower total cost	Higher total cost
Automatic savings	Savings only if you prepay

Table 7.4 shows an example of the money you could save by getting a fifteen-year loan. Not only does a fifteen-year loan enable you to save interest money, you also follow the counsel of prophets by getting out of debt quickly.

The following are some key terms and principles relating to mortgages that you should be familiar with before buying a home:

Amortization is simply the process of determining the amount and frequency of equal payments that will gradually repay a loan (including principal and interest) over the length of the loan.

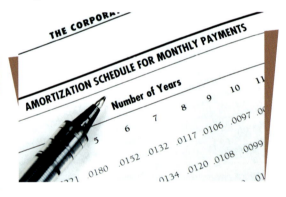

During the early years of a mortgage loan, the vast majority of the monthly payment goes to interest, not to principal. The interest portion of the monthly payment is calculated by multiplying the loan balance by the monthly rate of interest. The principal portion of the monthly payment is calculated by subtracting the interest portion from the monthly payment.

Mortgage insurance is required when the buyer of the home borrows more than 80 percent of the purchase price. This happens when the buyer makes a cash down payment of less than 20 percent of the purchase price. A lender takes greater risk in lending more than 80 percent of the purchase price to the homebuyer, as

Table 7.4 Fifteen-Year vs. Thirty-Year Mortgage Example

15-Year	30-Year
Loan Amount: $300,000	Loan Amount: $300,000
Amortization Period: 15 years	Amortization Period: 30 years
Interest Rate: 3.19%	Interest Rate: 3.95%
Monthly Payment: $2,099	Monthly Payment: $1,423
Total Interest: $77,868	Total Interest: $212,500
Difference in total amount of interest paid is $134,632!	

homeowners with less equity are more likely to default on the loan.

Payment Reduction Techniques

Joe J. Christensen warned, "How much house do we really need to accommodate our family comfortably? We should not endanger ourselves either spiritually or economically by acquiring homes which are ostentatious, feed our vanity, and go far beyond our needs."[9]

The principal amount of a loan will not change. However, there are things you can do to reduce the interest portion of the payments. Table 7.5 gives three common ways to reduce total interest paid to the lender over the life of the mortgage loan.

Mortgage Menu

Now that you are familiar with what a mortgage is, let's learn about different types of mortgages. But first, there are four key concepts that should guide your decision of how to finance a home.

1. Your time horizon: How long do you expect to have the mortgage, and how certain are you of that time horizon?

2. Your preference (if any) for low required payments: How important are lower payments in the initial years of the loan?

3. Your tolerance for interest-rate risk: Are you willing to assume the interest-rate risk of the loan? Where are interest rates now? Where do you expect them to go?

4. Your income and work status: Are you low income? Are you or have you been a member of the armed forces? If so, you may qualify for special mortgage programs.

Fixed rate mortgages have a constant (or fixed) interest rate throughout the life of the contract. This allows the borrower to be certain of payments, but the lender will be uncertain of the value of the payments as interest rates change. If the fixed rate mortgage is a first mortgage, the home is collateral for the loan. If the mortgage covers less than 80 percent of the appraised value, the home is the only collateral necessary. For mortgages greater than 80 percent of the appraised value, private mortgage insurance (PMI) is often required. The two most common types of fixed rate mortgages are 30-year and 15-year mortgages.

Adjustable rate mortgages (ARM), or variable rate mortgages, allow the interest rate to rise or fall with changes in mortgage interest rates over time. This effectively shifts the risks of the future from the lender to the bor-

Fixed rate mortgage

A loan which has a constant (or fixed) interest rate throughout the life of the contract. Monthly PI (principal and interest) remains fixed the duration of the loan.

Adjustable rate mortgage (ARM)

A loan which allows the interest rate to rise or fall with changes in mortgage interest rates.

Table 7.5 Mortgage Interest Reduction Techniques

Techniques	Benefits
Make a larger down payment	Reduces the initial loan amount
Have a good credit score	You qualify for a lower interest rate
Pay points	You get a lower interest rate
Shorten the length of the mortgage	You will have a lower interest rate and will pay less interest installments
Pay more than the normal monthly amount	Every extra dollar paid goes directly to principal (loan) reduction, which shortens the length of the loan and the total interest paid

Balloon mortgages

Mortgages where all remaining principle is due a certain number of years into the contract.

Graduated payment mortgages (GPM)

Mortgages with lower initial payments that increase over time.

Refinance

To finance a home again with a new loan and a new interest rate, must pay off old loan and closing costs.

Home equity loan

A loan which uses the equity in your house to secure your loan (to be avoided!).

Equity

Hypothetical amount of money you would have left if you sold your home and paid off your mortgage today.

Avoid home equity loans and home equity lines of credit like the plague!

rower. In return, the interest rate extended to the borrower is lower initially. There is usually a cap (+ 6%) which is the highest the interest rate can rise. Interest rates can also be adjusted lower if interest rates fall. For that reason, adjustable rate mortgages make more sense in times of high interest rates than in times of low interest rates.

Balloon mortgages are similar to standard mortgages. However, balloon mortgages have a due date three, five, or ten years into the contract when all remaining principal is due. Some are self-amortizing, while some are interest only. When the principal is due, the homeowner must either refinance or repay.

Graduated payment mortgages (GPM) are designed to allow younger people and those with a growing income to qualify for a home mortgage by initially reducing mortgage payments with contractual increases in the mortgage payments. Be cautious about entering into this type of mortgage because negative amortization could occur if your monthly payment is less than the interest-only amount would be.

Refinancing

If a homeowner has a high, fixed rate loan and market interest rates have decreased, the homeowner can **refinance** to a fixed rate loan with a lower rate of interest. The homeowner simply applies for a new loan (with a lower rate of interest) at the same bank or at a new bank and then continues to pay off the original loan amount.

On the other hand, a consumer with an adjustable rate loan may want to lock in a low, fixed rate loan. The benefits of a lower interest rate loan are lower payments every month and faster principal amortization. However, there may be closing costs (loan origination, appraisal, and legal fees), a prepayment penalty, and points on the new loan. Moreover, if the term of the new loan is greater than the number of years remaining on the original contract, the future payments are also a cost. In calculating the benefit of refinancing, the time value of money must be remembered. If one refinances for the remaining term of the original mortgage, then the sum of all costs of refinancing is a present value. The benefits occur over time because each month the monthly payment decreases.

Home Equity Loans

Also known as second mortgages, **home equity loans** and home equity lines of credit (HELOC) use the **equity** in your house (i.e., hypothetical amount of money you would have left if you sold your home and paid off your mortgage today) to secure your loan.

The benefits of a home equity loan are that you can usually borrow up to 80 percent of the equity in your home, and the interest payments may be tax-deductible. One disadvantage of this type of loan is that it limits your future financial flexibility. A home equity loan puts your home at risk: If you default on a home equity loan, you can lose not only your high credit score, but your home as well. There are few instances in which it is worth risking your family's financial wellbeing to accrue further debt. In addition, if the housing market declines you could owe more on your house than you could sell it for. This is called being upside-down in your mortgage and limits your flexibility to sell your home. Try to stay far away from home equity loans.

Avoid home equity loans and home equity lines of credit like the plague.

Types of Housing

When deciding where to live, it's important to weigh the different options and decide

which option best fits with your family's lifestyle and budget. Consider the following housing options:

- Single family housing: One house on one lot.

- Duplex: A lot with two dwellings under the same roof, but the lot is split into two separate legal parcels.

- Condominiums: You own your unit and are a shared owner of the surrounding property; you are required to pay a fee for the maintenance of the surrounding property to the condominium owners' association. Condominiums are much like apartments—the difference is that you are the owner.

- Cooperatives: The mortgage is with the cooperative and you "buy in;" your share of assessments, operating costs, and property taxes are paid to the cooperative; however, your portion of the cooperative's taxes and interest are tax deductible to you.

- Mobile homes: The price is attractive, but mobile homes have a history of depreciating; as such, they are often taxed as personal property rather than real property. Moreover, lenders will typically charge higher rates on mobile home loans.

Summary

President Gordon B. Hinckley counseled:

Be modest in your wants. You do not need a big home with a big mortgage as you

Dream Home Exercise

The home you live in makes a big difference to your family life. It is never too early to start thinking about your future family, where you would like to live with that family, the characteristics of the home you would like to live in, and to understand the amount of income required to purchase and maintain such a home. Try this exercise.

1. Imagine you and your future family in your dream home 15 years from now.
2. Write down the answers to the following questions:
   - Are you married?
   - How many children do you have?
   - In what city do you live?
   - How many bedrooms and how many bathrooms are in your dream home?
   - Any special features in your dream home?
3. Go to www.realtor.com and input the city, bedrooms, and bathrooms; select the home that best matches your dream.
4. On www.realtor.com go to mortgage calculator and determine what your monthly payment for that house will be.
5. Multiply the monthly payment times 5 to find the monthly gross income that will be required to purchase and maintain this home.

begin your lives together. You can and should avoid overwhelming debt. There is nothing that will cause greater tensions in marriage than grinding debt, which will make of you a slave to your creditors. You may have to borrow money to begin ownership of a home. But do not let it be so costly that it will preoccupy your thoughts day and night.[10]

In this chapter, we learned about buying a home. We discussed types of housing, the cost of housing, and how much house you can afford. We went through the nine steps of buying a home. Finally, we learned about mortgages, refinancing, and home equity loans. Remember, as with all debt, the goal is to pay off your mortgage and be debt free!

We hope that these big financial decisions now seem less intimidating and more exciting! As you apply the principles and practices taught in this chapter, we hope you will be better equipped to make these decisions wisely and claim the blessings of a home that is a "heaven on earth" rather than a home "from below."

Other Resources

➲ www.bankrate.com/mortgage.aspx

➲ www.realtor.com

➲ www.zillow.com

Notes

1. John Howard Payne, Home, Sweet Home, www.poemhunter.com
2. Bryan Sudweeks, *Open Learning World* (2011)
3. Carolyn H. Klopfer, *Home Can Be a Heaven on Earth*, 1985, https://www.lds.org/music/library/hymns/home-can-be-a-heaven-on-earth?lang=eng
4. Gordon B. Hinckley, "The Times in Which We Live," Oct 2001, https://www.lds.org/ensign/2001/11/the-times-in-which-we-live?lang=eng
5. Gordon B. Hinckley, "To the Boys and Men," Oct 1998, https://www.lds.org/ensign/1998/11/to-the-boys-and-to-the-men?lang=eng
6. James E Faust, "The Responsibility for Welfare Rests with Me and My Family," April 1986, https://www.lds.org/general-conference/1986/04/the-responsibility-for-welfare-rests-with-me-and-my-family?lang=eng
7. Luke 21:19
8. http://www.federalreserve.gov/econresdata/releases/mortoutstand/current.htm
9. Joe J. Christensen, "Greed, Selfishness, and Overindulgence," April 1999, https://www.lds.org/ensign/1999/05/greed-selfishness-and-overindulgence?lang=eng
10. Gordon B. Hinckley, "Living Worthy of the Girl You Will Someday Marry," April 1998, https://www.lds.org/ensign/1998/05/living-worthy-of-the-girl-you-will-someday-marry?lang=eng

9

Investing for the Long Term

Family Financial Security Using the Get-Rich-Slowly Plan

LEARN

- The differences between investing and speculating

- The seven principles of successful investing

- About the various asset classes

- To feel confident as you begin investing

The needs of a family are vast and varied. Some of these needs include providing for children, a home, transportation (cars), missions, university educations, weddings, travel to family events, your own mission as a couple, and retirement. That list is not comprehensive, and it doesn't even include wants such as skiing, renting a large campground for a family reunion, installing a lap pool and a hot tub in the back yard, or buying wave runners or a boat. Nor does it include your desire to bless others by anonymously giving to neighbors in need, supporting missionaries who cannot afford to support themselves, and donating to the BYU scholarship fund.

Let me give you an example of what family and extended family financial needs can look like when you are in your fifties and sixties. Tammy and I have twelve children. Seven are married, and they live in five states: Maryland, Kentucky, New Jersey, New Mexico, and Tennesssee. Five are unmarried teenagers or emerging adults. One of these children lives on his own, but the other four still live with us. Two children served full-time missions in Peru and Argentina from 2013 to 2015. The children are responsible for half the cost of their missions, but we contribute the other half. Each wedding costs thousands of dollars. Since 2013, eight new grandchildren have been born. For each grandchild we generally follow this same pattern: Tammy flies out to help when the baby is born and then I fly out for the baby blessing. These eight new grandbabies potentially represent sixteen round trip airfares. We have had three grandchildren turn eight, and trips for their baptisms also add up. Additionally, we have flown across the country to help out with health emergencies in our family. The list goes on and on.

You probably won't have twelve children, but I can guarantee that you will have significant financial needs with your family and your extended family as you grow older. The point I want to make is that finding a way to successfully acquire material resources for the long term is very important to your family. These resources make it easier to nurture a sacred family so that you can ultimately claim the blessing of eternal life with Heavenly Father and your loved ones. That's what investing is all about, "[f]or where your treasure is, there will your heart be also."[1]

The purpose of this chapter is to help you understand ways to invest money for the long term, so that when you have the opportunity to make significant expenditures to bless your children, your posterity, and other children of God, you have the resources to do so.

The parable of the ten virgins, five wise and five foolish, has both a spiritual and a temporal application. Each of us has a lamp to light the way, but it requires that every one of us put the oil in our own lamps to produce that light. It is not enough to sit idly by and say, "The Lord will provide." He has promised that they who are wise and "have taken the Holy Spirit for their guide" will have the earth given unto them.
—James E. Faust[2]

Investing vs. Speculating

"For it must needs be, that there is an opposition in all things." (2 Nephi 2:11)

Investing has a nefarious cousin who wreaks all kinds of havoc. This unscrupulous relative masquerades as investing but really is something much more sinister. Her name is *speculating*. She burns with the desire to become rich without work, to get something for nothing. She tries to entice all of us, and we must be firm in our resolve against her.

The key to understanding the difference between investing and speculating is a saying we want you to engrave in your heart: **If it sounds too good to be true, then it is too good to be true.** If they haven't already, many friends, relatives, or co-workers will come to you with "opportunities" that promise to make you rich. They will be very sincere and you will feel like you can trust them. But please remember this true financial principle related to investing: **Return on investment is positively related to risk.** To obtain greater than market-rate returns, you must take greater than market-rate risks, and such risks can bring upon your family devastating conflict and stress. After reading this chapter, we hope you will learn to politely decline any financial offers that sound too good to be true.

Speculation

Speculation is defined as any investment that promises a substantially greater than market-rate return. Wikipedia (yes, this is sometimes a valid source of information) defines it this way: "**Speculation** is the practice of engaging in risky financial transactions in an attempt to profit from fluctuations in the market . . . rather than attempting to profit from the underlying financial attributes . . . such as capital gains, interest, or dividends. Many speculators pay little attention to the fundamental value of a security and instead focus purely on price movements."[3]

The fundamental assumption undergirding speculation is that it allows you to get rich quickly—to make a lot of money in a short amount of time with little effort. This attitude is contrary to the LDS perspective that we should work for all we receive. President Gordon B. Hinckley wrote, "[W]ithout hard work, nothing grows but weeds. There must be labor, incessant and constant, if there is to be a harvest."[4]

Unfortunately, there are many speculators in the LDS community who recruit friends, neighbors, business associates, and ward members to schemes that promise large returns. Most of these are scams or extremely high-risk ventures. In a letter from the First Presidency, members of the Church were warned about "those who use relationships of trust to promote risky or even fraudulent investment and business schemes."[5]

I know of a young widow who invested part of the proceeds of her husband's life insurance settlement with a close friend, with the promise of a guaranteed high interest rate. Though the investment paid out for several years, one day the checks stopped coming. Soon thereafter, the company filed for bankruptcy, and the widow lost many tens of thousands of dollars. She felt betrayed that the sacred funds provided by her late husband had been lost in this way.

Please avoid speculation like the plague.

What to Do before You Speculate

Many families have bankrupted themselves because of risky investments. These financial losses have led to stress, anger, and bitterness and have damaged and sometimes destroyed family relationships. Before you even consider an investment that promises greater than market-rate returns, be sure you have done (or are doing) EVERYTHING on the following list:

THINGS YOU HAVE DONE:

- ❏ Freed your family from credit card debt and consumer debt
- ❏ Paid off your vehicles completely
- ❏ Paid off student loans
- ❏ Made your spouse an equal partner in investing

THINGS YOU ARE DOING:

- ❏ Contributing 10 percent of your income to tithing each month

Avoid speculation like the plague!

Speculation

The practice of engaging in risky financial transactions, often promising greater than market-rate return, in an attempt to profit from fluctuations in the market.

- ☐ Contributing at least 10 percent of income to a tax-advantaged, diversified, primarily stock-based IRA and/or 401(k) plan
- ☐ Contributing at least the value of two family meals to fast offering each month
- ☐ Meeting all the basic financial needs of the family for food, shelter, transportation, education, etc.
- ☐ Paying for adequate insurance (life, health, automobile, and home)
- ☐ Storing at least a 3-month emergency supply of money, food, water, and fuel (where possible)
- ☐ Meeting enough of the financial wants of the family to be happy (family vacations, entertainment, furniture, toys, etc.)
- ☐ Paying off your mortgage in a timely manner

If you have checked off everything on this list, then you have extra money that you are welcome to do whatever you want with, including investing in a risky deal. At that point, however, there is still opportunity cost. Even though you can afford to speculate, wouldn't you rather use that money for something more worthwhile? Let us add a comment about your own motivation. If your motivation for speculating is to make a lot of money with little effort, then realize that this motive is contrary to the laws of heaven. If your motivation is to acquire resources to bless God's children, good for you!

Investment

Investment
An asset or item that is purchased with the hope that it will generate income or appreciate in the future.

An **investment** is "an asset or item that is purchased with the hope that it will generate income or appreciate in the future. In an economic sense, an investment is the purchase of goods that are not consumed today but are used in the future to create wealth."[6]

Investing is distinct from speculating in several ways. The first is that an investment has a long-term orientation. Compared to speculating, it is a very slow, disciplined process of acquiring wealth to be used to bless your family and others. The second difference is that investing relies on true economic growth to fund its returns, while speculating tries to capture fleeting and temporary market fluctuations, not necessarily related to economic growth. Finally, in our worldview, investing is based on a stewardship perspective where returns are used to bless others while speculating has an individual perspective with the goal to maximize wealth for wealth's sake. Certainly this chapter is about investing, not speculating.

Wise investing has purposes beyond just getting a good return and making money. Here are some purposes we would like you to be aware of.

Investing helps you to do the following:

- meet your short- and long-term family goals
- demonstrate that you are a wise steward of God's possessions
- bring yourself to Christ, achieve your divine mission, and return with your family back to Heavenly Father's presence

Seven Principles of Successful Investing

Once you are ready to invest, you must recognize that there is not just one right way to invest. There are multiple methods of investing that depend on your budget, family goals, and investment plan. The key to successful investing is to know yourself and what you are trying to accomplish by investing. Whatever you decide to invest in and whatever phase of investment you are in, it is critical that you adhere to correct principles. Here are seven principles that, if followed, will help you to invest successfully.

Principle 1

Invest as a Full Partner with Your Spouse

Investing is not an end in itself; rather, it is a means for acquiring resources for you, your spouse, and your family to do God's work upon the earth. It is a divine stewardship. Consequently, you need to invest as a full partner with your spouse. You work together to document thoughtful and well-written financial goals. These goals are critical because they help you determine what you and your spouse want to accomplish with your investment program. When specific alternatives for investing are considered, both spouses consider the options, provide input, pray, and make the decision together.

You and your spouse also need to know your family budget. After basic needs are paid for, you must agree on how much you can afford to invest. We recommend that as soon as you are financially able, you invest at least 10 percent of your gross income in long-term, low-expense, tax-advantaged, diversified, primarily stock-based investments. You can remember the phrase, "10 percent to the Lord and 10 percent to long-term investments."

Principle 2

Understand Risk and Stay Diversified

Risk is inherent in all investment activities. Some common risks include inflation risk, company-specific risk, interest rate risk, financial risk, market risk, political and regulatory risk, exchange rate risk, and liquidity risk. The key to managing risk is to understand the different types of risk and to invest at a risk level that is comfortable for you and your spouse. If your investments are too risky, this may cause stress and conflict in your marriage and family.

It is important to understand the tolerance you have for risk. Are you able to watch and not panic when the stock market plummets 25 percent in a few months and the value of your portfolio has decreased $100,000? If the answer is no, you run the risk of selling your investments and permanently losing a lot of money. If you are risk-averse, you might be better off investing in less volatile instruments, like bonds. However, if the answer is yes, you will ride out the fluctuations in the market and reap a handsome long-term return a few decades from now.

Diversification is your best defense against company-specific risk. For example, if you invest in the stock of one company, you could win big if the company thrives—or you could lose everything if the company goes bankrupt. This is stressful, company-specific risk! However, if you invest in an S&P 500 mutual fund,

you actually own a little bit of 500 different large companies. If one of the companies goes under, it is of little consequence to you. You are still invested in 499 others. Diversification in the stock market completely alleviates company-specific risk. It helps you sleep better at night.

It is also advantageous to invest in several different **asset classes.** Asset classes are broad categories of investments with specific and similar risk and return characteristics. The three major asset classes are cash (or cash equivalents), fixed income (bonds), and equities (stocks).[7] Real estate and commodities (oil, gold, silver, etc.) are also considered assets. You may want your **portfolio** (the sum of all your investments) to include not only stocks but also bonds, cash, real estate, and commodities. Mutual funds or investments like them are available in all asset classes. We will talk more about asset classes later in the chapter.

Principle 3

Make Low-Cost and Tax-Efficient Investments for the Long Term

Watch your investment costs carefully, including costs for transaction fees, management fees, and taxes. Remember that when investing, a dollar saved is worth more than a dollar earned—you have to pay taxes on every new dollar you earn, but every dollar you save is already taxed and can earn interest. Every time you buy and sell, you are charged something. Be aware that frequent trading incurs significant transaction and tax costs; avoiding this will help you keep your costs low and increase the effective return of your investment. Look for investments that have low expenses and low fees.

In general, there are two kinds of diversified investment funds. **Actively managed funds** are managed by large teams of intelligent, well-trained, professional investors who spend all day every day doing research and trying to take advantage of opportunities to make money. They are trying to "buy low"

and "sell high" to make you as much money as they can. Unfortunately, every time they buy and every time they sell, there are transaction costs involved. Additionally, before you get your return you have to pay for their large salaries. **Passively managed funds** are managed by a few professionals who strategically invest your money using a "buy and hold strategy." It is possible that they may buy something for you and not sell it again for decades. Because of this, you have few transaction fees, and you have little to pay in the way of salaries and other overhead for the professionals. Actively-managed funds generally have a slightly better return on investment before expenses. However, after expenses, passively managed funds generally have the greater return on investment. If you are investing for the long term, we suggest you invest in passively managed funds.

You and your spouse should also defer or eliminate taxes on your investments as much as possible. The easiest way to do that is to invest in a 401(k) plan (a tax-advantaged retirement account set up by your employer, often with a match by the company) and/or an IRA (a tax-advantaged retirement account that you set up). Early in your career, it is generally best to invest in a Roth 401(k) and a Roth IRA. With Roth, you invest with after-tax money, so the government guarantees that forevermore the principal and all the gains will be completely tax-free. What a deal! We'll talk more about retirement planning later. If you have a very large salary and a high marginal tax rate you may consider a traditional

"I am going to max out my 401(k) contribution this year."

Asset classes
A group of financial assets with similar risk and return characteristics.

Portfolio
All of your various investments.

Actively managed funds
Funds that are managed by professional investors who constantly "buy low" and "sell high."

Passively managed funds
Funds that are managed by professional investors who invest money using a "buy and hold" strategy.

401k and/or IRA, where you get a tax break this year but pay the normal taxes when you decide to withdraw the funds later.

Avoid short-term trading or day-trading like the plague. In day-trading, the investor purchases selected stocks in the morning and then sells them before the end of the day. Short-term day trading is expensive and incurs a high level of transaction costs and taxes. I tell my students that day-trading is very much like gambling in Las Vegas, except for two things: (1) you generally lose more with day-trading than when you gamble in Las Vegas, but (2) if you happen to win big with day-trading, the Church will accept your tithing (they won't accept tithing on gambling winnings).

Avoid day-trading like the plague.

You will achieve your goals by investing for the long term. There are no "get-rich-quick" schemes that consistently work. If there were, everyone would use them, and we would all be rich!

Principle 4

Monitor Your Portfolio Performance

President Thomas S. Monson taught, "Where performance is measured, performance improves. Where performance is measured and reported, the rate of improvement accelerates."[8] How can you know how the investments in your portfolio are doing if you do not monitor their performance? To understand the performance of your investments, you will need to learn how to use benchmarks. **Benchmarks** are passively managed portfolios of financial assets that indicate how well your financial assets are performing by comparison. You can find these benchmarks on many different investing websites.[9] Set your own portfolio benchmarks and then monitor your portfolio performance on a monthly, quarterly, and annual basis.

Principle 5

Don't Try to Time the Market

Timing the market refers to the attempt to obtain greater than market-rate returns by buying when the market is low and selling when the market is high. These buy and sell decisions are informed by research, quantitative modeling, powerful computers, and traders' hunches. It is difficult, expensive, time-consuming, and just plain dumb to try to beat the market on your own. You are competing against hundreds of thousands of professional money managers who have much more time, money, and access to information than you have. Instead, it is more reasonable for you to engage in a "buy and hold" strategy where you invest broadly in diversified

mutual funds and in different asset classes. The best investments are tax-deferred or tax-eliminated retirement accounts (such as Roth and traditional 401(k) plans and Roth and traditional IRAs) because they reduce your tax liability.

Principle 6

Invest with High-Quality, Licensed, Reputable People and Institutions

When you need help investing, do not be afraid to ask for it. However, be sure to get help from good people whose actions and beliefs are consistent with the principles dis-

Benchmarks

Passively managed portfolios of financial assets that indicate how well your financial assets are performing by comparison.

 Avoid day-trading like the plague!

Timing the market

The attempt to obtain greater than market-rate returns by buying when the market is low and selling when the market is high.

Tax-deferred accounts

Accounts which allow you to invest without first paying taxes on the principal; you then pay taxes on both the principal and the earnings when you withdraw money at retirement.

Tax-eliminated accounts

Accounts which require you to pay taxes on the principal before you invest it, but you do not have to pay any taxes on the capital gains or future earnings.

cussed in this chapter. Make sure you invest with financial institutions and investment companies that have a tradition of meeting the needs of their investors. Work with good companies that offer good products. Be careful with your money and invest it wisely. Work only with licensed and registered advisors. In some circumstances, salaried financial planners or advisors may be a better choice than financial planners or advisors that are paid on commission. Salaried financial professionals may be more objective and have your best interest at heart.

Principle 7

Develop a Good Investment Plan and Follow It Closely

Develop a good investment plan that is consistent with your goals, your budget, and the principles discussed in this chapter. An **investment plan** is a detailed road map of your investment risk and return, investment strategy, constraints, and reporting and evaluation methodology. Think of your investment plan as a road map to successful investing. Follow this plan closely. If you plan wisely and invest accordingly, you will save yourself from heartache and problems in the future, and you will likely achieve your personal and family goals.

Asset Classes

Understanding asset classes is critical if you are to invest intelligently. Asset classes are broad categories of investments with similar specific risk and return characteristics. The three major asset classes include cash (and cash equivalents), fixed income (bonds), and equities (stocks). Real estate and commodities are also asset classes. We will discuss the first three to help you understand the benefits and risks of each specific asset class.

Cash (and Cash Equivalents)

The first and most common asset class is cash and cash equivalents. The major goals of this asset class are liquidity and preservation of capital. It includes money in savings, checking, and money market deposit accounts.

Investments in Certificates of Deposit (CDs), money market funds, and Treasury bills (T-bills) are also included in this category. Keeping cash in the cookie jar would also be included. There is little risk of losing principal since many of these investments are insured with the FDIC and the rest are secure. These are good investment assets for money you plan to use in less than a couple of years and when you don't want to risk the possibility of losing principal. For example, if you are saving for a

> **Investment Plan**
> A detailed road map of your investment risk and return, investment strategy, constraints, and reporting and evaluation methodology.

Table 9.1 Advantages and Disadvantages of Cash Assets

Advantages	Disadvantages
Liquidity: (cash or can be turned into cash quickly) Especially useful for your emergency fund	**Low rate of return:** Unlikely to keep up with taxes and inflation on the long term
Security: Principal is often insured by FDIC	**Fully taxable:** Make sure you take taxes into consideration when deciding to put money towards a cash asset
Guaranteed returns: Interest rates are guaranteed	

mission and you know you need the money in ten months, it would be wise to keep that money in a CD or other cash equivalent.

Fixed Income (Bonds)

Fixed income is generated by investing in bonds. A **bond** is a loan with a set interest rate purchased by an investor from a government or a company. The interest provides a safe, fixed income stream for the bondholder that is greater than the rate of inflation. Bonds are often used to finance retirement income. Because bond terms can range up to thirty years, they can provide a consistent and safe return for a long time. The typical return on bonds is lower than the return for stocks, but higher than the return for cash. It has been said that "Bonds will not make you rich but can keep you rich."

There are two major types of bonds. For **coupon bonds**, the bond issuer sells the bond for a set amount (**face value**) to the bond purchaser until the **maturity date.** The issuer makes regular interest payments to the purchaser until the maturity date. On the maturity date the issuer repays the face value of the bond to the purchaser.

For **zero-coupon bonds** the issuer sells the bond to the purchaser for a set amount that is less than the face value. During the term of the bond the issuer does NOT make regular interest payments. The issuer repays the face value to the purchaser on the maturity date. The difference between the purchase price and the face value is the return for the investor.

Zero-coupon bonds do not provide a steady income stream.

Bonds may be issued by a variety of entities and may be taxable or tax-free. **US Treasury bonds** have terms of up to 30 years and are backed by the full faith and credit of the United States. They are considered to be the safest investment on the planet. Other bonds, such as **corporate bonds** and bonds issued by US government agencies like Ginnie Mae (Government National Mortgage Association) are also taxable.

Corporate bonds are typically coupon bonds and are issued in $1,000 face value denominations with a fixed rate of interest. Corporate bonds are riskier than government bonds because if the company goes bankrupt, you lose the value of your bond. The riskier the company, the higher the interest rate. Bonds with high yields issued by companies in distress are called **junk bonds**. In general, you should not invest in junk bonds. You can get similar returns with less risk by investing in a diversified stock portfolio.

Municipal bonds are generally tax-free and are issued by state and local governments. A bond issued by a school district to build a new high school or a bond issued by a city to build a new water treatment plant are examples of municipal bonds. Those with high incomes (and high marginal tax rates) often find the after-tax return on municipal bonds to be higher than the return on taxable bonds.

Bond
A loan with a set interest rate purchased from a government or company.

Coupon bonds
Bond purchaser receives regular interest payments until maturity date.

Face value
Value of the bond when redeemed on the maturity date.

Maturity date
Date at which a bond is redeemed at face value.

Zero-coupon bonds
Bonds purchased at less than face value then sold at face value at the maturity date with no interim interest payments.

US Treasury Bonds
Bonds backed by full faith and credit of the United States.

Corporate bonds
Bonds issued by corporations.

Junk bonds
Bonds with high yields issued by companies in distress.

Municipal bonds
Tax-free bonds issued by state and local governments.

Short-term bonds
Bonds that mature in less than about four years.

Intermediate-term bonds
Bonds with a maturity of about four to seven years.

Long-term bonds
Bonds with a maturity of about seven or more years.

Inflation protected securities
Securities whose yield is linked to the rate of inflation as measured by a specific inflation index.

Bond mutual funds
Diversified funds in which you buy a share in thousands of different bonds in a changing portfolio.

Bonds can be issued with various lengths until the maturity date. **Short-term bonds** (or short-term bond mutual funds) include bonds that generally mature in less than four years.[10] Short-term bonds are less vulnerable to interest rate risk than long-term bonds, as there is a shorter time period before the bonds mature. Short-term bonds are generally considered good investments for anyone needing a dependable stream of income in an environment where interest rates are not likely to rise. **Intermediate-term bonds** (or intermediate-term bond mutual funds) are bonds with a maturity of about four to seven years.[11] Because of their longer maturity, they are more susceptible to interest rate risk (the risk that interest rates will rise during the period you own the bond). **Long-term bonds** (long-term bond mutual funds) are bonds with a maturity of seven or more years.[12] These bonds generally have the highest yields but are the most vulnerable to interest rate volatility. **Inflation protected securities** are securities whose yield is linked to the rate of inflation as measured by a specific inflation index. These bonds have the benefit that when interest rates rise, the yield on the bond rises as well.

Buying **bond mutual funds** is different than buying individual bonds. Mutual funds buy and sell bonds before they mature. Investing in a bond mutual fund means you are buying a share in thousands of different bonds in a changing portfolio, so you are more diversified than when you buy an individual bond. The income from a fixed-income mutual fund fluctuates as mutual funds buy and sell bonds. The market value of the mutual fund changes depending on whether the fund is selling bonds at a loss or at a gain. In general, bonds increase in value as interest rates go down, and decrease in value as interest rates go up. The longer the maturity of the bonds, the more the value of your bonds will increase or decrease as interest rates change. A typical long-term rate of return for bonds is around three to six percent per year.

Equities (Stocks)

The major goals of investing in this asset class are to provide growth and to earn returns that significantly exceed the inflation rate. Historically, the stock market has been the only major asset class to consistently outpace inflation over long periods of time. However, stocks are unstable on the short-term, so if you are investing for less than three to five years a smaller portion (if any) of your investments should be in stocks, due to their volatility. A key principle when you invest in the stock market is to avoid panic selling. When you own stock you can only actually lose money when you sell your stock for less than you paid for it. When the stock market drops 20% and you

Table 9.2 Advantages and Disadvantages of Bond Assets

Advantages	Disadvantages
Returns: Greater than cash; likely to beat inflation	Liquidity: Not as liquid as cash
Stable income stream: Excellent for retirees	Returns: Lower long-term returns compared to the stock market
Good for diversification: Returns are uncorrelated with stock market returns (when stocks go down, bonds may go up)	

panic and sell because you are afraid it will go down even further, *then* you actually lose that 20%. However, a healthier attitude if you are investing for the long term is to say to yourself, "Sure, the market has gone down 20%, but it always goes up and down. I'm going to hang tight." Then the market will recover, and you will continue on a track to earn 7% to 10% annual return on the long term.

An equity share is ownership in a business's earnings and assets. When you invest in equities (or stocks), you actually become part owner of the companies you invest in. If you bought all the shares of a company you would become the sole owner of that company. You get a proportionate share of the profits of the company by receiving **dividends** and you also benefit from increases in the company's share price. Mature companies are a likelier source of dividends—rapidly growing companies often prefer to reinvest profits and not offer dividends.

Shares of a stock are traded on a **stock exchange**. The New York Stock Exchange (NYSE) is by far the largest stock exchange in the world. About 2,800 companies trade their stock on the NYSE with a total market capitalization of about $21 trillion.[13] About 1.5 billion shares are traded each day.[14] The Dow Jones Industrial Average (DJIA) tracks the performance of 30 very large companies and is the most quoted number from the NYSE. The Standard and Poor's 500 Index (S&P 500) provides a more accurate gauge of the overall stock market because it includes more companies.

The second largest stock exchange in the world is the National Association of Securities Dealers Automated Quotations (NASDAQ). It lists about 3,100 companies with a total market capitalization of $8.5 trillion (2014). There is more daily volume on the NASDAQ (about 2 billion shares per day) than on the NYSE. The NASDAQ has also handled more than 1000 IPO's (Initial Public Offerings) for new companies since 2000. In general NASDAQ indexes provide higher long-term returns but with greater volatility than NYSE indexes.[15]

There are three separate types of stocks: growth, value, and blend. **Growth stocks** are companies whose earnings are expected to grow very rapidly. Frequently, these are companies developing new technologies or new ways of doing things. **Value stocks** are companies that are inexpensive in terms of the underlying fundamentals of the market. These are companies that have potential for good long-term returns through both appreciation and dividends. Growth and value stocks tend to perform in alternating cycles, so it makes sense to own both types. **Blend stocks** are stocks that include components of both growth and value stocks.

Stock mutual funds are funds that own stock in specific groups or types of companies. When you own shares in a particular company, you have company-specific risk. If that one company goes under, you lose your entire investment. When you buy into a mutual fund, you are buying a share in multiple companies to protect yourself from company-specific risk. What you actually own in the mutual fund changes over time depending on the fund manager's decisions. You are responsible for paying taxes on all distributions by the mutual fund, which are taxed at your level—not the fund's level. If your investment is through a Roth 401(k) or Roth IRA, you pay no taxes.

Stocks are often categorized as large-cap, mid-cap, and small-cap stocks. **Large-cap stocks** are from companies with a **capitalization** (what you could buy the company for if you bought all of the stock) of more than $10

Dividends
Money paid to shareholders on a regular basis.

Stock Exchange
A market in which securities (bonds, shares, and notes) are bought and sold.

Growth stocks
Companies whose earnings are expected to grow very rapidly.

Value stocks
Companies that are inexpensive in terms of the underlying fundamentals of the market.

Blend stocks
Stocks that include components of both value and growth stocks.

Stock mutual funds
Funds that pool investor money to purchase many different stocks in groups or types of companies.

Large-cap stocks
Stocks from companies with a capitalization of more than $10 billion.

Capitalization
What you could buy the company for if you bought all of its stock.

Table 9.3 Advantages and Disadvantages of Equity Assets

Advantages	Disadvantages
Excellent return on investments: When purchased as part of a diversified portfolio they offer highest return of the major asset classes (8 percent to 12 percent per year over the past eighty-five years)	**Market volatility:** The price of stocks can go up and down on the short-term, sometimes dramatically
Significantly beats inflation: Truly harnesses the power of compound interest	**Less stability of principal:** Compared to other asset classes, you can lose a lot of money on the short term

billion. **Mid-cap stocks** are from companies with a capitalization of $2 billion to $10 billion. **Small-cap stocks** are from companies with a capitalization of less than $2 billion.

International stocks (global stocks/emerging market stocks) are stocks of companies based entirely outside the United States. These can be of any size (small-cap, mid-cap, large-cap), of any type (value, growth, blend), and from any part of the world (outside the United States). Funds that contain a mixture of US and foreign holdings are called **global funds**.

History of Asset Class Returns

In order to make informed investments for the future, it is important to understand how the various asset classes have performed historically. Remember that an asset class is a group of financial assets with similar risk and return characteristics. Figure 9.1 shows the **geometric return** (a type of compound interest rate) and the standard deviation for each of the major asset classes. The greater the geometric return, the more money you make. The greater the standard deviation, the greater the risk you take of losing money in any given year. As you can see from the graph, over an eighty-five-year period the average yearly return rates are 12 percent for small-cap stocks, 10 percent for large-cap stocks (S&P 500), 6 percent for treasury bonds, and 4 percent for treasury bills. You will also notice that the greater the return, the greater the standard deviation, and consequently, the greater the risk and volatility.

Let's talk a little about volatility. Treasury

Mid-cap stocks
Stocks from companies with a capitalization of $2 billion to $10 billion.

Small-cap stocks
Stocks from companies with a capitalization of less than $2 billion.

International stocks
Stocks of companies based entirely outside the US or throughout the world.

Global funds
Funds that contain a mixture of US and foreign holdings.

Geometric return
The compound interest rate of an investment.

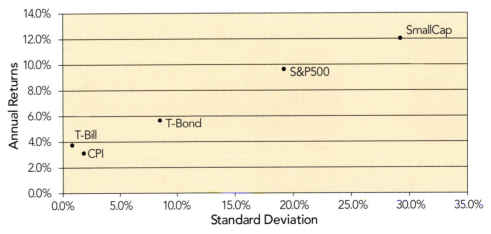

Figure 9.1 Risk and Return Relationship among Major Asset Classes

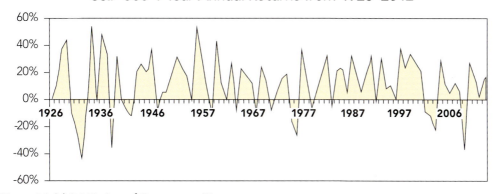

Figure 9.2 S&P 500 Annual Returns over Time

bills have made money every single year since 1927. They are a sure bet to be "in the black." Because of that certainty, the return is lower. On the other hand, large-cap stocks (S&P 500) have actually lost money nineteen out of the last eighty-five years (see Figure 9.2). Also, the range of returns and losses for stocks has been much greater.

The wide range of returns on stock seems to be risky. If you need your money in any particular year, it is risky. But when you hold stocks for a longer period of time, the risk diminishes. Notice in Figure 9.3 that if you take a 10-year perspective, there have only been two years (2008 and 2009) when the 10-year annual return was negative, and most of the time the 10-year return was positive, in the double digits.

Beginning to Invest

With this background information, let's move on to some practical advice for developing your own investment plan. In this section, we are taking a very basic approach. However, you would be surprised by the number of investors that do not follow these simple guidelines and priorities.

Six Guidelines for Basic Investing

1. PREREQUISITE

   Create a livable budget with funds for debt reduction and investing

My view is that you, whoever you are, should be investing for the long term every single month until you retire. However, you should invest responsibly. You should create a livable budget with expenses categorized

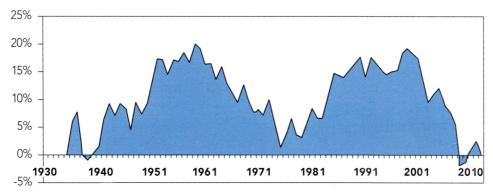

Figure 9.3 S&P 500 10-Year Returns over Time

within your income. This budget should include 10 percent for tithing and should meet all of the basic needs for everyday living (food, shelter, transportation, education, etc.). After these needs are taken care of, additional money should be allocated simultaneously to debt reduction and investment. In general, it is best to pay off credit card loans and other consumer debt before investing significant amounts. That said, I believe it is wise to invest small amounts ($10 or $20 per month) while you pay off your credit cards. In addition, if your company matches contributions to a 401(k) plan, you should invest at least to the percentage of the match, even if it slows paying off the credit cards. The 100% return on the company match to your 401(k) contribution dwarfs the 18% you have to pay on the credit card. In general, car loans and home mortgages can be paid off while you are also engaging in an investment program. Bottom line: get your financial house in order and invest responsibly.

2. Basics

Invest in an emergency fund and food storage

Money in the bank and food in the pantry should be considered essential investments. A good initial emergency fund includes enough money in your bank account to allow your family to survive for three months. It doesn't have to be three months of income, but it should be enough cash that you could survive for three months without an income. This emergency fund also becomes a buffer when unanticipated expenses occur (e.g., car repairs, appliance replacement, unexpected medical/dental expenses). In addition, we are counseled to invest in a three-month supply of "food that is part of your normal, daily diet."[16] This supply of food should be rotated periodically. It also provides a buffer in case something unanticipated happens.

3. Core

Invest in broad market index or core mutual funds

After you have your budget set up, your emergency fund in the bank, and your pantry full of food, you are ready to start investing in earnest. You should generally start by investing with a reputable investment firm to create a portfolio designed to capture the overall market. There are many reputable firms to choose from. A few of these are Fidelity Investments,[17] the Vanguard Group,[18] T. Rowe Price,[19] Homestead Funds,[20] and Northern Trust.[21] Fidelity Investments has an office just east of the University Mall in Orem, so you can talk to a real person face-to-face there. Homestead Funds caters to the small investor and allows you to invest with no minimum in mutual funds as long as you set up an automatic monthly investment from your checking account. Most other funds require a minimum initial investment of $500 to $5,000. If you are investing through a 401(k), you will use the investment service provided by your company. These funds are usually managed by large, reputable firms. Two apps—www.acorns.com and betterment.com—are easy ways to get started investing.

4. Diversify

Invest in additional asset classes and several specialized mutual funds

After you have made some basic investments and acquired more money to invest, you can branch out to a more balanced and sophisticated portfolio. Though there are many ways to do this, I will share just one. You can visit with your financial advisor about other options.

Dr. Craig Israelsen, the legendary mutual fund guru who previously taught at BYU, wrote an excellent book entitled *7Twelve: A Diversified Investment Portfolio with a Plan*[22] which outlines twelve separate investments in seven different asset categories in order to maximize growth while minimizing risk. The seven asset classes that he uses are US stock, non-US stock, real estate, resources, US bonds, non-US bonds, and cash. Your investments are equally distributed among twelve funds from these seven asset classes. Dr. Israelsen makes a convincing argument that this degree of diversification in the world economy provides the safest "get-rich-slowly" long-term investment plan. Because of the number of funds and the complexity of this plan, the investor needs a fairly substantial initial investment. If your investment funds are primarily in a 401(k) plan, you can accomplish diversification by opting for several different investment options.

5. Opportunistic

Invest in individual stocks and sector funds

If, after completing the first four steps, you still have extra funds to invest, you can move on to riskier investments, some of which border on speculating. Opportunistic investing should only be done with money you can afford to lose. When you invest in individual stocks or sector funds, you can win big or you can lose big. When you invest in individual stocks, it is better to hold them for at least one year because the gains will be taxed at a lower rate. One strategy involves doing your research and then investing in several individual stocks. It is possible that you may be lucky and beat the market.

6. Invest at your risk level

One of the key challenges of investing is to invest at a risk level that is comfortable for you and your spouse. Different investors can accept different levels of risk as they work to achieve their personal and family goals. If you choose to invest at lower risk levels, you will have a greater probability of not losing money, yet because of the lower risk, your returns are likely to be lower as well. There is a trade-off between risk and return. If your risk level is too low, you will need to save more money for retirement and other goals, as your returns will likely be less. If you take too much risk in your investing, there are obvious concerns. With higher risk, you have higher volatility but hopefully higher returns.

"Hold on, the market is shifting again."

If you invest at a higher risk level than you are comfortable with, you will be very concerned every time the market declines. This can cause detrimental stress if you are risk-averse. Interestingly, most investors are torn between fear and greed. When the financial markets decline, fear kicks in. We think that we should take our investments out of the market and that we will know when to put them back in before the market goes up again (this is called market timing). No investor can consistently time the market. Likewise, when the markets are going up, greed kicks in. We think we should put all our assets into one or two "sure things," which in reality are anything but sure. Your challenge, then, is to find the happy medium between fear and greed so that you can build a portfolio that will give you the amount of risk you are comfortable with and that will help you achieve your goals.

There is a general rule of thumb regarding risk: The closer you get to needing your invested money (such as during the years approaching retirement), the less risk you should have. With retirement investing, perhaps the majority of your investments when you are in your twenties and thirties will be equities. As you reach your forties and fifties, perhaps your portfolio should be weighted more towards lower-risk investments such as bonds and cash. One way to think of this is to take 100 minus your age, and that is the percentage of your portfolio that should be equities. That general guideline will help you decrease your risk as you get closer to retirement.

Final Cautions on Investing

Here are a few final cautions on investing:

- Do not go into debt to invest. This includes taking equity out of your home, buying on margin, or short-selling assets. Investing has enough risks of its own. Do not compound that with leverage.

- Beware of financial advisors who recommend shifting assets from one investment vehicle to another. Do not move your investments from one investment vehicle to another unless you fully understand all the costs and benefits.

- Beware of financial advisors paid on commission. Some advisors sell products based on their commissions, not what is best for you. Watch the turnover in your portfolio. A high turnover usually indicates problems and leads to lower returns.

- Listen to the Spirit. If it seems too good to be true, it probably is. Beware of members of your ward, friends, relatives, and others who will try to use their associations with you to have you buy their products. There are no guaranteed returns. If it sounds too good to be true, it is likely a scam.

- Finally, remember the wise counsel of M. Russell Ballard who said,

> There are no shortcuts to financial security. There are no get-rich-quick schemes that work. Do not trust your money to others without a thorough evaluation of any proposed investment. Our people have lost far too much money by trusting their assets to others. In my judgment, we never will have balance in our lives unless our finances are securely under control.[23]

Summary

You are ready to start investing! As you do, keep in mind the seven principles of successfully investing. Remember to stay far away from that monster called *speculation*, who brings risk, loss, and get-rich-quick catastrophes. Diversify your portfolio between various asset classes to diminish risk. Finally, follow the basic guidelines and priorities you have

learned in this chapter as you begin investing wisely. However small or large your income, consistently investing 10 percent of your income in long-term investments will bring your family financial security and help you meet your goals. Investing wisely and taking advantage of the power of compound interest is a way of demonstrating great financial stewardship of the resources with which your family is blessed. As President Gordon B. Hinckley said, "The gospel of Jesus Christ . . . [is] a greater investment than any. . . . Its dividends are eternal and everlasting."[24]

Notes

1. Luke 12:34
2. James E. Faust, "The Responsibility for Welfare Rests with Me and My Family," (Apr. 1986), https://www.lds.org/general-conference/1986/04/the-responsibility-for-welfare-rests-with-me-and-my-family?lang=eng.
3. "Speculation," Wikipedia, the Free Encyclopedia, https://en.wikipedia.org/w/index.php?title=Speculation&oldid=679572147.
4. Gordon B. Hinckley, "Farewell to a Prophet," Ensign (July 1994), https://www.lds.org/ensign/1994/07/farewell-to-a-prophet?lang=eng.
5. Ben Winslow, "Leaders Warn LDS against Money Scams," DeseretNews.com, http://www.deseretnews.com/article/695261200/Leaders-warn-LDS-against-money-scams.html?pg=all.
6. "Investment Definition," Investopedia, http://www.investopedia.com/terms/i/investment.asp.
7. "Asset Class Definition," Investopedia, http://www.investopedia.com/terms/a/assetclasses.asp.
8. Thomas S. Monson, Conference Report, (Oct. 1970), 107.
9. For example: www.Fidelity.com; www.Vanguard.com; www.HomesteadFunds.com.
10. Sue Stevens, "Bond-Fund Basics," Morningstar, http://news.morningstar.com/articlenet/article.aspx?id=172614.
11. Ibid.
12. Ibid.
13. http://www.businessinsider.com/global-stock-market-capitalization-chart-2014-11
14. "New York Stock Exchange: Company Listings," ADVFN, http://www.advfn.com/nyse/newyorkstockexchange.asp.
15. http://www.nasdaq.com/reference/market_facts.stm
16. "All Is Safely Gathered In: Family Home Storage," All Is Safely Gathered In: Family Home Storage, (2007) https://www.lds.org/manual/all-is-safely-gathered-in-family-home-storage/all-is-safely-gathered-in-family-home-storage?lang=eng.
17. www.Fidelity.com
18. www.Vanguard.com
19. www.TRowePrice.com
20. www.HomesteadFunds.com
21. www.NorthernTrust.com
22. Craig L. Israelsen, 7 Twelve: A Diversified Investment Portfolio with a Plan. First edition. Hoboken, N.J.: Wiley, 2010. http://www.amazon.com/dp/0470605278/?tag=mh0b-20&hvadid=3521451693&hvqmt=e&hvbmt=be&hvdev=c&ref=pd_sl_k2i1uem8l_e.
23. M. Russell Ballard, "Keeping Life's Demands in Balance," Ensign (May 1987), https://www.lds.org/ensign/1987/05/keeping-lifes-demands-in-balance?lang=eng.
24. Gordon B. Hinckley, Teachings of Gordon B. Hinckley. 567–68 First Edition. Salt Lake City, Utah: Deseret Book Co, 1997.

10

Retirement Planning

It's Never Too Early to Start

As a young person, it is easy to give nary a thought to retirement. That seems so far away! As a young couple in the late 1970s, Juanita and I were no exception. When Section 401(k) of the Internal Revenue Code was enacted in 1978, we were expecting our first beautiful baby girl. Things were very tight for us financially. We lived in a 300-square-foot trailer that we rented for $95 a month, and we were saving money for a down payment on a home. Even though my employer was going to match the first 2 percent of our contributions to this new-fangled 401(k), we wondered if we could afford the $40 per month we would have to contribute in order to receive the full match. We thought about it; we talked about it; we prayed about it; we played around with our budget; and, kicking and screaming, we finally signed up. Truth be known, this decision ended up being painless. We never missed the money because it was withdrawn before we ever saw the paycheck.

Looking back now, thirty-seven and a half years later, I am so glad we started investing back then. Through the miracle of compound interest, every single dollar we invested in 1978 is now worth about $32. By the time I retire in in 2023, every dollar invested back then will likely be worth about $64! By faithfully investing 10 percent of our income in tax-advantaged, low-fee, diversified, primarily stock-based mutual funds and index funds

LEARN

- What you can do now to begin to be prepared financially for retirement

- How many years you will and your spouse need retirement income

- How much income you will need per month during retirement

- What sources of regular income you can have in retirement, and how to determine if there is a shortfall

- How to determine if you want to leave an estate or use up most of your retirement before you die

- If you are on track for retirement saving

141

Start planning and investing for retirement today.

for thirty-seven and a half years, I now have a seven-figure sum that can be used to fund retirement for Tammy and me.

There is a moral to this story: you should be planning and investing for retirement today, even if you are only twenty years old! Whether you invest a little or a lot, start now!

Introduction

Ezra Taft Benson gave the following counsel: "Plan for your financial future. As you move through life toward retirement and the decades which follow, we invite all . . . to plan frugally for the years following full-time employment."[1]

People are living longer now than ever before. During the last century, average life expectancy in the United States increased from fifty-six to seventy-six for men and from fifty-nine to eighty-one for women—an addition of more than twenty years.[2] Experts project that as life spans continue to increase, the average individual will spend between twenty and thirty years in retirement. With fewer traditional pension plans available and smaller payouts from traditional government and private plans, retirement planning is an increasingly important part of family investment planning. Without adequate retirement planning, you and your spouse could be working as night watchmen when you are in your eighties just to make ends meet! Please, please start planning for retirement now!

Avoid putting off retirement planning like the plague.

In this chapter, we want to focus on information you need to know now so that you can make wise decisions in preparing for retirement in the future. We will address six questions that you will want to answer as you prepare.

Question 1

What can you do now to begin to be prepared financially for retirement?

To be prepared for retirement, you must start preparing now. Although you may be in school, perhaps struggling to get by on a meager income, you can still start by investing a small amount, even just $10 per month, into a Roth Individual Retirement Account (IRA). You can fund this account by shaving a couple of dollars off your food or entertainment budget every week. Simply by choosing not to eat out a couple of times every month, you may have something to invest. The principle is to get started investing earlier rather than later.

Divine Inheritence

God is a very wealthy personage. We all like to inherit from a wealthy parent and what could be more exciting than to inherit from God, to get everything that God has. Someone has said that thrift is a great virtue, especially in an ancestor. And God has been very thrifty, he has also been very wise and he has been very generous. To begin with, he created us in his own image and has endowed us with a set of his attributes and potentialities, the development of which is one of the purposes for which we live. He desires that every one of us should be rich. He has said: "... the fulness of the earth is yours ..." (D&C 59:16), and it pleaseth God that he has given all these things unto men to be used with judgment and thanksgiving. He has shared with us the fulness of the treasures of the earth and he desires to share with us the fulness of the treasures of heaven. He wants us to inherit the celestial kingdom and belong to that celestial order of which he himself is a member. And he has said that the greatest of all the gifts of God is the gift of eternal life in his presence.

—Sterling Sill[3]

Once you graduate from BYU and obtain a real job, you should begin investing at least 10 percent of your gross income each month into your retirement accounts. Where you invest is important. As we explained in the

previous chapter, if you are saving for retirement about forty years from now, it is best to invest in tax-advantaged, low-fee, diversified, primarily stock-based mutual funds and/or index funds. They will provide a return sufficient to allow you to claim the full blessings of the miracle of compound interest above and beyond inflation. Anyone who does that—whether a school teacher, attorney, plumber, social worker, or physician—can be financially independent when it's time to retire.

Because of significant tax advantages, you should invest your retirement dollars in the 401(k) offered by many employers. Companies are eliminating defined benefit retirement plans (these gave you a monthly pension for life in retirement) and replacing them with 401(k) matching funds. Oftentimes, companies match the first 5 percent (or more) of your contributions to the fund. To claim the match, you **must** make the contribution. You lose that free money if you don't invest! Don't miss out! It is almost always a wise decision to invest at least what the match is for your 401(k). In 2016, you could contribute up to $18,000 to a 401(k).[4]

Avoid losing free money from matches to your 401(k) like the plague.

If your company doesn't offer a **401(k)** (and even if it does), both you and your spouse can open up **Individual Retirement Accounts (IRAs)**. IRAs are like 401(k)s except instead of the company managing the funds, you manage your own funds through investments offered by financial firms. You can contribute up to $5,500 per year into your own IRA and your spouse can contribute another $5,500.[5]

The final fundamental thing you should be aware of for financial planning is the basic difference between a **Roth IRA/401(k)** and a **traditional IRA/401(k)**. With Roth accounts, you invest with after-tax dollars. Then, forever more, the principal and earnings are tax free. With traditional accounts, you can use your contributions as a reduction to income and save money on your taxes this year. Your earnings are tax free until they are withdrawn; however, when you withdraw your funds, both principal and earnings are taxed as regular income. All this means is that while you are young, until you make lots of income (e.g., $150,000 or more per year), you are generally better off with Roth than with traditional.

You might ask, what would I do to save for retirement now if I were a newly married junior at BYU and both my wife and I were working part-time jobs to try to graduate without student debt? I'll tell you what I would do: I would get started! I would invest $20 per month through automatic withdrawal from my checking account into a Roth IRA at www.homesteadfunds.com or betterment.com. I would select these funds because they require no minimum investment as long as you elect for automatic monthly withdrawals from your checking account. I would probably invest my contribution into their small company stock fund because, on the long term, it has the highest return. And then I would sleep with pleasant dreams knowing that I had started preparing for a long retirement in which my wife and I could serve missions, visit grandkids, and travel the world!

401(k)
A defined-contribution (DC) retirement plan offered to employees in which a specified amount of money is taken from both the employer and the employee on a regular basis and invested.

Individual Retirement Account (IRA)
A tax-advantaged retirement plan that is managed by the individual who owns the plan. Maximum contributions are $5500 per years until age 50. Money may not be withdrawn without penalty until age 59 ½.

Roth IRA/401(k)
A type of retirement plan in which contributions are taxed before they are put into the account and money is not taxed when it is withdrawn.

 Invest at least what the match is for your 401(k) and claim free money.

Traditional IRA/401(k)
A type of retirement plan in which contributions are not taxed and constitute an income adjustment when they are put into the account and money is taxed when it is withdrawn.

Question 2

For how many years will you and your spouse need retirement income?

To adequately fund your retirement you will need to know how many years to plan for. The answer to this question requires one simple subtraction equation, although it may be uncomfortable to think about. All you need to know is in what year you plan to retire and in what year you are likely to die, and then include a little cushion just to make sure you don't run out of money in case you live longer than you expect.

In what year do you and your spouse want to retire?

There are several financial factors to consider when answering this question. The earliest you can make unrestricted, penalty-free withdrawals from an IRA or 401(k) is age fifty-nine and a half. For traditional IRAs and 401(k)s, you must start taking distributions by the time you are seventy and a half. The earliest you can receive social security payments is age sixty-two, but if you do, the monthly benefit is considerably lower than if you wait a few years. The maximum monthly benefit from Social Security is at age seventy. The few companies that still have defined benefit pensions also have rules about age and the amount you receive. In general, you max out all of the monthly retirement benefits by waiting until age seventy to retire.

In what year do you and your spouse expect to die?

This is uncomfortable to think about because in our culture we typically avoid talking about death. However, you can get a fairly close estimate of when you are likely to die by going to an actuarial website. Actuaries predict when people will die, helping life insurance companies know how to have affordable rates and still make money. One interesting site is sponsored by Northwestern Mutual and is called "The Longevity Game."[6] In this game it asks you thirteen questions and then tells you how old you will likely be when you die. Another helpful, yet admittedly morbid, site is www.deathclock.com. It asks you a few questions and then creates your death date and a clock that counts down the seconds you have left to live.

Once you know the year you will retire and an estimated year of death, you simply subtract your retirement year from your death year and add a cushion (I suggest five years) to determine how many years you will need to fund retirement. In my case, I expect to retire in 2023. The Longevity Game tells me I will live until I am ninety-two, or until 2045. It says that Tammy will live until she is ninety-three, or until 2057. We do the math: 2057 minus 2023 equals 34, plus 5 for a cushion, and we realize we need to plan for thirty-nine years of retirement.

Question 3

How much income will you need per month during retirement?

This is dependent on many factors. The cost of living in the city where you retire makes a big difference. For example, if you retired in San Diego, the cost of living would be about 30 percent above the national average, mostly because of high housing costs.[7] However, if you retired in Idaho Falls, the cost of living would be about 15 percent below the national average, due in part to cheap potatoes![8] This means you would need $10,000 per month in San Diego to have the same standard of living that $6,500 per month would buy you in Idaho Falls.

The expense of the activities you want to engage in during retirement is also a factor. Do you want to explore the world and travel to exotic places, or do you want to be a homebody and explore your backyard? Do you have family members scattered across the country that you will want to visit for vacations and special occasions, or does all of your family live close by? Do you and your spouse want to serve a mission (or missions)? Do you want to have a monthly amount for charitable work and helping out children and grandchildren? These are all questions to consider.

One other important consideration is how much to plan for health care. Medicare covers major expenses, but Fidelity estimates that a couple entering retirement at age sixty-five should have $240,000 to cover "deductibles, co-payments, premiums for optional coverage for doctor visits and prescription drugs, out-of-pocket expenses for prescription drugs, and other expenses that Medicare doesn't cover, such as hearing aids and eyeglasses."[9] Assuming a retirement of twenty years, this translates into a $500 monthly expense.

Question 4

Beyond retirement investments, what sources of regular income will you have?

In planning for retirement, it is important to accurately estimate additional sources of income that you will have beyond your retirement investments. The most common of these is Social Security. Since it affects virtually everyone in the United States, we will examine it first.

Social Security

The Social Security Act was passed in 1935 as part of the New Deal during the Great Depression. Though it was designed to be a safety net, it is the primary source of retirement income for many of the 40 million Americans who are sixty-five and older. This is because many have not made wise investments into retirement accounts other than Social Security.

The Social Security program was designed to be a pass-through account. This means that the taxes you pay for Social Security (through the Federal Insurance Contribution Act, or FICA) are used to pay benefits to those who are currently retired, disabled, widowed, or orphaned. Because there are currently more people paying into Social Security than there are people receiving Social Security benefits, the tax reserves are maintained in interest-earning government bonds held by the Social Security Trust Fund. There was no investment or savings component to Social Security when it was originally set up because the government assumed that there would always be enough people in the working generation to pay for the retired generation's benefits. In 1935, there were 17 workers for each retiree who received benefits. Today, it is estimated that there are only 3.4 workers for each retiree who receives benefits. This is important to you because it is likely that your Social Security benefits will be reduced, either by a higher full-retirement age or by a reduction of the amount you will receive per month, or both.

Avoid relying entirely upon Social Security like the plague.

There are four main types of Social Security benefits: retirement, disability, survivors', and Medicare. These four main types are discussed in the following paragraphs.

 Plan to have additional sources of income beyond Social Security in retirement.

Retirement Benefits. For those who qualify, Social Security provides a lifetime monthly retirement benefit that is indexed with inflation. Eligibility and the amount of retirement benefits are dependent upon your work history and salaries. The full retirement age has increased to age sixty-seven, though you may choose to begin receiving reduced benefits anytime starting at age sixty-two. You can also delay receiving your benefits until age seventy to receive enhanced benefits. Someone with a long work history of good paying jobs would receive about $2,000 a month starting at age sixty-two, about $2,900 a month starting at age sixty-seven, or about $3,600 a month starting at age seventy. As you can see, the longer you delay receiving your retirement benefits, the more your monthly check will be. If you live much longer than the average person, you will receive much more total payout if you delay receiving your benefits as long as possible.

Disability Benefits. Workers who qualify for Social Security disability benefits are entitled to receive 100 percent of their primary insurance amount until one of the following situations occurs: the disability ends, the worker dies, or the worker attains full retirement age. The spouse's disability benefit is either 50 percent of the worker's benefit or the spouse's own Social Security benefit, whichever is larger.

Survivor Benefits. If the deceased worker was fully insured or currently insured, a lump-sum survivor benefit will be paid to eligible survivors. A monthly lump sum is available to the surviving resident spouse, nonresident spouse, or eligible children.

Medicare Benefits. Individuals who are at least sixty-five years old and who are eligible for Social Security retirement benefits on their own behalf are entitled to coverage under Medicare Part A. If the individual has applied for Social Security retirement benefits, no separate application is required. If the individual continues to work after age sixty-five and is not receiving Social Security benefits, an application must be filed in order for the individual to receive Medicare Part A coverage. Recipients of disability benefits are eligible for Part A coverage after they have been eligible for disability benefits for twenty-four months.

Employer-sponsored retirement plans

After Social Security, the second most common source of income for retirees is employer-sponsored retirement programs. Most companies offer retirement plans to their employees. They do this in hopes of attracting and retaining the best possible workers. Employers also receive some tax benefits by providing retirement plans. You can think of the payouts from these plans as a series of delayed payments you will receive during retirement for work you performed prior to retirement. Because they are tax-advantaged and include money contributed by the employer, employer-qualified retirement plans provide free money. Obtaining this money should be the highest priority for your retirement and investment funds. There are two main types of employer-sponsored retirement plans: defined-benefit plans and defined-contribution plans.

In a **defined-benefit plan (DB)**, all contributions are made by the employer. The benefit, or final monthly amount that will be received by the employee upon his or her retirement, is often guaranteed for life and based on the number of years of service and the final salary.[10] Because the employer is responsible for providing the final amount, he or she is the one that shoulders the risk of the investment plan. Defined-benefit plans are becoming less

---

Defined-benefit plan (DB)

A type of retirement plan in which all contributions are made by the employer and the benefit is guaranteed for life and based on the number of years of service and the final salary.

and less common. The percentage of employees covered by a DB plan fell from 38 percent in 1980 to 20 percent in 2008.[11] If you are fortunate enough to work for a company with a DB plan, a likely scenario would be to earn a lifetime benefit of approximately 1.5 percent per year of service multiplied by the average of your highest salaries. For example, if you worked for a company with a DB plan for thirty years and earned $10,000 per month during the last three years of employment, you would qualify for a lifetime pension of $4,500 per month (30 years × 1.5% × $10,000).

In contrast, with a **defined-contribution plan (DC)** contributions are made by both the employer and the employee, but the investments are chosen by the employee. The contribution amount is specified by a formula while the benefit amount is uncertain and varies according to payment amounts, the market, and the wise management of the employee. Because they place less risk on the employer than defined-benefit plans, defined-contribution plans are becoming more common. The percentage of employees participating in DC plans has increased from 8 percent in 1980 to 31 percent in 2008.[12] Most DC plans are 401(k) plans.

To understand the 401(k) plan offered by your employer, it is important to compare it to an Individual Retirement Account (IRA).

- 401(k): a retirement plan that is offered to all of the employees in a company or firm. It is typically used by mid- to large-sized companies. A 401(k) is managed by an administrator who takes a specified amount from both the employer and the employee (taking a portion of the employee's paycheck) on a regular basis. It has a clear structure and the opportunity for free money (from the contribution of the employer), but it also involves management fees. No withdrawals can be made while a person is still employed by the company. There is a cap of $18,000 per year for contributions (as of 2016).
- IRA: an individual retirement plan that is typically used by self-employed people. People who are not self-employed can also invest in an IRA apart from their employer-sponsored retirement plan, as long as their income is not too great. An IRA is managed by the individual who owns the plan, which allows that person to avoid management fees and gives them the freedom to contribute payments to the IRA on a flexible basis. There is a cap of $5,500 for contributions.

Both 401(k)s and IRAs have two options: traditional and Roth. In general the Roth option is preferable until you are making large sums of money. Here are some of the characteristics of Roth and traditional retirement accounts:

- Roth: contributions are taxed as ordinary income when they are put into the account. Contributions and earnings are not taxed when they are withdrawn. Since contributions are taxed before being invested, they may be withdrawn at any time without penalty. Earnings cannot be withdrawn before age fifty-nine and a half without incurring a penalty. No withdrawals are ever required.
- In traditional 401(k) plans and traditional IRAs, contributions are not taxed when they are put into the account. Contributions constitute a downward income adjustment for the year they are made. Contributions and earnings are taxed as ordinary income when they are withdrawn. Withdrawals cannot be made without a penalty before age fifty-nine and a half. Distributions may begin at fifty-nine and a half and *must* begin by seventy and a half using an actuarial formula predicting how much you need to withdraw year to get all your money taxed before you die.
- Penalties for early withdrawal may be waived when the money is used toward a down payment for a first-time home purchase, for educational expenses, or for

Defined-contribution plan (DC)

A type of retirement plan in which contributions are made by both the employer and the employee, but the investments are chosen by the employee; the contribution amount is specified by a formula, but the benefit amount varies according to payment amounts, the market, and the management of the employee.

unreimbursed medical expenses above 7.5% of the adjusted gross income.

Question 5

Do you want to leave an estate behind, or do you want to use up most of your retirement before you die?

The next question for retirement planning is whether you want to leave an **estate** to your descendants or to a charitable organization, or whether you want to use all of your money before you die. One of my relatives would say that his children and grandchildren needed to make their own way in the world, so he was going to use all of his money before he died. He would say that he wanted to "bounce his last check." He planned well, and by the time he died he had spent or given away everything except for his clothes, his old car, and a small dwelling.

If you want to leave an estate, you must decide how large you want that estate to be. This number will be the future value (FV) when you are calculating the amount of retirement you must save.

Estate

The money, property, and other assets owned by a person at the time of their death.

Question 6

How can you tell if you are on track for retirement saving?

Fidelity, one of the largest investment firms, has estimated a measure for being on track for retirement.[13] In this model, the goal is to have eight times your current salary saved by the time you retire. This is based on keeping an income stream of about 80 percent of pre-retirement income, factoring in Social Security income, and assuming a 5.5 percent return on investments (very conservative) and an inflation rate of 2.3 percent (probably accurate). To get to eight times the current salary, Fidelity offers the following retirement account benchmarks:

- Age 35 – one times current salary
- Age 45 – three times current salary
- Age 55 – five times current salary
- Age 67 – eight times current salary (beginning of retirement)

Because the rate of return is so important, it is essential to invest in the right places. In the first twenty years or so of investing, the criteria for a good retirement investment includes the following attributes:

- tax-advantaged
- low-fee
- diversified
- primarily stock-based
- mutual funds and/or index funds

Many financial institutions offer retirement investment plans that automatically invest your money according to the criteria listed above. The funds are often named by the year in which you plan to retire. For example the Fidelity Freedom® 2050 Fund is designed as an investment mechanism for those who expect to retire in 2046–2050.[14]

The criteria changes somewhat as you get closer to retirement. Stocks are riskier investments than bonds but produce higher returns on the long term. However, when you are close to needing money for retirement, it is a good idea to move to safer investments. A common rule of thumb is to have roughly 80 percent of your assets in stocks and 20 percent in bonds while in your twenties, and then adjust that ratio every five to ten years so that by the time you reach your sixties, you have about 60 percent of your assets in bonds or cash. For example, at age twenty-five you would have 25 percent in bonds and 75 percent in stocks; at age forty you would have 40 percent in bonds and 60 percent in stocks; at age fifty-five you would have 55 percent in bonds and 45 percent in stocks; and in retirement at age seventy you would have 70 percent in bonds and 30 percent in stocks.

With all of this information, you are in a position to start running some numbers related to retirement. The *Fundamentals of Family Finance Workbook* will help you learn how to do this with your financial calculator.

> *The first invitation is simple: I invite you to save money each week. The amount you save is not particularly significant; that is up to you. As you develop a habit of saving, you will benefit personally. And you may also have opportunities to assist others financially as a result of your diligence. Imagine the positive outcome of saving money weekly for six months, a year, 10 years, or more. Small efforts sustained over time can produce significant results.*
> —*Devin G. Durrant*[15]

Summary

Hopefully this chapter has helped you see that it is never too early to start planning and investing for retirement! You have seen that by investing in tax-advantaged, low-fee, diversified, primarily stock-based mutual funds and/or index funds from an early age, you will be financially prepared and your retirement years will be truly golden. We have answered six important questions that will help you determine financial needs associated with retirement.

The goal is not just to have a lot of money when you retire—it is to have sufficient resources to serve your family and God's other children. The goal is to be able to use your golden years to bring about much good in the world.

Other Resources

➲ www.deathclock.com

➲ https://www.fidelity.com/viewpoints/retirement/8X-retirement-savings

➲ www.homesteadfunds.com

Notes

1. Ezra T. Benson, "To the Elderly in the Church," (Oct. 1989), https://www.lds.org/ensign/1989/11/to-the-elderly-in-the-church?lang=eng, (emphasis added).
2. http://www.infoplease.com/ipa/A0005140.html
3. Sterling W. Sill, "A Fortune to Share," (Oct. 1973), https://www.lds.org/general-conference/1973/10/a-fortune-to-share?lang=eng
4. http://www.irs.gov/Retirement-Plans/Plan-Participant,-Employee/Retirement-Topics-401k-and-Profit-Sharing-Plan-Contribution-Limits
5. http://www.irs.gov/Retirement-Plans/Plan-Participant,-Employee/Retirement-Topics-IRA-Contribution-Limits
6. http://media.nmfn.com/flash/longevity-game/game.html
7. http://www.kiplinger.com/slideshow/real-estate/T006-S001-most-expensive-u-s-cities-to-live-in/index.html
8. http://www.kiplinger.com/slideshow/real-estate/T006-S001-10-cheapest-u-s-cities-to-live-in/index.html

9. http://www.aarp.org/health/medicare-insurance/info-12-2012/health-care-costs.html
10. http://www.ssa.gov/policy/docs/ssb/v69n3/v69n3p1.html
11. http://www.ssa.gov/policy/docs/ssb/v69n3/v69n3p1.html
12. http://www.ssa.gov/policy/docs/ssb/v69n3/v69n3p1.html
13. https://www.fidelity.com/calculators-tools/planning-guidance-center
14. https://fundresearch.fidelity.com/mutual-funds/summary/315792416
15. Devin G. Durrant, "My Heart Pondereth Them Continually," (Oct. 2015), https://www.lds.org/general-conference/2015/10/my-heart-pondereth-them-continually?lang=eng

11
Tips for Frugal Living

How to Minimize Your Family's Expenses

LEARN

- Practical tips for frugal living that will help your family decrease your expenses

- Strategies to save money on food, transportation, household expenses and recreation

At the heart of successful family finance is the principle of living within your means. Most families, at one time or another, have difficulty following this principle. If you find your family in this situation, there are basically two options for getting back on track. One option is to increase your income. You can ask for a raise in your present job, take a second or third job, apply for a new job in your current field that pays more, or get additional education or training to qualify you for a job in a different field with greater remuneration. Increasing your income, though sometimes viable, generally takes time and can prove very stressful, especially when taking on additional work.

The second way to move from deficit spending to living within your means is to decrease your expenses. You have more control over the spending side of the family finance equation than you do over the income side and can often make choices that have immediate and positive impacts on the family budget. You can decide to cancel cable; you can decide to sell one of your cars; you can decide to reduce the frequency of eating out; you can decide to ride your bike instead of driving your car; you can decide to have the thermostat set at 78 degrees instead of 72 degrees in the summer time. There are myriad decisions you can make to reduce spending. This chapter is designed to give you tips for frugal living—practical advice designed to minimize your family's expenses. We will look at specific ways to reduce the amount that you and your family spend on food, household goods, vacations, and holidays.

Saving Money on Food

Providing sufficient healthy food for the family is a basic responsibility that you and your spouse have. Whether we like it or not, each member of the family needs to eat almost every day (except perhaps on fast Sunday). In fact, most family members need to eat three, four, or more times per day (especially if you have teenagers). The cost for fulfilling this responsibility can vary dramatically from one family to the next. According to the United States Department of Agriculture Center for Nutrition Policy and Promotion, the typical budget for food for a family with two parents and four children under the age of ten ranged from $1,169.81 per month ($15,237.72 per year) for the "thrifty" plan to $2,519.82 per month ($30,237.84) for the "liberal" plan.[1] That is a very wide range and, in either case, a lot of money. However, there are many opportunities to save money on food while at the same time providing more healthy food alternatives for your family.

One easy way to save money and make food more healthy is to prepare meals from raw ingredients instead of eating prepared items. Let me give you an example. I devour a 2-ounce bowl of delicious steamy oatmeal each morning. If I were to purchase that most excellent oatmeal served in a fine china bowl at the Marriott Hotel, the cost would be about $8. If I buy the oatmeal in a Styrofoam cup from McDonald's, the cost is less than $2. If I buy instant oatmeal that comes in individual pouches in a colorful box with a Quaker man smiling contentedly at me and then prepare my breakfast in the microwave, the cost is lowered to less than $0.50 per serving. If I buy the same pouches with the Western Family label, the cost is reduced to less than $0.30 per serving. If I buy a 3-pound round tub of old fashioned oatmeal with that same smiling Quaker man, the cost goes down to less than $0.10 per serving. Finally, if I buy a 25-pound sack of old-fashioned oatmeal from the food storage section at Maceys, the cost is less than $0.05 per serving.

When we prepare food from raw ingredients bought in bulk, we often save a lot of money. It is ironic that food in its raw form is not only the least expensive, it is also the most nutritious. Of course, you pay for these monetary savings and improved nutrition with the time it takes to prepare the food. However, parents can include children in meal preparation, which can help strengthen family bonds.

Here is another example. I love fresh whole wheat bread. I can get an excellent, nutritious, fresh loaf from Great Harvest for $5.50. However, the cost for the raw ingredients to make it in my own kitchen from scratch is only $0.69 ($0.50 for your own freshly-ground bulk whole wheat from your year's supply, $0.05 for the yeast, $0.01 for the salt, $0.03 for the oil, and $0.10 for the electricity). Of course, many parents don't have time to make homemade bread. In the Hill home, we taught our children how to make bread. We provided the ingredients and paid our children

$2 per loaf for fresh whole wheat bread. The child could do two batches in about two hours and make $20, providing us with ten loaves of fresh bread at $2.67 per loaf.

Here are a few other ways to decrease the amount you spend on food for your family each month:

- **Remember H.A.L.T.** Don't go shopping when you are hungry, angry, lonely, or tired. Research has shown that if you go grocery shopping when you are hungry, you are likely to buy more and also to buy items that are less healthy (more sweets and high-calorie items).[2]

- **Make a menu and write out a shopping list.** Know what you are going to buy before you enter the supermarket. One helpful practice is to make a menu for the meals you are going to prepare and then create a shopping list from that menu. Another practice is to keep a shopping list on the refrigerator and write items on the list as you notice the need. My wife, Tammy, goes so far as to organize the shopping list by the different areas of the supermarket to make the shopping trip shorter and more efficient.

- **Take advantage of loss leaders and use ad match.** A loss leader is an item that the store sells at below-cost in order to get you inside the store. The idea is that the store may lose money on the one item, but they'll make money on all of your other purchases. Often, the loss leaders are featured in shopping ads. You can go to a store that ad matches (like Walmart) and then get all of the loss leaders from all of the stores. There are a number of websites[3] that identify the loss leaders in all the stores for free or for a small fee.[4]

- **Buy store brands.** Name brands (e.g., Kraft) and store brands (e.g., Western Family) often only differ in the packaging and advertising. Buying the store brand instead of the name brand will save you 10 percent or more on the item.

- **Reduce the number of trips to the supermarket.** You can reduce expenditures by going to the store once a week instead of multiple times whenever you have a need. This also saves you time, gas, and wear and tear on your car.

- **Pay cash.** A study by Drazen Prelec and Duncan Simester of the Sloan School of Management at MIT reveals that shoppers spend up to 100 percent more when using a credit card versus cash.[5] One strategy is to put an amount of cash in the food shopping envelope each week (perhaps $100 or $150 or $200). Take the cash with you on your weekly shopping trip. When the cash is gone, you stop shopping for the week and wait until the next week to continue.

- **Buy in bulk and prepare meals from raw ingredients.** Bulk food usually costs less per unit. In the Provo area, there are often case lot sales. By purchasing a case of food (e.g., tuna, tomato sauce, cream of chicken soup), you can often save 20 percent or more on your purchase. Before buying, be sure to check the price against the single unit price to make sure you are getting a good deal.

The skill of wisely shopping for food can be very beneficial to the long-term financial health of the family. Let me lay it out for you in dollars and cents. Let's say that instead of spending $1,500 a month for food for your family of six, you are able to be frugal and only spend $1,000 a month. Let's do a little time value of money calculation and figure out how much it would be worth if you invested the $500 per month savings each month in a tax-advantaged, diversified, primarily stock-based mutual fund yielding 10 percent per year. In 30 years, it would be worth $1,130,243.96. Need I say more?

Saving Money When You Go out to Eat

Food costs much more if bought in a restaurant instead of a supermarket, and yet American families are spending more and more money eating out. The total amount spent in restaurants nearly doubled during the past fifteen years from $379 billion in 2000 to $709 billion in 2015.[6] In January 2015, for the first time in history, Americans spent more money in restaurants than they did in grocery stores.[7]

It is a national craze to go out to eat frequently. And it is very easy to spend a lot of money going out to eat if you are not careful. One way to decrease expenses significantly is to reduce the amount spent on restaurant meals. Here are some suggestions:

- **Bring your own lunch to work.** Unless you are networking, there is little value in taking the time to buy lunch when you are at work. Bring your lunch. It is healthier, less expensive, and takes less time. The average worker in the United States goes out to eat for lunch twice per week and spends $936 each year doing so.[8]

- **Share a meal with your date.** In the United States, restaurants are known for their large portion sizes and calorie count. For example, at Outback Steakhouse one meal that includes one-half of a Bloomin' onion for an appetizer, a classic blue cheese wedge salad, an 8-ounce filet mignon with loaded mashed potatoes, a mini shake, and a slice of carrot cake runs about 3,637 calories and about $50.[9] Tammy and I learned to leverage this by sharing not only the appetizer but the entire meal. That cuts both the cost and the calorie count in half. The shared meal always satisfies us, and we save a lot of money and calories.

- **Order ice water, not soda.** Fountain drinks have the biggest profit margin of any food item in the restaurant. A 20-ounce soda that costs you $1.99 costs the restaurant about $0.10 to $0.13.[10] You can save big by not ordering soda. It isn't good for you anyway.

- **Go out for a late lunch instead of dinner.** If you go out to eat at 3:30 p.m. and order from the lunch menu, you will get the same food as dinner, but it will cost less. Sometimes the portion size is a little bit smaller, but you don't need the larger portion size, do you? It will also be less crowded, so you can talk more easily with your date or family members. In addition, eating the main meal earlier in the day aids your digestion, makes it easier to sleep,[11] and promotes weight loss.[12]

- **Use coupons/savings cards and books.** There are countless options for obtaining coupons to reduce the cost of a restaurant. Many two-for-one options are available in newspapers and online. Avoid two-for-one offers that require you to buy a drink, and look for the true blue two-for-one offers with no strings attached. Here is one word of advice: When buying two-for-one, make the tip as if you were paying full price. The waiter or waitress had to do just as much work as if you had paid full price. Don't skimp on the tip!

Saving Money on Transportation

Our transportation choices have a big impact on the family budget. In 2013, the average American family spent just over $750 per month ($9,004 per year) on transportation costs.[13] There is room in that number for savings. Here are some suggestions:

- **Buy a low-mileage, late-model used car instead of a new car.** A new car loses a significant amount of its value in the first year. For example, the 2014 Hyundai Genesis lost 38 percent of its value in the first year.[14] Using very conservative assumptions, the 2014 Genesis would still have about 92 percent of its useful life remaining in 2015, and yet the cost would only be 68 percent of the new model. Many websites make it easy to shop for a late-model, low-mileage used car.[15 16 17 18]

- **Pay cash for your vehicle.** If you make a car payment to yourself each month and then pay cash for your car, you will have earned interest rather than paid interest to the car dealership. You can also invest this money for greater returns.

- **Look at the total cost of ownership.** A car will cost you much more than just the sticker price. You also need to account for the cost of gasoline, repairs, insurance, and service. Several Internet sites can give you the total cost of ownership for various models of new and used cars.[19 20]

- **Get an inexpensive car for male teenage drivers.** Male teenage drivers have astronomical insurance rates. You save your family a lot of money by rating your sons on a vehicle that doesn't have collision or comprehensive insurance on it.

- **Service your car on time.** The most important thing you can do to lengthen the life of your vehicle is to change your oil on time, every time. A general rule of thumb is to change the oil every 3,000 miles or 3 months, whichever comes first. Clean oil is essential to extend engine life, and the engine is the most important part of a car to safeguard. Synthetic oil is generally better than traditional petroleum-based oil at protecting your engine and is less expensive over the long term because you only have to change it half as often.[21]

- **Shop around for auto insurance.** Automobile insurance is required in the United States, and the price of insurance varies dramatically from company to company. Shop around to get a good price for your car insurance.

- **Bundle trips.** You can save a surprising amount on gas and wear-and-tear on your car if you do some planning and bundle several purposes with one trip. For example, plan to go to the grocery store after taking your daughter to soccer practice. Carpooling is another example of this principle. Instead of all parents driving their kids to mutual every time, carpool so that several children ride together.

- **Walk and bike places.** Walking or biking not only saves money but is also good for your health. Where feasible, walk to church and ride your bike to work.

Saving Money on Household Expenses

Household expenses—the cost of goods and services in the home—consume a significant amount of money each month. Here are some suggestions for reducing those costs:

- **Get rid of cable.** Cable can cost more than $100 per month. You might consider canceling cable and using an HD antenna and streaming services for your entertainment. We canceled cable a couple of years ago and got a $39.95 HD antenna. We were surprised that it picked up more than a dozen stations on the air for free in full HD. We haven't missed the cable, except during some live sporting events.

- **Get rid of your landline.** There is little reason to have a landline anymore. You can replace all of its functions with cell phones or an Internet phone.

- **Cut your family's hair.** Parents who cut their children's hair can save a bundle, especially in a large family. For example, in a family with six children, you can save almost $1,000 per year in haircuts by cutting their hair at home. Using the time value of money, if you invested that $1,000 per year savings in a tax-advantaged, diversified, primarily stock-based mutual fund that averaged 10 percent increase per year, you would have $164,494.02 after thirty years. Go buy those clippers from Walmart!

- **Lower your thermostat in the winter, and raise it in the summer.** Every degree higher in the winter or lower in the summer will save you 3 to 5 percent on your heating or air conditioning bills. That can add up to hundreds of dollars every month. Likewise, be conscious of when you open and close doors and windows in your home. In the summer, open them when the temperature outside is cooler than inside to cool down the house. Use common sense.

- **Choose cell phone plans wisely.** Cell phone plans vary dramatically from carrier to carrier. Be smart about the plan you choose. Family plans are often much less expensive per phone than individual plans.

- **Turn off electronic devices.** When you are not using an electronic device, do not waste power by leaving it on. Be sure to turn off televisions and computer monitors when not in use. It saves even more money to unplug electronic devices when they are turned off.

- **Shop at garage sales in nice neighborhoods early in the day.** Many household items (especially toys, yard equipment, sporting equipment, and baby things) can be purchased for less money at garage sales. Many sellers are just trying to get rid of their junk, which may be your treasure. You may want to focus on garage sales in nice neighborhoods. Also, go before the sale is officially open; if you are the first one there, you'll get the nice stuff at a good price. Another way to save money at a garage sale is to offer one half of the asking price. Many times the seller will accept your offer.

- **Look online.** Websites like ksl.com and craigslist.com both have thousands of items, many at a fraction of the cost of store-purchased items. This is a good source for baby-related purchases. I have a daughter who bought a double jogging

How Frugal Living Can Be a Blessing

By Ashley LeBaron, Family Finance Research Assistant

I have personally experienced how frugal living can bless families. My parents live a wonderful balance of frugality (toward things that don't matter in the long-run) and generosity (toward things that do matter in the long-run). My parents are great at spending their money on things that we value as a family. These values include strengthening familial relationships, gaining perspective-expanding experiences via travel, and investing in education. Because of my parents' wise use of their resources, I have gained an appreciation for money. Money itself may be meaningless, but the things you can do with well-managed money are truly wonderful.

Strengthening Familial Relationships

I am the fourth of five close-knit siblings, the four oldest of which now live away from home. We also live in four separate time zones. In these years of emerging adulthood, my older siblings and I don't have much money to spend on plane tickets, so we wouldn't see each other very much if not for our parents' help. My parents decided long ago to put family first, and I see that demonstrated in the way they finance how our family gets together. I see them sacrificing some of their own personal wants in order to do this. We continue to enjoy close, loving sibling bonds because we are able to be together multiple times a year.

Gaining Perspective-Expanding Experiences via Travel

Growing up, my friends always assumed that my family was filthy rich because we traveled often. That is not true. My dad sought out and created work opportunities in other countries so that we could experience and appreciate other peoples and cultures. This is something that my family values. My parents made a conscious decision to use their money on these experiences, while my dad drove a dumpy old Toyota Corolla for twelve years. We were not traveling because we had endless resources; we were traveling because we had saved and sacrificed in order to do so. To me, these international experiences have been life-changing and literally priceless.

Investing in Education

It is common knowledge that, generally, the more education you have, the more you are paid (not to mention the other countless benefits of education). Education, then, is simply an investment in your future. My parents have always stressed the importance of this, and they have always demonstrated their support. My parents paid for my needs and modest wants in high school so long as I continued to excel scholastically, and because of that support, I was able to focus on my studies and now enjoy a full-ride scholarship, saving me thousands of dollars each semester. My parents paid for my housing and living expenses my first year of college so that I could focus on building a good GPA foundation in order to keep my scholarship and be a desirable candidate for graduate school. I am so grateful that they have lived frugally, which has put them in a financial position to lend this help. Their support of my educational pursuits has blessed me and will continue to pay off for the rest of my life.

My parents have taught me that while money is not the most important thing in life, it can help make possible some of the most important things. That is why living frugally is a blessing so long as it enables you to spend money on what your family values. Frugal living is only meaningful so long as we use our acquired resources to bless our families and build God's kingdom.

stroller online for a fraction of the cost of a new stroller.

- **Shop at Deseret Industries or other thrift stores.** Similar to garage sales, these stores often have used items at a fraction of their new cost. In addition, by shopping there you are supporting a job training and placement program.[22]

- **Set a waiting period before making major household purchases.** It is easy to give way to impulse household purchases that can rack up balances on our credit cards. You might consider setting a waiting period for any purchase over a certain amount, say $100. This allows you to see if you really need that item and limits expensive impulse purchases.

Saving Money on Recreation

The Family: A Proclamation to the World names "wholesome recreational activities" as one of the foundational principles upon which successful marriages and families are based. Many vacations can qualify as wholesome recreation, and research has shown that they generally enhance family adaptability and cohesion.[23] Vacations are generally a good thing for families. However, not all vacations are created equal. Surprisingly, some vacations that cost the least are those that strengthen families the most. For example, camping and backpacking are among the least expensive vacation alternatives but provide an experience that promotes family adaptability while treating what has been called Nature Deficit Disorder (NDD).[24] A family of six may save thousands of dollars by choosing to go camping in national parks instead of flying to Orlando to go to Disney World and Universal Studios. And it may also be that a camping trip would strengthen that family more than a trip to Disney World.

Here are some other suggestions for making your recreational dollars go further:

- **Leverage timeshare presentations.** Once you reach a certain income bracket, you will have many opportunities to attend timeshare presentations. Often, these marketing tools enable you and your family to stay at the sponsoring resort for two to three days for free, on the condition that you and your spouse both attend a timeshare sales presentation for about two hours. Doing this enables you to stay in a nice place at little or no cost to you. All you have to do is be comfortable saying "no" at the end of the sales presentation.

- **Use reward miles from your credit card to pay for air travel.** Many credit cards offer you the perk of accruing airline reward miles toward future travel. If you choose and use your credit card wisely, this can add up to two or three free roundtrip tickets per year. These free tickets can make the difference between a vacation being affordable or not.

- **Be flexible to go at the last minute.** Unused cruise tickets and hotel rooms are often sold at a large discount at the last minute. You can stay informed of these deals via many websites including www.travelzoo.com, www.greatvaluevacations.com, www.skyauction.com, www.travelocity.com, and www.hotels.com, to name a few.

- **Stay with family members.** If you enjoy renewing extended family ties, staying with family members around the country can be satisfying and save you money. Be

aware that if you stay with a family member, they may come and visit you as well!

- **Vacation at home.** Often, we do not take advantage of all the wonderful vacation opportunities in our own backyards. Tammy and I recently canceled an international trip and vacationed from home instead. We used www.tripadvisor.com and found highly-rated restaurants and tourist destinations to visit in Utah County. We had a blast and stayed in the best accommodations—our own home!

- **Go to the dollar theater.** If you like to see movies in a theater, just wait a few weeks and you can save 70 to 80 percent on the ticket price by going to the dollar theater. Avoid getting popcorn; the popcorn at the dollar theater costs more than the movie tickets.
- **Make good use of the library.** Instead of buying books, check them out of the library. The library also has low-cost DVDs and an online lending library.

Summary

To make it easier to joyfully live within your means, you can either increase your income or decrease your spending. In this chapter, we examined practical tips for frugal living. There are many ways to cut your expenses, such as spending less on groceries, cutting the cost of going out to eat, saving money on transportation, reducing household expenditures, and stretching your vacation dollar.

Prophetic Counsel on Frugality

The February 1998 issue of the Ensign contains a message from (then) Elder Eyring entitled "The Family." The following is an excerpt from this message that relates to principles addressed in this chapter. I hope you read this and the rest of his address, for it is prophetic counsel.

[T]here are important ways in which planning for failure can make failure more likely and the ideal less so. Consider these twin commandments as an example: "Fathers are to … provide the necessities of life … for their families" and "mothers are primarily responsible for the nurture of their children." Knowing how hard that might be, a young man might choose a career on the basis of how much money he could make, even if it meant he couldn't be home enough to be an equal partner. By doing that, he has already decided he cannot hope to do what would be best. A young woman might prepare for a career incompatible with being primarily responsible for the nurture of her children because of the possibilities of not marrying, of not having children, or of being left alone to provide for them herself. Or she might fail to focus her education on the gospel and the useful knowledge of the world that nurturing a family would require, not realizing that the highest and best use she could make of her talents and her education would be in her home. Consequently, because a young man and woman had planned thus, they might make what is best for a family less likely to be obtained.

Surely they are both wise to worry about the physical needs of that future family. The costs of buying a home, compared to average salaries, seem to be rising and jobs harder to hold. But there are other ways the young man and the young woman could think about preparing to provide for that future family. Income is only one part of it. Have you noticed husbands and wives who feel pinched for lack of money choose for a solution ways to make their family income keep rising but soon find that the pinch is there whatever the income? There is an old formula which goes something like this: Income five dollars and expenses six dollars: misery. Income four dollars and expenses three dollars: happiness.

Whether the young man can provide and, after work, return home to his family at a reasonable hour, and whether the young woman can be there to nurture children, can depend as much on how they learn to spend as on how they learn to earn. President Brigham Young said it this way, speaking to us as much as he did to the people in his day: "If you wish to get rich, save what you get. A fool can earn money; but it takes a wise man to save and dispose of it to his own advantage. Then go to work, and save everything, and make your own bonnets and clothing." (Journal of Discourses, 11:301)

In today's world, instead of telling young couples to make bonnets, President Young might suggest they think carefully about what they really need in cars, clothes, recreation, houses, vacations, and whatever they will someday try to provide for their children. And he might point out that the difference in cost between what the world says is necessary and what children really need could allow the margin in time that a father and a mother might need with their children in order to bring them home to their Heavenly Father.

Even the most frugal spending habits and the most careful planning for employment may not be enough to ensure success, but those things could be enough to allow us the peace that comes from knowing we did the best we could to provide and to nurture.[25]

However, I would like to conclude this chapter with a caution. There are some who take frugality to an extreme. While it is a virtue to live within your means, any virtue taken to an extreme can become a vice. Don't miss out on meaningful experiences because of unnecessary frugality. Money, when used wisely (emphasis on *used*), can be a great blessing to our families and others. We must remember that we are stewards of our resources and that they are meant to be used to bless God's children. They are not meant to be hoarded. As you try to live frugally, keep a stewardship perspective and use your frugality in order to acquire resources to bless God's children.

Notes

1. "USDA Food Plans: Cost of Food." United States Department of Agriculture Center for Nutrition Policy and Promotion, http://www.cnpp.usda.gov/USDAFoodPlansCostofFood/reports.
2. Notifications, Desktop, Profile, Settings, and Logout. "Confirmed: It's A Bad Idea To Go Grocery Shopping Hungry." *The Huffington Post*, http://www.huffingtonpost.com/2013/05/06/grocery-shopping-hungry-high-calorie-foods_n_3225089.html.
3. See http://www.pricematchwithrachel.com/.
4. See also http://www.dealstomeals.com/.
5. Erik Folgate, "You Spend More Money When You Use A Credit Card." Money Crashers, http://www.moneycrashers.com/you-spend-more-money-when-you-use-a-credit-card/.
6. "Restaurant Industry Sales." *National Restaurant Association*, http://www.restaurant.org/Restaurant/media/Restaurant/SiteImages/News%20and%20Research/Industry%20dashboard/Annual-sales-for-Dashboard-2015.jpg.
7. "Americans' Spending on Dining Out Just Overtook Grocery Sales for the First Time Ever." Bloomberg.com, http://www.bloomberg.com/news/articles/2015-04-14/americans-spending-on-dining-out-just-overtook-grocery-sales-for-the-first-time-ever.
8. "Lunchtime: Americans Spend Nearly $1K Annually Eating Out For Lunch." *Forbes*. http://www.forbes.com/sites/halahtouryalai/2013/09/25/lunchtime-americans-spend-nearly-1k-annually-eating-out-for-lunch/.
9. "Outback Steakhouse Nutrition Information." https://www.outback.com/nutrition.
10. "How Much Would I Need to Drink for a Restaurant to Lose Money on a $2 Fountain Soda?" *Quora*, https://www.quora.com/How-much-would-I-need-to-drink-for-a-restaurant-to-lose-money-on-a-2-fountain-soda.
11. "Taste: What You Eat Can Affect Sleep." *National Sleep Foundation*, https://sleepfoundation.org/bedroom/taste.php.
12. Garaulet, M., P. Gómez-Abellán, J. J. Alburquerque-Béjar, Y.-C. Lee, J. M. Ordovás, and F. a. J. L. Scheer. "Timing of Food Intake Predicts Weight Loss Effectiveness." International Journal of Obesity (2005) 37, no. 4 (April 2013): 604–11. doi:10.1038/ijo.2012.229.
13. Daniel Wesley, "How The Average U.S. Consumer Spends Their Paycheck." *CreditLoan*, http://www.creditloan.com/blog/how-the-average-us-consumer-spends-their-paycheck/.
14. "New Study Reveals 10 Best Cars to Buy Used Rather Than New." *Autotrader*, http://www.autotrader.com/best-cars/new-study-reveals-10-best-cars-to-buy-used-rather-than-new-234955.
15. Visit www.carmax.com to search for late-model, low-mileage used cars.
16. Search www.lowbooksales.com for used cars.
17. See also www.autotrader.com for another source.
18. Visit www.cargurus.com as a fourth option for finding a good used car.
19. See www.edmunds.com.
20. See also www.kbb.com.
21. "Why Would I Upgrade to a Synthetic Motor Oil?" *HowStuffWorks*, http://auto.howstuffworks.com/synthetic-motor-oil.htm.
22. "Deseret Industries | Shop." Deseret Industries, https://deseretindustries.org/shop?lang=eng.
23. M. A. Widmer, R. B. Zabriskie, and R. Loser, (2005). "Wholesome Family Recreation." In S. K. Klein and E. J. Hill (Eds.), Creating Home As A Sacred Center: Principles for Everyday Living (Provo: BYU Academic Publishing, 2005), 221–232.
24. M. A. Widmer and S. T. Taniguchi, "Wholesome Family Recreation: Building Strong Families." In A. Hawkins, D. Dollahite, & T. Draper (Eds.), Successful Marriages and Families: Proclamation Principles and Research Perspectives (Provo: BYU Studies Press, 2012), 225–236.
25. Henry B. Eyring, "The Family", Ensign (Feb 1998), https://www.lds.org/ensign/1998/02/the-family?lang=eng.

12

Work and Family

Providing for and Nurturing Your Family in Harmony[1]

LEARN

- Strategies that can help your family experience greater joy as you juggle the demands of work, family, and church

- To focus on the most important things

"The Family: A Proclamation to the World" teaches that we are responsible to both provide for and nurture our families in the context of the gospel of Jesus Christ.[2] To provide for a family, it is essential that we obtain employment that provides adequate income and that we manage our money wisely. However, the time and energy we invest in providing may make nurturing difficult. Being fully involved as a spouse and parent on top of adequately providing and being a reliable employee can feel like the weight of the world on your shoulders.

> *The happiest people I know are those whose life-style centers around the home. Work is very important, and success in one's profession or business is also essential to happiness, but remember what we say so often: "No other success can compensate for failure in the home."*
> — *N. Eldon Tanner*[3]

As we struggle to juggle our employment, our home duties, and our church callings, we may often feel stressed and unbalanced. We wrestle with the decision of whether to work late or leave on time to attend a child's activity. We agonize about whether or not to miss a previously planned family outing because an unexpected church assignment has come up. We wonder if we should stay up late to go the extra mile in preparing a Sunday lesson or to go to bed and get much needed rest. We wonder if we should study for a final when our help is needed with a sick child. Sometimes it seems like work, home, and church are in a tug of war, each fighting for our personal time and energy. Juggling these responsibilities may eventually exhaust us and cause us to lose interest in the very things we love most. We may even begin to feel inadequate, pessimistic, and discouraged.

Perhaps it is beneficial to view the situation from a different perspective. Recent social science research proposes that work, family, and other life domains can actually be complementary—not competing—priorities. Success on the job often contributes to our success outside of work and vice versa. A recent international study reveals that relationships and social interactions, physical and psychological benefits, and improved skills are some aspects of work that can enhance home life, and it also works the other way around.[4] The key to harmony is to invest our time and money in activities that enhance multiple domains that we value in our lives. Regularly making the time and spending the money to engage in family relationship-building activities can be thought of as a long-term investment, like the stock market, which will yield long-term blessings of family unity.

This concept of enhancement—sometimes called *life harmony*[5]—utilizes a musical metaphor. Just as the different melodies in a well-composed piece of music unite in harmony, the different facets of our life can also coordinate in peace. Using the perspective of life harmony, we no longer see work, family, and church as fighting for our limited time and money. We see mortality as a great symphony, with the many different responsibilities in our own lives as instruments united harmoniously to the glory of God.[6] The way we manage and consecrate our financial resources is a great orchestrator of these instruments.

There is no single formula for creating a life where we successfully provide for and nurture our families. However, there are a variety of strategies that can help us no matter our circumstances. Employing any of these strategies can help us experience greater joy as we bring the demands of job, family, and church into greater harmony. In this chapter, we focus on suggestions in seven areas: (1) enhance energy, (2) increase quality time, (3) learn to bundle, (4) focus on the most important things, (5) work flexibly, (6) simplify your life, and (7) center on the Savior.

1. Enhance Energy

Research has documented that it is the depletion of energy—rather than time spent on the job—that is the main factor in whether people feel like there is conflict between work and the rest of their lives.[7] It is very possible that an invigorating job requiring fifty hours per week may have a less negative impact on the home than a depressing job requiring forty hours per week. When we feel that our employment is sapping our strength, there is little energy left for service at home or in the church.

One way to increase our energy without reducing work hours is to make a list of all the things we do at work that either drain or energize us. To create more work-family harmony,

"Sorry you missed his concert ... but here is an encore."

we may arrange to do the energizing things right before we go home so that we can carry more of that energy home to our families. For example, if I were an engineer who loves design work and hates paperwork and meetings, I might choose to get onerous paperwork tasks done earlier in the day and save the energizing design work for the hours right before I go home.

Another way to increase energy is to choose to make time to do things that are personally renewing. Physical exercise often creates physical energy. Peaceful music may soothe our souls. Talking to a friend can be energizing. A short nap is often invigorating. Having a few minutes alone in quiet solitude can rejuvenate our hearts. Taking time for rejuvenating activities may appear to only add more to a to-do list full of high-priority tasks, but such moments can add the extra physical and spiritual strength we need to accomplish everything. Even the Savior took time for this kind of replenishment.[8] It is important to see personal renewal as an investment, not as a waste of time.

An often overlooked means of increasing energy at work is prayer. We are repeatedly counseled in the scriptures to "pray always,"[9] but prayer may be forgotten while on the job. One father has related that he prays frequently at work, sometimes on his knees and sometimes silently, and is blessed with spiritual light (energy) that guides him in how to be more effective in his job. As the Spirit helps him solve work problems, he feels he has more time and energy for his family and church service. Indeed, we are counseled in the scriptures to "cry over the flocks of your fields, that they may increase."[10]

The commute to and from work can also be a time of energy renewal rather than depletion. One mother reviews scriptures she has memorized as she walks to work. She arrives on the job with a clear and active mind. One father listens to conference talks as he drives home from work. By the time he greets his family, he has forgotten about aggravating experiences during the work day and is ready for his most important work.[11] After the incessant demands of many jobs, we often need a slower tempo for renewal before returning to our homes.

As we open our minds to better see ways we can enhance energy, we may discover activities that foster harmony in our lives without requiring additional time. We may find ourselves with less fatigue, conflict, and stress while actually doing more. Additionally, we may find that as we seek physical and spiritual renewal, we allow ourselves access to the enabling power of the Atonement, helping us on a day-to-day basis to accomplish more than we thought we could on our own.

2. Increase Quality Time

In many cases, we need to be available for extended lengths of time in order to meet the immediate concerns and needs of our children, making quality time the product of quantity time. Important interactions happen during lengthy periods of unstructured time. However, not all time is created equal. To obtain life harmony, we must find ways to put each moment to its best use. When Elder Dallin H.

Oaks was in his third year of law school and involved in church responsibilities, he had to make the most of the limited time he had with his daughters. He recalls,

> My favorite play activity with the little girls was "daddy be a bear." When I came home from my studies for a few minutes at lunch and dinnertime, I would set my books on the table and drop down on all fours on the linoleum. Then, making the most terrible growls, I would crawl around the floor after the children, who fled with screams, but always begged for more.[12]

There is no doubt this was quality time!

In his occupation as an airline pilot, President Dieter F. Uchtdorf was required to travel away from home for long periods of time. He found family harmony by seeking quality time. His son Guido remembers, "When Dad returned home, we played, we talked, and we laughed together." Guido added, "That was quality time!"[13]

Family mealtime is a great opportunity for high-quality family time. President Ezra Taft Benson taught, "Happy conversation, sharing of the day's plans and activities, and special teaching moments occur at mealtime because mothers and fathers and children work at it."[14] A life harmony study among a subsample of United States IBM employees who are parents revealed that regular family mealtime protected individuals from conflict between work and family life when they had to work long hours.[15] In addition, extensive social science research has documented that regular family meal time is associated with less adolescent risk for a variety of internalizing behaviors such as depression, weak self-esteem, suicidal thoughts, attempted suicide, withdrawn or distressed behavior, and behavioral problems.[16,17,18]

To be together for mealtimes is a challenge, especially in large families. It requires careful planning. One family holds a family council each Sunday and carefully selects a dinnertime each evening when everyone can be there. The time varies according to the activities of the week. Another family chose to share the big meal of the day at 3:00 pm each afternoon, right when the children came home from school. In this family, the father came home early from work for dinner with the family and then finished his workday at home via telecommuting.

Bedtime may also be a time of extraordinary quality. Children rarely want to go to sleep when parents want them to, but will often give parents undivided attention at bedtime. In an experiment consisting of 405 mothers and their infants or toddlers, it was found that having a consistent bedtime routine can lead to better sleep for children and a better mood for their mothers.[19] Parents can read or tell stories, pray, cuddle, sing songs, read the scriptures, and many other things. This is also an ideal time to teach the gospel. The peaceful feelings associated with bedtime stay with children throughout the night. Likewise, these bedtime interactions with children may be just what a parent needs to forget the frustrations of the day and to sleep peacefully.

The specific ways to increase quality time are innumerable. One may focus on creating time for carefree play with the children, or carefully plan a time when all family members can be available for family dinner, or make it a priority to be available during the bedtime hour. The specifics may vary, but the principle is the same: when we make the effort to engage in meaningful activities with those we care about, we are better able to provide for and nurture our families in harmony.

3. Learn to Bundle

Bundling, according to life harmony research, is when one activity simultaneously serves purposes in two or more aspects of life.[20] Successful bundlers are often able to do two or more things at the same time harmoniously. In many cases, each facet of the activity is of greater value because it is bundled than if it were done as its own activity. For example, when a couple chooses to walk together, they may get needed exercise, relax and be rejuvenated, share ideas about church callings, express their affection, talk about their children, brainstorm solutions to problems at work, and so on. This one bundling activity is of great value because it may contribute to so many facets of life.

Bundling can also be a benefit to the family budget and contribute to personal time. For example, if you have to take your son to and from soccer practice on the other side of town, you may choose to bundle that trip. Instead of two round trips, you could bring your daughter with you, drop off your son, and pick up some things at a nearby Home Depot with her while your son is at practice. By doing so, you would get one-on-one time with your daughter, save the travel time, save gas, and get the shopping done.

A few years ago my wife Tammy gave me a tandem bicycle for my birthday. This has proved to be an ideal tool for bundling. We often ride together on a bike path up a beautiful canyon next to the Provo River. By doing so, we can both get as much exercise as we each want. (If you get tired, you can just put your feet up!) We stay close, so it easy to talk to one another and strengthen our marriage as we exercise. We are invigorated by the beautiful scenery on the trail. We greet and sometimes talk with members of the community. The list could go on and on. Riding a tandem bike with a family member accomplishes so much more than riding alone.

Another example of bundling is when a parent takes a child with them to run errands. A mother may take her child with her to purchase groceries. While shopping, she has the opportunity to connect with her child one-on-one and engage in relationship-building conversation. She can also teach principles of provident living by showing her child how to save money by comparison shopping.

In today's world, many parents provide transportation for their children to school and many other activities. This may be an excellent opportunity to bundle travel time with meaningful conversation. Elder Robert D. Hales counseled parents, "As you drive or walk children to school or their various activities, do you use the time to talk with them about their hopes and dreams and fears and joys? Do you take the time to have them take the earplugs from their MP3 players and all the other devices so that they can hear you and feel of your love?"[21]

We may also bundle church service time with family time. A bishop with a young family in a ward with numerous widows related that he brings one or more children with him each time he makes a non-confidential visit. The widows have learned to love his children, and the children are able to see their father ministering.

When we do two or more things at the same time in harmony, we give that time period greater value. As we examine our lives, we will find many such activities that will enable us to provide for and nurture our families in harmony.

4. Focus on the Most Important Things

Bundling does not always work. There are many times when it is better to set firm boundaries and not let the drumming of paid work overpower the gentle melodies of home life. Keeping the Sabbath day holy, as free as possible from the stresses of employment, may be a key to focused harmony. Bob Egan, a successful IBM executive, told my work and family class at BYU that he made a promise never to work on a Sunday, and he never has. He said it feels good to tell his children, "Sunday is a special day, a day different than other days of the week. Daddy doesn't go to work on Sunday."

Weekly family home evening is also sacred family time around which firm boundaries should be set. Outside friendships, work, and church service should not encroach upon this activity. This might be a great time to turn the phones off completely, avoiding even the intrusive buzz of an incoming text message. It is a time to say "no" to activities (however worthy they might be) that intrude upon a faith-promoting family home evening.

Family vacation may be another time for muting work completely. In today's wireless world of smart phones, tablets, iPads, and laptops, it is easy to let work bring dissonance to the delicate tunes of vacation renewal. A few years ago, I took my wife and three of our children to enjoy the Big Island of Hawaii for an eight-day vacation. I brought my laptop with the thought that I could log on a few minutes each day and keep up with my e-mail. However, the few minutes turned into a few hours each day. It seemed that even when playing with the kids at the beach, I would become distracted by thinking about a work project or by becoming irritated because of something I read in an e-mail. It is true that where the mind is, the heart is sure to follow. A few days into vacation, my boss firmly demanded (via e-mail) that I join an important 9:00 a.m. conference call the next morning. After replying that I would attend, I realized that the 9:00 a.m. call in New York would be 3:00 a.m. Kona time. Sitting in on that tense conference call in the wee hours of the morning, with the sound of the waves crashing in the background, was the straw that broke this camel's back. I asked myself, "What am I doing? I'm supposed to be on vacation!" So after the call I locked up the laptop, put away the calling card, and crawled back into bed. I made a resolution: from then on I would throw off my "electronic leash" whenever I went on vacation.[22]

Part of focusing on the most important things is recognizing that the family takes priority over other life domains. The First Presidency wrote, "However worthy and appropriate other demands or activities may be, they must not be permitted to displace the divinely-appointed duties that only parents and families can adequately perform."[23] Sometimes we erroneously place church service arbitrarily above family responsibilities. President Dieter F. Uchtdorf taught, "Even some programs of the Church can become a distraction if we take them to extremes and allow them to dominate our time and our attention at the expense of things that matter most. We need balance in life."[24] Certainly our employment and church callings are important and should be fulfilled diligently. However, on occasion, we may need to remember what Elder Dallin H. Oaks counseled: "We have to forego some good things in order to choose others that are better or best because they develop faith in the Lord Jesus Christ and strengthen our families."[25]

5. Work Flexibly

Research has consistently shown that those who provide for their families in jobs with workplace flexibility are better able to nurture family members. Workplace flexibility is defined as "the ability of workers to make choices about when, where, and for how long they engage in work-related tasks."[26] Some examples of workplace flexibility include telecommuting (working electronically from home), flextime (being able to modify start times, meal breaks, and ending times), part-time (working reduced hours for reduced pay), and leaves (taking time off without pay for family responsibilities).

A large body of research documents the benefits of this flexibility to both work and family life. For example, one study in a large multinational corporation compared 279 mothers working part-time in professional positions with 250 mothers working full-time. Those working part-time reported that they used their extra discretionary time to care for and nurture their dependent children. They reported less work-to-family conflict as well as greater work-family success, childcare satisfaction, and family success.[27]

Another study compared 441 telecommuters who worked primarily from home to 4,315 workers who worked primarily from the office. Those who worked from home reported greater job motivation, career opportunity, work-life balance, and personal/family success. They also reported that they were less likely to be thinking about leaving the company.[28] Several other studies have revealed that those who have workplace flexibility are able to work longer hours without experiencing work-family conflict.[29, 30]

Over the years, I have personally used each of these options to facilitate work and family harmony. The strategy that probably helped the most was when I worked from home for IBM instead of commuting to and from the office each day. In 1990, I became one of IBM's first telecommuters. For nearly ten years, I worked from my home in Logan, Utah, more

than 2,000 miles from my co-workers in New York. This enabled me to live in a quiet community, forego the stressful forty-five-minute commute each morning and evening, and be at home within earshot of my family for most of our waking hours. I found myself much more involved in the everyday activities of the home and much more in tune with the individual needs of my children. I also found that the flexibility and autonomy of telework enabled me to do my job more effectively and efficiently.

However, working with so many children in the background sometimes made it difficult to maintain professional boundaries between work and home life. Let me share one humorous story of mine on telecommuting that appeared in a *Wall Street Journal* article[31]:

> One morning while I recorded my daily voice mail greeting, my wife Juanita was folding clothes in the laundry room across the hall. My six-year-old daughter Emily had just taken a shower upstairs and could not find the clothes she wanted to wear. She came downstairs draped in nothing but a towel. When Juanita saw her, she said in a loud, giggly female voice, "Look at you! You have no clothes on!" After several colleagues commented with a chuckle about my voice mail greeting, I listened to it, and this is what I heard:
>
> Male Voice: This is Dr. Jeff Hill with IBM Global Employee Research . . .
>
> Giggly Female Voice: Look at you! You have no clothes on!

Male Voice: I'm not available right now . . .[32]

The plethora of electronic tools available in the digital age opens up many possibilities for when, where, and how long work is performed. Most large companies and many smaller ones offer these flexible work options. Whether it is flextime, telecommuting, part-time work, or leaves, a key component for achieving life harmony is to choose to work flexibly. Those who are successful at this choose to work when it makes sense to work and to be with family members when it makes sense to be with them.

6. Simplify Your Life

Voluntary simplicity—deliberately choosing to accumulate fewer possessions and engage in fewer activities than possible—aids in creating life harmony.[33] The key to accomplishing this financially is to distinguish between needs and wants. We should first plan to meet our needs and then simplify by purchasing fewer items that are simply wants. Elder L. Tom Perry counseled, "In our search to obtain relief from the stresses of life, may we earnestly seek ways to simplify our lives."[34] King Benjamin's counsel is applicable to many of us today: "And see that all these things are done in wisdom and order, for it is not requisite that a man should run faster than he has strength." [35] In following this counsel, Elder Neal A. Maxwell challenged every member of the church to find an activity they didn't need to do anymore, and then stop doing it.[36]

Many of us seek diligently to please and help those around us. Sometimes we agree to do too many things that are not part of our primary mission. If we really want to focus on those activities with value, then we need to

learn how to kindly but firmly say "No."

That may be easier said than done, especially for those of us who want to please others. I have learned a simple way to do this. When someone asks me to do something, I respond, "Thank you very much for this invitation. I appreciate it. Let me think it over and I'll get back to you tomorrow." If, after consideration, I decide it is an invitation I'd rather not accept, I think of others who might want to do it. Then when I get back to the person, I say something like, "I thank you again for the invitation, but with what's going on right now, I am not going to be able to accept. However, you might want to contact Thom Curtis or Wally Goddard. One of them might be interested, and they would probably do a better job than I would." Using such a dialogue, I can say no without a twinge of regret.

In order to obtain life harmony, we must also look for ways to compose a life of modest means. We live in a materialistic world. With our many materials and pursuits, we may run the risk of obscuring the simple but powerful life melody we hope to compose. One important way to simplify life is to follow the coun-

Avoiding Materialism

Out of necessity, most of us are involved in earning money and acquiring some of the world's goods to be able to sustain our families. It requires a good part of our time and attention. There is no end to what the world has to offer, so it is critical that we learn to recognize when we have enough. If we are not careful, we will begin to chase after the temporal more than the spiritual. Our pursuit for the spiritual and eternal will then take the backseat, instead of the other way around. Sadly, there appears to be a strong inclination to acquire more and more and to own the latest and the most sophisticated.

How do we make sure that we are not drawn down this path? Jacob gives this counsel: "Wherefore, do not spend money for that which is of no worth, nor your labor for that which cannot satisfy. Hearken diligently unto me, and remember the words which I have spoken; and come unto the Holy One of Israel, and feast upon that which perisheth not, neither can be corrupted, and let your soul delight in fatness."

—Elder Michael John U. Teh [37]

sel of the prophets to stay out of debt. Elder Joseph B. Wirthlin promised great blessings to those who pay an honest tithing, spend less than they earn, learn to save, honor financial obligations, and teach children sound financial principles.[38]

A family may work together to simplify life by reducing the number of demands outside the home. This will eliminate some low-value activities, making room for activities of greater worth. For example, a father may choose to go golfing with the office group every other week instead of every week. A bishop may decide to reduce the length and frequency of ward leadership meetings. A Relief Society instructor may choose to spend a little less time making fancy handouts for her lesson. Youth may choose to reduce the number of extracurricular activities that they are engaged in during the school year and the amount of time they spend "hanging out." Though the ways to simplify life vary, remember the principle of reducing the number of low-value activities and the time spent engaging in them.

7. Center on the Savior

Perhaps the most important key in successfully providing for and nurturing our families in harmony is to center on the Savior. President Howard W. Hunter emphasized, "I am aware that life presents many challenges, but with the help of the Lord, we need not fear. If our lives and our faith are centered on Jesus Christ and his restored gospel, nothing can ever go permanently wrong."[39] The concept of life harmony is embodied in the scripture, "And we know that all things work together for good to them that love God, to them who are called according to his purpose."[40] When the primary focus of our life is to become a disciple of Jesus Christ, everything else—employment, home, and church—falls into place.

We create harmony as we center on the Savior by building spiritual patterns in the home.[41] There are many ways of doing this. Many families have a pattern of beginning each

The Mexican Fishing Village Story

Author Unknown

An American entrepreneur, father of two young children, was standing on the pier of a small coastal Mexican village when a small boat, containing just one fisherman, docked. Inside the small boat were several large yellow fin tuna. The American complimented the Mexican on the quality of his fish.

"How long did it take you to catch them?" the American asked.

"Only a little while," the Mexican replied.

"Why don't you stay out longer and catch more fish?" the American then asked.

"I have sufficient to support the needs of our home," the Mexican said.

"But," the American then asked, "What do you do with the rest of your time?"

The Mexican fisherman smiled and with a twinkle in his eye said, "I do a lot at home, señor. I play with my niños, lend a hand with the comida, and then take a siesta with my wife, Maria. After helping the kids with their homework, we stroll to the plaza in the evening where we listen to the guitar and sing with our amigos. I have a full and wonderful life, señor."

The American scoffed, "I am a Stanford MBA and could help you. You should spend a lot more time fishing, and with the proceeds you could buy a bigger boat, and with the proceeds from the bigger boat you could buy several boats. Eventually you would have a fleet of fishing boats. Instead of selling your catch to a middleman, you would sell directly to the consumers, eventually opening your own can factory. You would control the product, processing, and distribution. You would need to leave this small coastal fishing village and move to Mexico City, then LA, and eventually New York, where you would run your expanding enterprise."

The Mexican fisherman asked, "But señor, how long will this all take?"

The American replied, "Not long, maybe fifteen to twenty years."

"But what then, señor?"

The American laughed. "That's the best part. When the time is right, you would sell your company stock to the public and become very rich; you would make millions."

"Millions, señor? Then what?"

The American said slowly, "Then you would retire and move to a small coastal fishing village where you could do a lot at home. You would play with your grandkids, help with the comida, take a siesta with your wife, and stroll to the plaza in the evenings where you could listen to the guitar and sing with your amigos . . ."[42]

day by reading and discussing the scriptures, followed by family prayer, per the counsel of our church leaders. We have also been counseled to hold a meaningful family home evening every week.

Elder David A. Bednar gave several suggestions about how to center our lives on the Savior by being "more diligent and concerned at home."[43] He counseled parents to frequently bear their testimonies in informal settings in the home. He also advised parents to be consistent in these spiritual patterns. He said, "Our consistency in doing seemingly small things can lead to significant spiritual results."[44]

There are numerous other small and simple things that can be done to more effectively center on the Savior. Priesthood blessings provide a way for fathers to partner with the Savior in rearing children in love and righteousness. Beginning and ending a sincere fast together as a family is another way to be centered on Christ. Parents can also read faith-filled inspirational stories at bedtime. The key, whatever the specific path, is to create an environment that centers on the Savior.

We center on the Savior when we bless the poor with our financial resources. Elder Jeffrey R. Holland eloquently taught that we are to "do what we can to deliver any we can from poverty that holds them captive and destroys so many of their dreams."[45] Indeed, Elder Holland continued, "when we are in the service of our fellow beings, we are only in the service of our God."[46]

Summary

Providing for and nurturing our families in harmony may appear to be an unrealistic ideal when it seems the best we can do is "struggle to juggle" our extensive demands. However, utilizing strategies such as enhancing energy, increasing quality time, learning to bundle, focusing on the most important things, working flexibly, simplifying our lives, and centering our lives on the Savior can lighten the burden and bring greater joy and purpose to the work of life. As we seek life harmony, we will be more able to both provide for and nurture our families and compose of our lives a magnificent symphony.

Notes

1. Substantial portions of this chapter were originally published in E. J. Hill (2014), Finding life harmony as we struggle to juggle. In B. L. Top and M. A. Goodman (Eds.), *By divine design: Best practices for family success and happiness.* (pp. 1-22). Provo, UT: Religious Studies Center and Deseret Book.
2. E. J. Hill, S. Allen, J. I. Jacob, A. F. Bair, S. L. Bikhazi, A. Van Langeveld, G. Martinengo, T.T. Palmer, & E. Walker (2007), Work-family facilitation: Generating theory using a qualitative assessment. *Advances in Developing Human Resources, 9*(4), 507-526.
3. First Presidency and Council of the Twelve Apostles, "The Family: A Proclamation to the World," (Nov. 1995).
4. S. D. Friedman, P. Christensen, & J. DeGroot (1998), Work and life: The end of the zero-sum game. *Harvard Business Review*, 76(6), 119-129.
5. E. J. Hill, & R. Anderson (2004), Life harmony: Helping clients find peace in a busy life. *AMCAP Journal, 29,* 143-151.
6. E. J. Hill, and G. Martinengo (2005), Harmonizing paid work and home life. In S. K. Klein and E. J. Hill (Eds.), *Creating home as a sacred center: Principles for everyday living* (pp. 273-282). Provo, UT: BYU Academic Publishing.
7. D. S. Carlson, M. E. Kacmar, and L. P. Stepina (1995), An examination of two aspects of work/family conflict: time and identity. *Women in Management Review, 10,* 17-25.
8. See Matthew 14:23
9. See 3 Ne 18:15, 3 Ne 18:18, D&C 93:49,

D&C 93:50, D&C 90:24, Luke 21:36, 2 Thes 1:11, 2 Ne 32:9, D&C 10:5, D&C 19:38, D&C 20:33, D&C 31:12, D&C 32:4, D&C 61:39, D&C 88:126, D&C 90:24

10. See Alma 34:25
11. E. J. Hill (2012), Lecture in MBA 549: Work and Family class, Brigham Young University, Provo, Utah.
12. Dallin H. Oaks, "The Student Body and the President", (September 1975), *BYU Speeches*, http://speeches.byu.edu/reader/reader.php?id=6076.
13. Russell M. Nelson, "President Dieter F. Uchtdorf: A family man, a man of faith, a man foreordained," (July 2008), https://www.lds.org/ensign/2008/07/president-dieter-f-uchtdorf-a-family-man-a-man-of-faith-a-man-foreordained?lang=eng.
14. Ezra Taft Benson, "To the mothers in Zion; address given at a fireside for parents," (Feb. 1987).
15. J. Jacob, S.M. Allen, E. J. Hill, N. L. Mead (2008), Work interference with dinnertime as a mediator and moderator between work hours and work and family outcomes. *Family and Consumer Sciences Research Journal 36*(4), 310–27.
16. M. E. Eisenberg, R. E. Olson, D. Neumark-Sztainer, M. Story, & L. H. Bearinger (2004), Correlations between family meals and psychosocial well-being among adolescents. *Archives of Pediatrics and Adolescent Medicine, 158,* 792–96.
17. B. H. Fiese, K. P. Foley, & M. Spagnola, (2006), Routine and ritual elements in family mealtimes: Context for child well-being and family identity. In R. W. Larson, A. R. Wiley, and K. R. Branscomb (Eds.), *Family mealtime as a context of development and socialization* (pp. 67–89). Ann Arbor, MI: Wiley Periodicals, Inc.
18. S. L. Hofferth, & J. F. Sandberg, (2001), How American children spend their time. *Journal of Marriage and the Family, 63,* 295–308.
19. J. A. Mindell, L. S. Telofski, B. Weigand, & E. S. Kurtz (2009), A nightly bedtime routine: Impact on sleep in young children and maternal mood, *Sleep, 32*(5), 599–606.
20. K. Sandholtz, B. Derr, K. Bruckner, and D. S. Carlson (2002), *Beyond Juggling* (San Francisco, CA: Berrett-Koehlers).
21. Robert D. Hales, "Our Duty to God: The Mission of Parents and Leaders to the Rising Generation," (April 2010), https://www.lds.org/general-conference/2010/04/our-duty-to-god-the-mission-of-parents-and-leaders-to-the-rising-generation?lang=eng.
22. E. J. Hill, (1999, November 25). Put family first – work will be there when you return. *Deseret News.* C08.
23. The First Presidency, "Letter from the First Presidency," (Feb. 1999), https://www.lds.org/liahona/1999/12/letter-from-the-first-presidency?lang=eng.
24. Dieter F. Uchtdorf "We Are Doing a Great Work and Cannot Come Down," (April 2009), https://www.lds.org/general-conference/2009/04/we-are-doing-a-great-work-and-cannot-come-down?lang=eng.
25. Dallin H. Oaks, "Good, Better, Best," (Oct. 2007), https://www.lds.org/general-conference/2007/10/good-better-best?lang=eng.
26. E. J. Hill, J. G. Grzywacz, S. Allen., V. L. Blanchard, C. Matz-Costa, S. Shulkin, & M. Pitt-Catsouphes (2008). Defining and conceptualizing workplace flexibility. *Community, Work, and Family, 11,* 149–63.
27. E. J. Hill, V. Martinson, & M. Ferris (2004). New-concept part-time employment as a work-family adaptive strategy for women professionals with small children. *Family Relations, 53*(3), 282–92.
28. E. J. Hill, M. Ferris, & V. Martinson (2003). Does it matter where you work? A comparison of how three work venues (traditional office, virtual office, and home office) influence aspects of work and personal/family life. *Journal of Vocational Behavior, 63,* 220–41.
29. E. J. Hill, A. J. Hawkins, M. Ferris, & M. Weitzman (2001). Finding an extra day a week: The positive effect of job flexibility on work and family life balance. *Family Relations, 50*(1), 49–58.
30. E. J. Hill, J.J. Erickson, E. K. Holmes, & M. Ferris (2010). Workplace flexibility, work hours, and work-life conflict: An extra day or two. *Journal of Family Psychology, 24*(3), 349–58.
31. S. Shellenbarger (1997, September 24), Work and family: These telecommuters just barely maintain their office decorum, *The Wall Street Journal,* p. B1.
32. S. Shellenbarger, (1997, September 24).
33. B. Brophy (1995, December), Stressless—and simple—in Seattle. *U.S. News and World Report, 11,* 96–97.
34. L. Tom Perry, "Let Him Do It with Simplicity," (Oct. 2008), https://www.lds.org/general-conference/2008/10/let-him-do-it-with-simplicity?lang=eng.
35. See Mosiah 4:27

36. Neal A. Maxwell, "Take Especial Care of Your Family," (April 1994), https://www.lds.org/general-conference/1994/04/take-especial-care-of-your-family?lang=eng.
37. Michael John U. Teh, "Where Your Treasure Is," (April 2014), https://www.lds.org/general-conference/2014/04/where-your-treasure-is?lang=eng.
38. Joseph B. Wirthlin, "Earthly Debts, Heavenly Debts," (April 2004), https://www.lds.org/general-conference/2004/04/earthly-debts-heavenly-debts?lang=eng.
39. Howard W. Hunter, The Teachings of Howard W. Hunter, 1997, (Salt Lake City, UT: Bookcraft).
40. See Romans 8:28
41. K. Newell, & L. D. Newell (2005). Building spiritual patterns in the home. In C. H. Hart, L. D. Newell, E. Walton, & D. C. Dollahite (Eds.), *Helping and Healing our Families* (pp. 152–56). Salt Lake City, UT: Deseret Book.
42. Adapted from: http://www.noogenesis.com/pineapple/fisherman.html.
43. David A. Bednar, "More Diligent and Concerned at Home," (Oct. 2009), https://www.lds.org/general-conference/2009/10/more-diligent-and-concerned-at-home?lang=eng.
44. See note 42
45. Jeffrey R. Holland, "Are We Not All Beggars?" (Oct 2014), https://www.lds.org/general-conference/2014/10/are-we-not-all-beggars?lang=eng.
46. See Mosiah 2:17

13

Marriage and Money

Successfully Sharing Your Family's Financial Stewardship as a Couple

LEARN

- Financial questions to discuss while dating

- Effective and efficient ways to finance the engagement and the wedding

- Principles and practices for successfully sharing your family's financial stewardship as a married couple

Melissa was exhausted. She woke up tired every morning and could hardly move until she had an energy drink. She felt fatigued all the time and often went to bed totally drained. Although Melissa loved her newborn, he wreaked havoc with her sleep schedule. When she married handsome and fun-loving Michael last year, she had no idea that the transition to family life would be so challenging or so exhausting. Melissa and Michael had to adapt in many ways, but their greatest trials concerned money.

Melissa was a saver, and Michael was a spender. Melissa had made her first budget at age eleven and had lived within her own budget ever since. She was responsible; she paid all the bills on time, she balanced her checkbook, and she carefully considered every purchase. After she was married, she would consult with her husband on every major purchase. Michael, on the other hand, grew up in a wealthy family and was used to buying what he wanted. He wasn't careful with their money and would often make purchases that Melissa considered foolish. Even worse, he didn't have the courtesy to consult with her before making those purchases.

When they were first married, they were very happy, and Melissa was able to overlook Michael's financial carelessness. He was just so good-looking and fun to be around! However, as the stress, expense, and fatigue of working, finishing school, studying, and having a baby set in, it became much more difficult to stay calm. The result was numerous volatile arguments which often degenerated into shouting matches and name-calling. One time it got so loud that their neighbors knocked on their door to see if someone needed help. Right now Melissa is wondering if she made a mistake marrying Michael. She has an appointment to see the bishop on Tuesday night.

Introduction

Money really matters to a husband and wife and to their marital relationship. When couples act as equal partners in the economics of the home and leverage their individual talents, financial challenges can generally be avoided, and when they do occur, they can become stepping stones to deeper love and respect. However, when the couple lacks financial skills, cannot cope with financial differences, or is unequally yoked, financial difficulties are often associated with family stress[1] and even divorce.[2] Elder Marvin J. Ashton quoted a study by the American Bar Association that indicated that "89 percent of all divorces can be traced to quarrels and accusations over money."[3] Dr. Bernard Poduska reflected, "The saying 'married for better or worse, or until *debt* do us part' seems to reflect today's marital realities more accurately than does the traditional vow."[4] It is not surprising that economic trials can be at the heart of marital difficulties because how you spend money reflects your priorities and what you value. It can send a message that you value things more than you value your spouse, and that message can poison a relationship.

The purpose of this chapter is to outline principles and practices for successfully sharing your family's financial stewardship as a couple. First, we will look at dating and finances. Then we will examine financing the engagement and the wedding. Finally, we will discuss some principles and practices for handling money matters joyfully as a married couple.

Dating and Finances

When you are ready to get married and are actively seeking an eternal spouse (you know who you are!), it is important to consider the way a potential partner handles money. Just like you would want to see how a potential eternal mate interacts with children before getting engaged, you should also carefully evaluate how a potential spouse deals with economic matters.

Here are some financial questions to answer about your potential spouse, either by observation or direct questioning, before getting engaged.

Are you a saver or a spender?

In many marriages, one partner is a saver, and the other partner is a spender. Both play an important role. Early in a marriage, it is a great blessing when the saver can help the spender stay within the budget. Later in the marriage, if the family is doing well financially, the spender can take the lead in budgeting for some special expenditures that would strengthen relationships: perhaps a second honeymoon or a nice family vacation. Couples fare better financially when at least one of the spouses is a saver and neither is materialistic.[5, 6]

What is your net worth?

Net worth is simply the total value of your assets minus the total value of your liabilities (debts). It is not necessary to know the net worth of your potential mate to the penny. However, it is essential to know if your future fiancé is bringing a large amount of debt into the marriage. I heard of a couple at BYU who were married in the temple and, the week after the honeymoon, the wife found out her new husband had more than $100,000 in debts. How do you think she felt? She was as angry as a horned lizard! She felt deceived and

betrayed. The transparency you have in your finances is a reflection of the trust you have in your relationship. It took this wife a long time to regain trust in her husband. Debt is not necessarily a relationship show-stopper, but it should certainly be disclosed before engagement.

What is your attitude about debt?

Look for someone who desires to minimize and eventually eliminate debt. If a potential mate is fine with carrying a balance on credit cards, buying furniture on revolving credit, purchasing a new car with a 72-month contract, getting as many student loans as possible, and obtaining the latest fashionable clothes on credit, then that person is waving a big warning flag in front of your face. Be careful! It is better for a potential spouse to be financially wise than to be drop-dead gorgeous!

What is your attitude about financial help from family?

Of course, it's fine to have some financial help on occasion, but it is healthiest for a new couple to be as financially independent as possible from his parents and her parents. If a potential spouse expects family support on a long-term basis, be careful!

What is your credit score?

Your credit score affects the amount of interest you will pay on a home loan, an auto loan, or even the premium for auto insurance. When you apply for a mortgage, the credit score of both partners will be considered. You can obtain your credit score in minutes for free from www.creditkarma.com or www.mint.com. If you are young, either a high score or no score is acceptable. However, if your prospective mate has a low score (in the 500s or lower), this is a warning flag that that person has not handled money well in the past, and it may be difficult or expensive to get credit until that score is improved.

Do you currently have and live within a budget? If so, what are your living expenses each month?

If the answer is "yes" to the first question, you know you have someone very special, because many students do not even have a budget. If the answer to the second question is "less than budget," then you know you have someone who is careful with money and will probably help your marriage avoid financial pitfalls.

How are you paying for your college education?

The answer "mostly with student loans" is a warning flag. It's hard to get off to a good start financially when you are saddled with paying off student loans for ten, fifteen, or more years. Fortunately, graduating BYU students (along with graduates from Utah State) have the lowest average student loan debt of any university in the United States (BYU average of $15,509 vs. national average of $25,250).[7] It is impressive when someone is debt-free and especially impressive if he or she put themselves through college debt-free independent of his or her parents (through scholarships, savings, and work).

How do you foresee sharing finances and assets with your spouse after marriage?

In general, an attitude of equal partnership with finances is best. You are looking for someone who expects to have joint checking accounts and both partners' names on deeds and titles. If you are expecting to be a stay-at-home parent, be very wary of someone who expects to have a greater say in the finances because he or she is "earning the money."

How many children do you desire in your family?

The specific number may not be as important as whether or not the desire is for a large, medium-sized, small, or child-free family. This matters financially because the latest figures show that in the United States, on average, it costs parents $245,000 to raise each child to age eighteen,[8] an amount that does not include the cost of an LDS mission. On the other hand, a desire for a large family may indicate family-centeredness and, when accompanied with a saver's mentality, this may be absolutely wonderful! I know this from experience.

What is your expectation about who is going to earn the money in your family?

It is important to understand if there is an expectation of a traditional earner situation with a full-time employed husband and a stay-at-home wife or whether both partners are expected to be employed to provide family income. There are many options in this regard, and decisions are often emotionally-charged. It is important to talk about this before getting engaged. On this topic, Elder Quentin L. Cook taught,

> These are very emotional, personal decisions, but there are two principles that we should always keep in mind. First, no woman should ever feel the need to apologize or feel that her contribution is less significant because she is devoting her primary efforts to raising and nurturing children. Nothing could be more significant in our Father in Heaven's plan. Second, we should all be careful not to be judgmental or assume that sisters are less valiant if the decision is made to work outside the home. We rarely understand or fully appreciate people's circumstances. Husbands and wives should prayerfully counsel together, understanding they are accountable to God for their decisions.[9]

What do you think about tithing and other donations?

You are probably dating or probably will date someone who wants to be married in the temple, so you can assume that they consider themselves a full tithe-payer. However, there are many ways that tithing is interpreted, and it is nice to know what those are. Do you pay tithing on the "gross" paycheck or on the "net" (after Social Security and taxes have been taken out)? Do you pay tithing on gifts and scholarships? These questions have no right or wrong answers. The bishop will not ask any of these specific questions in the temple recommend interview. He will only ask, "Are you a full tithe-payer?" It is up to you to answer, and it's nice when the husband and wife are on the same page in this regard.

Financing the Engagement and the Wedding

The Engagement Ring

Purchasing an engagement ring is the first major financial decision that you will make related to your marriage. Will you follow gospel-based financial principles when you buy the diamond? Nowhere have the brethren indicated that an engagement ring should be purchased with borrowed money. It is much better to save and sacrifice and pay cash for a smaller ring than it is to go into debt to buy a larger ring. Many couples start with a smaller ring and then get a second ring after they are well-established financially. If your future spouse is expecting you to go into debt for a large engagement ring, that could be a warning flag. Be careful!

Since buying an engagement ring is a major purchase, it is generally wise that both the bride and the groom have a say in the ring. One way to make this possible is for the engaged couple to go ring shopping together and decide on several possible selections. Then the groom can surprise the bride with the specific selection. Here is another word of caution: the ring decision is something you should make without undue outside influence. If one of your parents is giving too much input, politely ask them to "mind their own business." ☺

The Wedding Budget

The average cost of a wedding in the United States is now $31,213![10] The most expensive place for a wedding is in Manhattan ($76,328), and the least expensive, not surprisingly, is Utah ($15,257). And I would suspect that the least expensive county for marriage in the least expensive state is Utah County. Wedding costs include everything spent by everyone: the bride and the bride's family, and the groom and the groom's family. LDS weddings are less expensive because the temple, sealer, bishop, and stake president do not charge for their services, and there is no need to pur-

chase alcoholic beverages for the guests. There are no really accurate figures available, but I would estimate that a typical LDS wedding costs about $6,000 to $18,000. The decisions you make related to wedding expenditures are indicative of the principles you will follow later on in the marriage.

The first principle you should follow is to avoid debt. When it comes down to it, what is the minimum amount you must spend for a temple wedding? The venue is free, the sealer is free, and the interviews are free. The only expense that you must make is the purchase of a wedding license. If you get married in Utah County (in the Mount Timpanogos, Provo, Provo City Center, or Payson temple), the cost is $40.[11] Everyone can afford that! There is no need to go into debt. Have the best wedding you can within the resources you have. If you can't afford it, just don't do it! Learn to say no!

The second principle is to jointly create

and stick to a budget. Usually it is best if the bride and groom sit down with both sets of parents to create a budget. Different families do this in different ways. In some cases, a parent, usually the mother of the bride, does most of the work and is responsible for most of the budget. In other families, the bride and groom are given a budget. In my family, we give our child a check and give them total responsibility for how they spend it. Whether they have a reception or not is up to them. If they have it in a reception center or a church cultural hall is their choice. Whatever money they have left, they can keep to help them get off to a good start.

Here is one other bit of financial advice: Don't over-spend on the honeymoon. That special time right after the wedding is not designed for elaborate sightseeing; it is designed to have a quiet, private time together to get to know one another as husband and wife. For the honeymoon, "less" is often "more." A quiet, private, inexpensive getaway is often better for the marriage than an elaborate, expensive tour of some sort. Save that for an anniversary.

Principles for Handling Money in Marriage

Principle 1: Equal partnership

The Family: A Proclamation to the World states: "Husband and wife are obligated to help one another as equal partners."[12] There is perhaps nowhere that equal partnership is more important than in marriage. Equal participation in financial decisions by both husband and wife is an important part of this equal partnership. Both husband and wife should agree before major purchases are made. Every financial decision of substance should be made by consensus and if consensus cannot be achieved, the purchase should not be made.

Principle 2: Total trust and transparency

Trust is a large foundation stone for a healthy marriage. The way a couple manages money is indicative of their trust level. In general, there should be total transparency in finances. The couple should write checks out of the same checkbook. Both names should be on the deed to the house, on the home mortgage, on the titles to the cars, on the utilities, on the cell phone plan, on the credit cards, on everything. Besides trust, there is another reason for this transparency: Credit scores are achieved individually and both credit scores are considered when a married couple applies for a mortgage. Having official joint responsibility for finances will positively build the credit score of both.

There is one caveat to this principle: In remarriage, where significant assets are involved, it is often advisable to have a pre-nuptial agreement in which the assets from the former marriage are secured for the children of that marriage. For example, when Tammy and I were married, we made a pre-nuptial agreement. Everything that Juanita and I had accrued in twenty-nine years of marriage (e.g., home equity, 401(k) accounts, and other investments) was kept for my eight children and me. Everything that Mark and Tammy had accrued in eighteen years of marriage was kept for Tammy and her four children. In this way, the children felt secure. Blending a family is hard enough, but by doing this, there couldn't be the rationale of "she married Dad for his money." However, all of our financial gains after the day of the wedding were kept in common (joint checking account, 401(k), etc.).

Principle 3: Reduce and eventually eliminate debt

Both partners should agree on how they will reduce and eventually eliminate debt. The saver in the marriage will have an easier time eliminating debt than the spender. However, it is essential that both partners agree to avoid credit card debt and consumer debt like the plague. They should also work together to pay off car debt and student loans and eventually pay off the mortgage. They should rejoice together when the last payment is made and they are debt-free forever.

Both partners should avoid credit card debt and consumer debt like the plague.

Principle 4: Counsel with the Lord in all thy financial doings

As husband and wife, you should counsel with the Lord in all your doings, and finances are no exception (see Alma 37:33, 36–37). After you've made your best effort at creating a livable budget, place it before the Lord and pray as a couple for approbation. Before you buy a new car, pray together to receive a confirmation that this major purchase is acceptable. Before putting earnest money down on a home purchase, pray for divine approval. God cares about every aspect of your life, including your finances. Your finances are a stewardship from Him. Be sure to make Him a part of all your financial doings. He won't necessarily tell you what to do, but He will often give you impressions if you are about to make a big mistake.

Practices for Handling Money in Marriage

Practice 1: Do your budget together, and review it frequently

Create your monthly budget together, track it together, and modify it together. This budget is your family financial roadmap. It is

where, together, you give each dollar a name. It should reflect the needs and wants of both spouses and the children. In marriage relationships, both husband and wife should have a say in budget creation. One spouse may be the "hands on" person for the budget (e.g., entering expenditures into a spreadsheet, monitoring mint.com, etc.). However, there should be a frequent reporting of the budget status. Tammy and I review our weekly calendar after church every Sunday afternoon. Right afterwards, we review where we are on our monthly budget. By reviewing it frequently, we can apprise ourselves of course corrections if we are spending too much money.

Practice 2: Make major purchases together

It follows from the principle of equal partnership that all financial decisions of substance should be made by consensus—both husband and wife should agree on the purchase. Failure to heed this counsel has been the cause of many divorces. For example, I heard of a husband who spontaneously purchased a new Harley-Davidson motorcycle. Their family was on a tight budget already, and when the wife realized what the monthly payment for this foolish purchase meant, it was the last straw. She left him.

Practice 3: Agree to spending limits

Each partner in the marriage should agree to the family budget and to a spending limit

Both partners should avoid credit card debt and consumer debt like the plague!

beyond which the approval of the other spouse is required before the purchase is made. This limit may be very low early in the marriage, even as low as $10. Later on, after the family has been financially wise for years, that limit may rise to several hundred dollars or more.

Practice 4: Sleep on it

Another helpful practice is to never make a major purchase on the spot. It is so easy to get carried away with irrational emotions when you see a car, house, or boat for the first time. It is advisable to "sleep on it" and make a final purchase decision the next day or later. The husband and wife then have time to look objectively at the purchase, absorb the cost of the purchase, consider the pros and cons of the purchase, and contemplate the opportunity cost for what else they might do with that money that would be of more worth. In this relaxed scenario, both the spender and the saver can make their cases. It also provides time for the couple to pray and, in some cases, fast about it before making the final decision. When both the husband and the wife have fully discussed the purchase and have received a confirmation from the Spirit, buyer's remorse is less likely, and couples are less likely to blame one another if the purchase doesn't work out well.

Practice 5: Deal with financial disagreements constructively (remember H.A.L.T.)

All couples have disagreements about finances. These disagreements are normal and are to be expected. The key is to make the discussions engendered by these disagreements productive rather than allow them to spiral towards anger, bitterness, and contempt. Spiraling disagreements over finances contribute to stress and even divorce. One way to make financial discussions productive is to remember the H.A.L.T. principle. Be very careful when you discuss finances if either spouse is hungry, angry, lonely, or tired. Hunger contributes to anger. Referring to a study of 107 couples he conducted at Ohio State University, Dr. Brad Bushman found that low blood sugar levels made disagreements contentious. He commented, "If couples have a sensitive topic to discuss, it would be really smart to do it over dinner or better yet after dinner. They should definitely not do it on an empty stomach."[13]

Practice 6: Mad Money

As a general principle, be transparent in financial matters: Both spouses should know and have a say in family income and expenditures. However, individuals may vary quite a bit in what purchases they believe are worthwhile or unwise. Contention can ensue over even small items if the two spouses disagree. One way for you to limit this contention over small purchases is to implement the practice called *Mad Money*. This practice dictates that each spouse should have a monthly amount of money over which they have total control. This money is "off budget," and there is no accountability to the other spouse for how it is spent. The monthly amount of this Mad Money may vary as financial circumstances change.

Let me share an experience of how Mad Money helped my first wife and me avoid conflict. Juanita was considerably more frugal than I was. I still remember her getting after me one afternoon for buying two hot dogs for my son and me at a football game. "I could have fed our whole family (of nine) a good dinner for what you spent on those two hot dogs!" she said. And she could have! But it still irked me. I worked hard, and I felt I should be able to buy some hot dogs at the stadium if I wanted. Anyway, we reduced this contention when we

started allowing each other $50 per month in Mad Money. Now, if I wanted something inexpensive that Juanita considered frivolous, I could just go ahead and get it and not worry about it (as long as I didn't spend more than $50 Mad Money in a month). Mad Money is an idea worth trying!

Summary

Fortunately, the story of Melissa and Michael, mentioned at the beginning of the chapter, has a happy ending. After listening carefully to Melissa, their wise bishop counseled with both of them together. It was clear that Michael loved Melissa dearly and wanted their marriage to thrive. Their bishop, a faculty member in the BYU School of Family Life, suggested they take the Family Finance class together and they agreed. Melissa's sister agreed to watch the baby. In class they learned to budget together, to respect each other in purchases, to allow for Mad Money, and how to minimize and eliminate debt. Now they are getting more sleep, they have more money, and things are going well with their marriage.

Money does matter in marriage. In this chapter, we have discussed questions you should ask before getting engaged. We then talked about financing an engagement ring and a wedding. Finally, we proposed principles and practices for how to manage money in marriage. Money can be such a blessing in our lives! When spouses are equal partners and handle their money responsibly, money can be a tool, not a vice. Like all things in life, money is another opportunity for couples to work together and grow closer together. We hope these principles, practices, and tips will help you on your journey together.

Other Resources

- http://www.bankrate.com/finance/personal-finance/couples-cash-money-management-with-your-partner.aspx
- www.creditkarma.com
- www.mint.com
- http://www.focusonthefamily.com/marriage/money-and-finances/money-management-in-marriage/money-and-marriage

Notes

1. C. G. Gudmunson, I. F. Beutler, C. L. Israelsen, J. K. McCoy, and E. J. Hill, "Linking financial strain to marital instability: Examining the roles of emotional distress and marital interaction," *Journal of Family and Economic Issues* (2007): 28(3), 357-376, doi: 10.1007/s10834-007-9074-7.
2. J. Dew, S. Britt, and S. Huston, "Examining the relationship between financial issues and divorce," *Family Relations* (2012): 61(4), 615–28, doi: 10.1111/j.1741-3729.2012.00715.x.
3. https://www.lds.org/bc/content/shared/content/english/pdf/welfare/33293_000_One_Money_English.pdf.
4. B. Poduska, *Till debt do us part: Balancing finances, feelings, and family,* (Salt Lake City, UT: Deseret Book Company, 2000).
5. J. S. Carroll, L. R. Dean, L. L. Call, and D. M. Busby, "Materialism and marriage: Couple profiles of congruent and incongruent spouses," *Journal of Couple & Relationship Therapy: Innovations in Clinical and Educational Interventions* (2011): 10(4), 287–308.
6. L. R. Dean, J. S. Carroll, and C. Yang, "Materialism, perceived financial problems, and marital satisfaction. *Family and Consumer Sciences Research Journal* (2009): 35(3), 260-281, doi: 10.1177/1077727X06296625.
7. http://money.cnn.com/2011/11/03/pf/student_loan_debt.
8. http://money.cnn.com/2014/08/18/pf/child-cost/.
9. Quentin L. Cook, "LDS Women Are Incredible!" (April 2011), https://www.lds.org/ensign/2011/05/lds-women-are-incredible?lang=eng.
10. http://www.prnewswire.com/news-releases/

the-knot-the-1-wedding-site-releases-2014-real-weddings-study-statistics-300049675.html.
11. http://www.utahcounty.gov/Dept/ClerkAud/Marriage.html.
12. "The Family: A Proclamation to the World," *Ensign* (Nov. 1995), 102. See also https://www.lds.org/topics/family-proclamation?lang=eng.
13. http://www.bloomberg.com/news/articles/2014-04-14/hungry-spouses-lash-out-as-low-blood-sugar-spurs-anger.

14

Children and Money

Teaching Financial Responsibility to Your Offspring

LEARN

- Effective practices for teaching your children sound financial principles

By Ashley B. LeBaron, Christina M. Rosa, Carly Schmutz, Alex K. Gunnerson, Nicholas A. Jones, Travis J. Spencer, Jarna N. Knickerbocker, and E. Jeffrey Hill

Throughout this textbook, we have tried to teach you gospel principles and financial skills to help you live joyfully within your means. You have the responsibility of teaching your own children these same principles and skills. If you do so from the time they are young, you will raise financially independent young adults who will successfully navigate their way through the economic landscape. If you fail to teach these principles, your children may depend upon you and your financial resources to support them for the rest of your life. This is a high-stakes game. Winners may very well enjoy their golden years serving missions and visiting grandkids who live in financially secure homes. Losers may see many of these blessings evaporate. We invite you to be diligent in teaching your children gospel principles and practical skills of family finance.

> *"Train up a child in the way he should go: and when he is old, he will not depart from it."*
> *(Proverbs 22:6)*

Marital intimacy problems and financial problems are often the result of a failure to communicate. Sex and money—it seems like they are often lumped together. For some reason, parents have difficulty talking with their children about sex. Because of this, children often get erroneous ideas from their friends and from the media about sex and its purposes. Our society pays a big price for this communication failure: early sexual activity, sexually transmitted diseases, unwanted pregnancy, births to unwed mothers, etc. Likewise, many parents have difficulty talking with their children about money. Because of this, children often get erroneous ideas from their friends and from the media about finance and its purposes. Our society pays a big price for this communication failure as well: frivolous spending, large credit card debt, the student loan crisis, high bankruptcy rates among the young, etc. As Dave Ramsey says, "Children are sponges—they are going to absorb whatever is around them, so we need to be intentional about what surrounds them." We must overtly teach our children about finances (as well as about sex).

In this chapter, we focus on how to teach financial responsibility to your children so they do not contribute to the financial crises of this epoch. Many of you do not have children yet, but we believe that by carefully studying these principles, you will be prepared to teach them in the future. Most of this chapter will be built around a qualitative research study conducted at BYU in 2015 entitled *Effective parental practices for teaching children sound financial principles: Retrospective perceptions of financially-capable emerging adults*.[1] For this study, the BYU research team focused on financial principles and practices taught to children by their parents, especially *how* these were taught, both overtly and subconsciously. The team gathered 224 essays and conducted 53 interviews with BYU students. These students were asked to specifically identify what their parents taught them about finances and how they did it. Using thematic content coding, the researchers distilled more than three dozen themes which they then consolidated into eight general financial principles. Within each principle, they also identified specific practices of *how* parents successfully instill these principles. This chapter is organized around those eight principles and associated practices.

Principle 1: Open Financial Communication in the Home

Effective parents communicate openly about their finances with their children. They make finances a regular, comfortable topic of family conversation. They instill confidence that their children can make good financial decisions.

Effective parents often use the everyday activities of the home as a context to freely talk and teach about finances. One student remembered his parents talking openly about finances around the dinner table:

> [My parents] would talk about the stock market, and they would talk about how to distribute their wealth. My mom would talk about how she wanted to purchase some financial instruments, but my dad would disagree, and then he would tell her the reason, and then they would talk about things like that. . . . A lot of the time it would be brought out at the dinner table. . . . They talked about interest rates on savings accounts, and they talked about just the economy.

Another theme that arose was how parents would be open enough to sensitively share financial difficulties with their children. Another student said the following:

> My parents are also fairly open about our family's finances. When my dad lost his

job, they held a family council in which we prioritized our needs from our wants in order to deal with the change of income. They also told us that they had ordered my mom's dream car—a green Mini Cooper with two white racing stripes—but that they wouldn't be going through with it because of our recent unemployment. This taught me to be responsible and adaptable to changing financial situations.

Family Matters

Tammy and I were newlyweds (with twelve children) when we found ourselves in a real financial crunch: one of our investments, which brought in $750 per month, suddenly failed. Without warning, our after-tax spendable income dropped significantly. We decided to be totally open with the children about this misfortune and to include them in figuring out what we could do about it. We held a special family council to deal with this issue. Prior to the council, Tammy and I wrote down $2,300 of monthly expenditures that weren't absolutely essential. These expenditures included things like cable ($150), keeping the thermostat higher in winter and lower in summer ($100), cell phones ($150), the newspaper ($10), EFY ($100), additional contributions to the new car fund ($100–$400), etc. We talked about each possibility as a family, and then every person privately made a list of what he or she would cut to make up for the $750 per month loss. I found I was out of step with the rest of the family in several matters. Everyone wanted to cut the newspaper, except me. No one wanted to cut the cell phones, except me. Once we got everyone's input, we cut according to the recommendations: we stopped the newspaper, adjusted the thermostat, waited to get a new car, cut cable, etc. I believe this experience helped my children understand what you sometimes have to do to live within your means.

Natural teaching moments will occur if you work on your finances in a place where your children can see you. Several students commented that they learned a lot as their parents took the time to explain what they were doing when working on family finances. One student said,

> I remember seeing my dad spend hours on the computer calculating taxes and other financial documents. Some nights I would just pull up a chair and ask him a bunch of questions about what he was doing. I learned a lot about what all the financial terms meant and how he decided where to put all of his money. I still call my dad very frequently to ask his opinion about what I should be doing now to secure my financial assets for the future.

Principle 2: Save and Sacrifice

Effective parents teach their children to save and sacrifice for what they want. They do not spoil their children nor foster a sense of entitlement. They make their children wait to make purchases until they have the money.

Media advertising and marketing campaigns teach our children to crave what they want and to demand it right now. As a parent, you must teach your child the virtue of patience. When you are at the store and your son sees a PlayStation that he wants, tell him, "That's great. When you have saved enough money to buy the PlayStation, I'll bring you back, and we can get it."

A few years back, CNN quoted a study on college students at the University of Illinois at Urbana–Champaign. The researchers found that of those young adults with good financial skills, "Nearly all said their parents had gotten them into the habit of saving as young

children, suggesting saving is a behavior that comes from experience, not knowledge."2

A student in our BYU study recalled that her parents would buy things she *needed* for her, but they encouraged her to save her own money to purchase things she *wanted*.

> As I grew older and started earning money by babysitting and mowing lawns, my parents encouraged me to be a little more financially independent. When I wanted to buy something that was not exactly a need, my parents would tell me they did not have the money in their budget to allow for me to have the item, but that I could get money from my savings jar and purchase it myself. Later, when I wanted to go to Especially for Youth (EFY) over the summer, my parents and I compromised on the cost. They saw how important it was to me to go to EFY and that I did not have $400 to pay for it all. They told me they would pay for the whole event and I could pay them back as I got the money, up to $200. As a fourteen-year-old girl, I learned that I could rely on my parents for financial support if it was absolutely needed, but I was still responsible for myself.

Another student talked about how his parents taught him to save and sacrifice for what he and the family wanted:

> I recall several times when my parents would discuss with us kids how the electricity bill or water bill was a little high and we needed to lower it. They made a goal to go to Disneyland and told us that if we helped cut down our spending costs, we would be able to go. My mom and dad often reminded us to turn off the lights when we left a room, put on a jacket before turning the thermostat up in the wintertime, and take shorter showers to save water.

It is essential for parents to teach the habit of saving. One way to teach this is by requiring that children divide their earnings into three categories: *tithing*, *savings*, and *spending*. Some have a Mason jar for each category. Others have a nice savings box that they bought at Deseret Book. Some simply go with envelopes. The mechanics differ, but the principle is the same. The proportions may vary (10 percent tithing, 40 percent savings, 50 percent spending; 10 percent tithing, 70 percent savings, 20 percent spending; 10 percent tithing, 20 percent savings, 70 percent spending; etc.). Whatever your method, teach this basic principle: you should first discharge your debt to the Lord (tithing), then you save, and then you are able to spend what's left. Here is what one of the participants in the BYU study wrote:

> While growing up, my parents taught me to save consistently by having my siblings and [me] put aside 20 percent of all the money we received as gifts or earned by working. Because of the consistency of saving, it was never a question whether or not I was going to save money. My parents taught me that saving was a part of receiving money. I was very grateful they helped me learn the principle of saving because now, ten years later, I can see the benefits.

Principle 3: Work Hard

Effective parents teach their children to work—both with and without pay. They foster a spirit of entrepreneurship by encouraging their children to earn money themselves outside the home.

It is important to teach your children the connection between work and money. Because of the behavior of some parents, some children

come to believe that money automatically appears when they want something. You must teach your children to work for what they want. Begin while they are young. Elder Marvin J. Ashton wrote,

> One of the greatest favors parents can do for their children is to teach them to work. Much has been said over the years about children and monthly allowances, and opinions and recommendations vary greatly. I'm from the 'old school.' I believe that children should earn their money needs through service and appropriate chores.[3]

Rachel Cruze, daughter of financial celebrity Dave Ramsey, wrote, "I learned early on that work creates discipline, and when you have discipline in your life, you are a healthier person."[4] Underscoring the importance of work, Dave Ramsey wrote, "You should view teaching your children to work in the same way you view teaching them to bathe and brush their teeth—as a necessary skill for life."[5]

It is important to teach your children to see the connection between work and money—that money is the reward for honest labor. Giving your children a weekly allowance may blur the connection between labor and financial reward. Rachel Cruze offers an interesting perspective on allowances: "When speaking of money, 'allowance' shouldn't even be in your children's vocabulary. Use the word 'commission,' and explain how money comes from work."[6]

Several participants in the BYU study of young adults mentioned practices that taught this principle. One of the students described how hard work taught her the value of money:

> One of the most valuable lessons that my parents taught me was the importance of hard work. When I was little, they gave me opportunities to earn small sums of money from doing some of the tougher chores around the house. We had our regular chores that we did, but Mom assigned small amounts (like $0.50 or $1) to extra chores such as washing the cars, washing out the trash cans, and deep cleaning the oven or fridge. Working from the time I was young really helped me to value my hard-earned money. I am much less likely to spend on things that I don't really need because I have worked hard for what I have.

Another of the BYU study participants recalled how his mother taught him to plan and save for purchases:

> My mom took advantage of the time when I obsessed over Pokémon cards to teach me about saving. Each week I would fold laundry for $0.25 a basket until I had enough money to buy my beloved Pokémon cards. Together, we worked out how much money the cards cost, how many quarters it took to pay that much, and how many weeks it took to save that much. For months, I folded four baskets of laundry each week for four weeks, so that by the end of the month, I could claim the cards I worked and saved for.

It is great to give children the opportunity to earn money within the home. However, fostering ways to help them earn "green" dollars by working outside of the home can be very beneficial. Here is what happened in one family:

> Well, I started mowing the lawn with my dad when I was four. I had a lawn mowing business when I was eight, and I've had a job ever since.... So my brother and I actually started it. We just printed off about 200 fliers and took them around the neighborhood and put them around on people's doors. Then the next week we had twelve lawns to mow.

While it is important to give children the opportunity to do some chores for money, it is essential for children to learn to do their part without pay. Here is how one student put it: "They gave us chores. We didn't get paid for chores. So they taught us to really be motivated to work rather than just for the pay."

Principle 4: Live Within Your Means

Effective parents teach their children to be frugal, live within their means, and avoid debt.

Teach your children to live joyfully within their means. Children must come to understand that money is finite and that when it's gone, it's gone. If a child wants something but doesn't have the money for it, the parent should not buy it. Children should have to work and save and sacrifice until they have sufficient to buy what they want. Students in our study reported many ways their parents taught this. One student describes how being given a certain amount of money for school supplies can help children learn to live within their means.

> Every summer, about two weeks before a new school term started, my mom would take my siblings and me to Walmart. Before we started shopping, she would give each of us $40. We were told we could spend this money on school supplies, clothes, or whatever else we needed for school but were cautioned that we would have to be careful about how we spent it because we would not be given more. I still have a clear memory of staring up at a new SpongeBob backpack the year before starting second grade, weighing in my mind whether or not I could reuse school supplies from the previous year so I would have enough money to purchase the backpack. It was through experiences like this that my parents taught me about how to use money.

Another person in the study told of her mom's powerful example of living within her means:

> [Because] my mom was so frugal growing up, I was very aware of how much stuff cost. Like I would never get a soda or drink when we would go out to eat, which was hardly ever. We'd just get water. I was just very aware of how much stuff cost just because I could see that my mom did that. So even though I never knew where

my dad's paycheck went, I knew that "Oh, cable costs money." Having internet costs money or another phone line. I was just very aware at a very young age because my parents told us "Oh, this costs money."

This study also revealed that parents were creative in showing how to live within your means. One student remembered the following:

> I learned that you really don't need to spend a lot for nice things. You just need to be creative sometimes! We spent so much time painting things, refinishing furniture, creating furniture and toys for our Barbies and pets, and finding free stuff.

Principle 5: Use a Family Budget

Effective parents set, live within, and share their household budget with their children.

Many parents are reticent about sharing too much about the family budget with their children. However, Elder Robert D. Hales taught, "We help our children learn to be provident providers by establishing a family budget.

We should regularly review our family income, savings, and spending plan in family council meetings."⁷ Perhaps it is good to share more rather than less. One student remembered a creative way that her parents included the children in the family budgeting discussion:

> One time in particular, our parents decided to teach us about finances by putting my younger sister and me in charge of planning out how we were going to spend the family's money for next month. We were the parents for the night. They brought out an envelope of money and then let us go to town. As my sister and I started planning out all of the fun we would have—toys we would buy, treats we would splurge on, etc.—my parents asked if we wanted to keep living in our home, if we wanted our lights to stay on, if we wanted heat and food to eat, cars to drive, and so on. It quickly became apparent that we didn't have quite as much money as we had hoped to spend on any and every wish we had! We learned a valuable lesson about planning how to spend money in the future, in addition to learning that "real life" costs money.

Help your children budget their own money while they are young. One student described how his parents taught him budgeting at an early age:

> I remember my parents giving us a small cardboard bank that had self, tithing, and saving slots on it. We were taught to save 10 percent of our income for tithing, and then save some money, and we could use the rest to spend.

When children are older, parents can teach them more adult-like budgeting skills. One student remembered how her dad taught these skills:

> Later in my life, I asked my dad to teach me the basic principles of budgeting. So one day, we sat down at the kitchen table, took out a piece of paper, and wrote out a fake budget plan. He started with the initial gross income, then taught to always first pay the Lord (tithing) and yourself (savings). Next, he asked me to list off some other categories important in a budget. After I gave suggestions and he added more, our list consisted of things like rent, utilities, groceries, clothes, entertainment,

Bill Cosby teaching budgeting: https://www.youtube.com/watch?persist_safety_mode=1&safety_mode=true&v=L7soJdOhKZM

miscellaneous, etc. He explained to me the importance of the entertainment and miscellaneous categories, so as not to leave them out. Finally, he stressed the importance of actually living within the budget.

Rachel Cruze suggests five foundations for a teen's budget:

1. Save a $500 emergency fund.
2. Get out of debt (and stay out of debt).
3. Pay cash for a car.
4. Pay cash for college.
5. Build wealth and give.

The value of The Five Foundations is that they teach teens how to prioritize their budgets. They lay out a sensible, goal-based plan that aligns with their monthly budgets and shows them where they're heading.[8]

checks (yes, they still need to know how to do this), and take responsibility for their money in a more adult manner."[9]

Rachel Cruze's statement was supported by student interviews in our BYU study. One student reported the following experience:

> They [my parents] also taught me the principle of saving by establishing a bank account for me when I was twelve years old. My parents helped me understand that all the money I wanted to save, I could put in this bank account and then I could use for education later on. Because of this lesson, I was able to put my money in a savings account in the bank and let it compound interest. By the time I went on my mission, I had saved enough to pay for half of my mission.

Another student described a similar experience:

> My dad took me to the bank, and we set up two certificates of deposit, and I remember him trying to explain to me what it was.

Parents need to help children learn to be responsible with debit cards and credit cards.

Principle 6: Provide Real-World Financial Experience

Effective parents provide real-world experiences with money and financial institutions.

It is important that parents teach children to deal with real financial institutions outside of the home. Rachel Cruze states, "Keeping up with a checking account as a teenager can teach them so many lessons. They'll learn how to interact with a bank, check their account online, actually reconcile their account, write

The Hill-Mulford Family Bank

By E. Jeffrey Hill

There are many ways parents can teach children that money matters and how to live joyfully within their means. One practice my family adapted from Richard and Linda Eyre was to establish a family bank.[10] We call it the Hill-Mulford Family Bank. Until they graduate from high school, our children may invest their money in and borrow money from this family bank. Money invested earns 10 percent interest per month, compounded monthly. Money borrowed costs 10 percent interest, compounded monthly. This arrangement quickly teaches children that it is wise to save money and allow it to earn interest and that it is unwise to borrow money and pay interest. But there was a problem: the children learned this lesson so well that we had to limit the balance to avoid bankruptcy. We calculated that, due to the miracle of compound interest, our eight-year-old who invested five dollars per month in the Hill-Mulford Family Bank would have more than four million dollars by the time high school graduation came along. We decided to limit savings and loans to $100. At that point, the money is withdrawn and can be taken in cash or deposited into a real bank.

After beginning to teach a family finance class at BYU and learning so much about the retirement value of a 401(k), we decided to make another Hill-Mulford financial offering. We call it the Hill-Mulford Family 401(k). It has many of the same characteristics as an employer-sponsored traditional 401(k). In the workplace, contributions to a 401(k) are matched by the employer for retirement, earn a return, and cannot be withdrawn early without a substantial penalty. Our family 401(k) is designed to help our children save for missions and for education.

As parents, we match our children's contributions until they graduate from high school. We guarantee a return of 1 percent per month on the family 401(k) balance (in line with what a return would be on a diversified, primarily-stock based mutual fund). The children can only withdraw the money in the family 401(k) for expenses associated with missions or higher education. The maximum balance in the family 401(k) is $10,000. In order to make sure we fund the family 401(k) with real money, we keep a separate investment account in the outside financial world that has at least the balance of the combined family 401(k) balances. We are hopeful that our children's experience with the family 401(k) will help them learn to fully utilize the employer-sponsored 401(k) when they begin working full-time, as well as provide a savings plan for future missions and higher education expenses.

Children see people pulling out pieces of plastic from their wallets at the store and getting whatever they want. Children need to know what debit and credit cards are and how to use them. Here is how one student reported being taught about debit and credit cards:

> My parents taught me about credit cards and how to watch your balance on them by getting me a debit card when I was eighteen. Starting with my debit card helped me develop skills to better manage a credit card. My parents would explain to me about their credit card when we went to different stores. Because they explicitly told me how they use their credit card and how they manage their balance, I feel confident in my ability to have a credit card and never get in credit card debt.

By using financial transactions in the home, you can teach your children what will happen when they conduct a real transaction with a real bank. For example, one BYU student reported the following experience:

> My parents taught me that whenever they loaned me money, they also expected me to pay them back. Sometimes they would write down on a piece of paper the exact amount I owed them and had me sign the paper saying I would pay them back. The little things they did to help me understand what a loan from the bank would be like (by facilitating that experience in the home) really helped me have experience.

Several students expressed appreciation that their parents had taught them how to make real investments with real financial institutions in their teenage years. One student described the following experience about investing:

> Once I was in high school, he [my dad] also involved me in the process of investing money. When he had a meeting with his financial manager, he would invite me to join them for a couple of minutes to discuss my finances. I remember my dad telling me he thought it would be a good idea to take $1,000 of my savings and invest it. Then the three of us discussed some options, and my dad and I ended up making a decision together. This taught me that saving is not the only thing to do with your money. It also taught me that it's important to consult with people who are wiser than you and to look at a lot of options before making a decision.

Principle 7: Give Freely of Your Resources

Effective parents teach their children to freely give to institutions and people in need.

Many students in the BYU study explained how their parents taught them to contribute tithing. This student learned about tithing through a family home evening lesson.

> At a young age, my parents taught a family home evening lesson about tithing. I was about seven or eight years old when they gave each of my siblings and me two glass jars. They gave us markers and let us decorate them, labeling one "Savings" and the other "Tithing". They taught us that one-tenth of all that we earn is for the Lord. I eagerly put coins and dollar bills in my savings jar and learned how to calculate and put 10 percent of my savings in the Tithing Jar. It was a very simple way my parents helped me visualize tithing and keeping track of how much I earned.

Parents can require that their children pay

tithing on money they earn, especially when a parent is involved in the money-earning process. One BYU student in our study remembered how his dad taught him about tithing:

> I remember a memory from when I might've been five years old in which we were cleaning a side alleyway of a mini-mall. When finished, we got paid some money, and my dad gave me some of the money for helping. I remember being upset when he told me I'd have to pay money in tithing. I had just worked hard for that money! While early on my parents didn't make a lot of money, they always paid their tithing, and we've never been left wanting for money.

Teach your children to serve by being an example of anonymous service. May we all be like this student's father and teach our children through example!

> I know that my dad is very good at saving money. And he was always just very, very generous. If someone ever needed something, he would never say anything. I would learn that my dad was generous through other people.

A Hill of Generosity

Tammy is an excellent example to our children of being generous. At Christmas, she seems to have a knack for knowing who among our friends could use a little extra help. She talks with the kids about how we might assist, and together we decide on the plan. Sometimes it's a gift, most often it's cash, but it's always anonymous. We think of creative ways to get the money to the families safely and anonymously. —Dr. Hill

Principle 8: Example is the Best Teacher

Effective parents model the application of sound financial principles. Example is the best teacher.

Be the kind of person you want your children to become, and then be around enough for it to rub off. This is particularly important when it comes to money. Unfortunately, many couples choose not to share financial information with their children, a decision that is not particularly healthy. We encourage you to instead model your financial decisions and teach your children by example, like the parents in the following stories shared by BYU students.

One student observed wise financial decisions while living at home: "I watched my parents talk about financial decisions together, shop at thrift stores, buy the generic brand cereal, share hamburgers and fries instead of buying each of us happy meals, and rarely buy new clothes for themselves."

Another student learned about the importance of saving from a family discussion: "I still remember the day when my parents paid off our house. They explained to my siblings and me what that meant and how they did it. My parents told us that they had diligently saved, and they encouraged us to do the same when we have our house."

Lasting Impressions

Parents can make a big impression upon their children when they share successes related to getting out of debt. I still have fond memories of my dad calling me over as he wrote the checks for the monthly bills. I remember him writing the mortgage check and then writing a second check. He asked me, "Jeff, do you know why I am writing another check to the bank for our house?" I didn't have a clue. He told me, "I'm doing it so we can pay back the bank faster so we don't have to owe anybody anything." I still remember that experience more than fifty years later. —Dr. Hill

Another BYU student shared how his parents were examples of wise investing: "I think [my dad] and my mom, the first thing they do in the morning is read scriptures, and the second thing they do is look at stocks, and then they go eat breakfast. I guess him being wise in his investment kind of shows me the importance of investing. . . . I feel like the sooner you invest, the better off you're going to be."

Summary

Parents who talk openly with their children about the family's finances; who teach their children to save their money, work hard, and live within their means; who use a family budget, provide real-world experience, and give freely; and who teach by example, will likely raise children who will grow up to be financially-empowered emerging adults. This is an essential task. The stakes are high.

Here are some closing words by Dave Ramsey:

> The psalmist said, "Like arrows in the hand of a warrior, so are the children of one's youth" (Psalm 127:4). This is a great word picture to remind us that our children are to be released into the world. If they are strong and true, they will fly straight just like an arrow that is properly formed. It is gratifying to pull back a bow, let an arrow fly, and watch it strike the bull's-eye. Unfortunately, in our soft and wimpy culture, we are not releasing arrows; we are releasing boomerangs. We throw them out, and they come right back.[11]

May all of you take seriously your responsibility to teach gospel-based principles and practical financial skills to your children so that they can fly straight as an arrow and successfully navigate their financial futures.

Notes

1. LeBaron, A. B., Rosa, C. M., Schmutz, C., Gunnerson, A. K., Jones, N. A., Spencer, T. J., Knickerbocker, J. N., & Hill, E. J. (2015, April). Effective parental practices for teaching children sound financial principles: Retrospective perceptions of financially-capable emerging adults. Poster presented at the annual conference of the Utah Council of Family Relations, Logan, UT.
2. Stephen Gandel, "Everything You Know About Kids and Money Is Wrong," CNN Money, July 18, 2006, http:// money.cnn.com/ magazines/ moneymag/ moneymag_archive/ 2006/ 08/ 01/8382223/ as quoted in Ramsey, Dave; Cruze, Rachel (2014-04-16). Smart Money Smart Kids: Raising the Next Generation to Win with Money (Kindle Locations 3349-3351). Lampo Press. Kindle Edition.
3. Marvin J. Ashton, "One for the Money," (September 2007), https://www.lds.org/ensign/2007/09/one-for-the-money?lang=eng.
4. Ramsey, Dave; Cruze, Rachel (2014-04-16). Smart Money Smart Kids: Raising the Next Generation to Win with Money (Kindle Locations 256–57). Lampo Press. Kindle Edition.
5. Ramsey, Dave; Cruze, Rachel (2014-04-16). Smart Money Smart Kids: Raising the Next Generation to Win with Money (Kindle Locations 268–69). Lampo Press. Kindle Edition
6. Ramsey, Dave; Cruze, Rachel (2014-04-16). Smart Money Smart Kids: Raising the Next Generation to Win with Money (Kindle Locations 333–34). Lampo Press. Kindle Edition.
7. Robert D. Hales, "Becoming Provident Providers Temporally and Spirtually," (April 2009), https://www.lds.org/general-conference/2009/04/becoming-provident-providers-temporally-and-spiritually?lang=eng
8. Ramsey, Dave; Cruze, Rachel (2014-04-16). Smart Money Smart Kids: Raising the Next Generation to Win with Money (Kindle Locations 1458–61). Lampo Press. Kindle Edition.
9. Ramsey, Dave; Cruze, Rachel (2014-04-16). Smart Money Smart Kids: Raising the Next Generation to Win with Money (Kindle Locations 1480–82). Lampo Press. Kindle Edition.
10. Eyre, Linda, and Richard M. Eyre. 3 Steps to a Strong Family. New York: Simon & Schuster, 1994.
11. Ramsey, Dave; Cruze, Rachel (2014-04-16). Smart Money Smart Kids: Raising the Next Generation to Win with Money (Kindle Locations 2864–68). Lampo Press. Kindle Edition.

15

Consecration

Learning to Share Your Financial Resources Effectively

"Many people spend most of their time working in the service of a self-image that includes sufficient money, stocks, bonds, investment portfolios, property, credit cards, furnishings, automobiles, and the like to guarantee carnal security throughout, it is hoped, a long and happy life. Forgotten is the fact that our assignment is to use these many resources in our families and quorums to build up the kingdom of God."
—Spencer W. Kimball[1]

LEARN

- Your responsibility to use your resources wisely for God's purposes.

- The spiritual, temporal, individual, and familial reasons for you to learn about family finance.

- The eternal principles upon which a financial stewardship perspective is based.

- How to share your financial resources effectively.

- To feel a desire to build your financial home upon the rock of the gospel of Jesus Christ and live joyfully within your means for the rest of your life.

As we near the end of our sojourn called family finances, it is time to stop for a moment, look back, and gain perspective on what we have learned. Fundamentally, we would have you "remember, remember that it is upon the rock of our Redeemer, who is Christ, the Son of God, that ye must build your [financial] foundation; that when the devil shall send forth his mighty winds [of economic downturn], yea, his shafts [of layoffs] in the whirlwind, yea, when all his hail and his mighty storm [of inflation and high interest rates] shall beat upon you, it shall have no power over you to drag you down to the gulf of misery and endless wo [also known as debt and financial insecurity], because of the rock upon which ye are built [whereon you pay 10 percent of your income to the Lord and 10 percent to long-term savings], which is a sure foundation [allowing for responsible budgeting and living joyfully within your means], a foundation [of adequate insurance and wise investments], whereon if men build they cannot fall [if they consecrate everything to the Lord]."[2] As a summary, this chapter will review material from the beginning of the book (the why's and

what's of family finance) and elucidate how we can effectively share our financial resources with God's children.

Family finance can generally be viewed in one of two ways: from an eternal perspective or from the world's materialistic perspective. The eternal perspective assumes that all material resources are owned by God and that we are stewards over those resources so that we may bless His children. The world's materialistic perspective is any perspective that leaves God out of the equation. The perspective you choose will make a big difference in the way you manage your money and your life. Perhaps family finance, from an eternal perspective, is simply the temporal application of spiritual principles. Perhaps the way you use agency in relation to your financial stewardship is at the heart of our mortal probation.

The Why's

In order to answer the question "Why should I learn about family finance?" you must first reflect on inspired doctrine.

Spiritual: To bring you to Christ

The ultimate purpose of everything God does is to bring us to Christ. If God's work and glory is to bring to pass the "immortality and eternal life of man,"[3] and if the only way you can have eternal life is through Jesus Christ,[4] then the purpose of all God does, including encouraging you to wisely manage your finances, is to bring you to Christ. The ultimate purpose of paying a full tithe and being generous with your offerings is to bring you to Christ. The ultimate purpose of budgeting is to bring you to Christ. The ultimate purpose of paying your taxes and obtaining adequate insurance is to bring you to Christ. The ultimate purpose of investing in long-term, low-fee, tax-advantaged, diversified, primarily stock-based investments is to bring you to Christ. If somehow you miss this message, you will have missed the major message of this book.

Temporal: To help you become a wise steward

The Lord said, "For it is required of the Lord, at the hand of every steward, to render an account of his stewardship, both in time and in eternity. For he who is faithful and wise in time is accounted worthy to inherit the mansions prepared for him of my Father."[5] It may be that the way you magnify your financial stewardship in mortality will be indicative of the stewardships you will receive in the eternities.

Some individuals believe that money is somehow dirty or tainted. It is true that "the *love* of money is the root of all evil,"[6] but that only applies when we put money above other, more important things. Money is not the most important thing, but that doesn't mean it is not important. I believe that on judgment day you will be asked about your financial stewardship. I don't believe you will be asked about your net worth or about how much money

you made, but rather about how you managed that stewardship and used it to bless others.

Individual: To accomplish your divine mission

You have a sacred mission to perform here on earth, magnifying your "divine nature and destiny."[7] Your mission will require material resources. As you fulfill your financial stewardship faithfully, you can acquire resources to consecrate to the work God has for you to do.

On a personal note, both Tammy and I felt that her gifts for teaching and connecting with others could be used to bless God's children. We pondered and prayed and both felt very good about her going back to school and getting a master's degree in marriage and family therapy. The two-year program that would give her the training she needed cost about $40,000. If we hadn't had the money, she couldn't have gone back to school without incurring a large debt. Because we had been wise financial stewards, we were able to make the investment to help Tammy accomplish her divine mission. Now she is counseling and helping many families, as well as teaching hundreds of students in classes at BYU.

Family: To return with your family back to Heavenly Father's presence

An eternal perspective of home finances strengthens your eternal marriage and is a conduit for positive parenting. President David O. McKay reminded us that "No other success can compensate for failure in the home."[8] You will be disappointed in life if you gain the riches of the world and lose your spouse and family in the process.[9] When we choose to use our financial resources to strengthen our families, we choose to return with our families back to God's presence.

Let me share another example. We have a tradition in our family in which the graduating seniors get to go on a senior trip. The trip usually costs a few hundred dollars, and they have a lot of fun. Surprisingly, my son Ryan Mulford asked if I would take him on a fishing trip to Alaska for his senior trip (instead of going with his friends on a cruise). I don't fish,

and this trip would be much more expensive than a cruise; however, the offer brought tears to my eyes. Ryan is Tammy's son. It's often difficult to connect with stepchildren, so his desire to go fishing with me was touching. I thought about it, and we decided to go fishing in Alaska along with two other sons (one Mulford and one Hill). The total cost was ten times what a cruise with his friends would have cost; however, it was a decision that brought us all together and was a real highlight in our lives. I believe this decision brought us closer to returning to Heavenly Father's presence.

The What's

The second important question for you to consider is, "What are the eternal principles upon which this financial stewardship perspective is based?"

Principle 1: Ownership

The Psalmist wrote, "The earth is the Lord's, and the fullness thereof; the world, and they that dwell therein."[10] We know from scriptures that the Lord is the creator of the earth;[11] the creator of worlds, men, and all things;[12] the supplier of our breath;[13] the giver of our knowledge;[14] the giver of our life;[15] and the giver of all we have and are.[16] Nothing you have is your own—it is all God's. Therefore, you should not feel proud of the things you acquire.

When we realize that everything we have belongs to God, it changes our perspective. For example, imagine you and your family were very hungry and had ten beautiful apples, but you didn't know when you might get more apples. Then imagine that I came up to you and asked for one of your apples. You might give me one, or you might not. However, now imagine that you and your family were very hungry and had *no* apples. Imagine that I came up to you and gave you ten beautiful apples. I ask for just one of those apples back. What would you do? You would give me the apple, of course. Can you see how understanding the principle of ownership—understanding that everything belongs to God—can change your whole perspective?

Principle 2: Stewardship

Because God owns everything, you have a responsibility to use your resources wisely for His purposes. You should first meet the needs and appropriate wants of your family and then consecrate the rest to bless God's other children. Being blessed with material things in life should not only be seen as a blessing but also as a responsibility, for "unto whom much is given much is required."[17] The Lord expects us to be wise stewards so that our financial resources grow for consecration to God's purposes. Focusing on the parable of the talents is instructive:

> For the kingdom of heaven is as a man travelling into a far country, who called his own servants, and delivered unto them his goods. And unto one he gave five talents . . . Then he that had received the five talents went and traded with the same, and made them other five talents. . . . After a long time the lord of those servants cometh, and reckoneth with [him]. And so he that had received five talents came and brought other five talents, saying, Lord, thou deliveredst unto me five talents: behold, I have gained beside them five talents more. His lord said unto him, Well done, thou good and faithful servant: thou hast been faithful over a few things, I will make thee ruler over many things: enter thou into the joy of thy lord.[18]

If we are wise stewards with our material possessions on earth, it is more likely that we will be able to joyfully return to our Heavenly Father's presence.

Principle 3: Agency

Your financial stewardship enables you to make choices. President David O. McKay wrote, "Next to the bestowal of life itself, the right to direct that life is God's greatest gift to man."[19] The blessing of agency is an unconditional gift from God. The choices you make with money are at the heart of mortality's test. Will you choose to waste your resources upon transitory pleasures, or will you choose to serve others and build up the kingdom of God? Will you choose to act on impulse and burden yourself with debt, or will you act prudently so that money becomes a tool for family joy and not the cause of stress and worry? How you use the gift of financial resources shows what you really believe and how much you really love God and His Son, Jesus Christ.

Principle 4: Accountability

The Lord counseled, "For it is required of the Lord, at the hand of every steward, to render an account of his stewardship, both in time and in eternity."[20] The first three principles outlined above are God's gift to you. The fourth principle of accountability, if followed wisely, can be your gift back to God. You will be required to give an account of your stewardship to Heavenly Father over the blessings you have received.

This principle of accountability is also important within the family setting. Husband and wife are accountable to each other for their choices to live within their budget and stay out of debt. Children are accountable to their parents for their financial choices as well.

> ## The Power to Save
>
> [T]here is a state of human misery below which no Latter-day Saint should descend as long as others are living in abundance. Can some of us be content living affluent life-styles while others cannot afford the chlorine to purify their water? Can we ignore the most basic temporal needs of our brothers and sisters and profess belief in President Joseph F. Smith's statement that "a religion that has not the power to save people temporally … cannot be depended upon to save them spiritually"? —Glenn L. Pace [21]

Sharing Your Financial Resources Effectively

In this class, we have taught principles which, if followed on the long term, are likely to help you acquire significant financial resources. Obtaining those resources is just the beginning. A fundamental, eternal question associated with your financial stewardship is whether or not you will be generous and share your resources with others. Our final message to you in this book will outline some principles and practices that will help you be generous and share your resources with others.

Putting Riches in an Eternal Perspective

In the following parable, the Savior teaches us a poignant lesson about finances:

> And he spake a parable unto them, saying, The ground of a certain rich man brought forth plentifully: And he thought within himself, saying, What shall I do, because I have no room where to bestow my fruits? And he said, This will I do: I will pull down my barns, and build greater; and there will I bestow all my fruits and my goods. And I will say to my soul, Soul, thou hast much goods laid up for many years; take thine ease, eat, drink, and be merry. But God said unto him, Thou fool, this night thy soul shall be required of thee: then whose shall those things be, which thou hast provided? So is he that

layeth up treasure for himself, and is not rich toward God.²²

The point of this parable isn't that the rich man acquired material resources. The point is that he did so in order to be comfortable, to "eat, drink, and be merry."²³ The point is that he should have obtained that wealth in order to bless God's children.

President Spencer W. Kimball taught about the importance of stewardship:

> In the Church, a stewardship is a sacred spiritual or temporal trust for which there is accountability. Because all things belong to the Lord, we are stewards over our bodies, minds, families, and properties. (See D&C 104:11–15.) A faithful steward is one who exercises righteous dominion, cares for his own, and looks to the poor and needy. (See D&C 104:15–18.)²⁴

Let's now look at some practices that will help us effectively share our resources with others.

Be a Diligent Full-Tithe Payer

Tithing is the primary financial law upon which economic blessings are predicated.²⁵ If you pay a full tithing (10 percent of your income or increase²⁶) and are generous with offerings, the windows of heaven will be opened to you.²⁷ Writing the first check of each month to the Church for tithing is a reflection of your faith.

Be Generous with Fast Offerings

We should be diligent in keeping the law of the tithe: This means paying a full tithe, no more and no less. Fast offerings are different. They provide a means to be as generous as we want to be in helping the poor. In some ways, our fast offerings may be even more indicative of a generous heart than tithing. President Spencer W. Kimball taught:

> Each member should contribute a generous fast offering for the care of the poor and the needy. This offering should at least be the value of the two meals not eaten while fasting.
>
> Sometimes we have been a bit penurious and figured that we had for breakfast one egg and that cost so many cents and then we give that to the Lord. I think that when we are affluent, as many of us are, that we ought to be very, very generous. . . . I think we should . . . give, instead of the amount saved by our two meals of fasting, perhaps much, much more—ten times more when we are in a position to do it.²⁹

Be Generous with Other Offerings

On the "Tithing and Other Offerings" contribution slip, there are several categories for generous contributions besides tithing and fast offerings. We've categorized these into the following categories: missionary work and blessing the poor.

Be Generous by Contributing to Missionary Work

General Missionary. A contribution to the General Missionary Fund helps those of

> ## Swimming Against the Current
>
> Perhaps our most pivotal moments as Latter-day Saints come when we have to swim directly against the current of the culture in which we live. Tithing provides just such a moment. Living in a world that emphasizes material acquisition and cultivates distrust for anyone or anything that has designs on our money, we shed that self-absorption to give freely, trustingly, and generously. By this act, we say—indeed—we are different, that we are God's peculiar people. In a society that tells us money is our most important asset, we declare emphatically it is not. —Jeffrey R. Holland²⁸

humble means throughout the world serve missions. This need is particularly acute with the increasing number of missionaries serving from the less-developed areas of the world. President Thomas S. Monson encouraged us to contribute to this fund: "To help maintain this missionary force, and because many of our missionaries come from modest circumstances, we invite you, as you are able, to contribute generously to the General Missionary Fund of the Church."[31]

Ward Missionary. A contribution to the ward missionary fund enables you to contribute to the missionary account of any missionary serving from your ward. All missionaries and their families in the United States and Canada are required to contribute $400 a month toward their missions. By contributing to the ward missionary fund, you are able to help the missionaries and their families.

There are advantages to contributing to the missionary through the fund rather than to the family directly. First, you are sure the money goes toward the missionary work. Second, you also qualify for a tax deduction. You would not qualify for a tax deduction if you gave the money directly to the family.

Be Generous by Blessing the Poor with Your Resources

We have a special responsibility to bless the poor with our resources. The prophet Jacob provides us with some excellent counsel about riches and how they should be used to bless those in need:

> But before ye seek for riches, seek ye for the kingdom of God. And after ye have obtained a hope in Christ ye shall obtain riches, if ye seek them . . . for the intent to do good—to clothe the naked, and to feed the hungry, and to liberate the captive, and administer relief to the sick and the afflicted."[32]

Humanitarian Aid. Contributions to the Church's Humanitarian Aid Fund "allow the Church to help people throughout the world by providing relief and help so people

The Lord's Blessings Poured Out

We might conclude that since we pay tithing with money, the Lord will always bless us with money. I tended to think that way as a child. I have since learned it doesn't necessarily work that way. The Lord promises blessings to those who pay their tithing. He promises to "open ... the windows of heaven, and pour ... out a blessing, that there shall not be room enough to receive it" (Malachi 3:10). I testify that He fulfills His promises, and if we faithfully pay our tithing, we will not lack for the necessities of life, but He does not promise wealth. Money and bank accounts are not His richest blessings. He blesses us with wisdom to manage our limited material resources, wisdom that enables us to live better with 90 percent of our income than with 100 percent. Thus, faithful tithe payers understand provident living and tend to be more self-reliant. —Carl G. Pratt[30]

may help themselves."[33] These funds are often donated to those affected by large-scale disasters. When disasters occur, LDS Charities "sends food, clothing, medical supplies, and other emergency relief assistance to bless the lives of those with urgent needs."[34] Since 1985, the Humanitarian Aid fund has assisted more than 23 million people in 163 nations.

There are many other worthwhile possibilities for contributions to Church funds in order to bless the poor. We will mention two additional funds.

Perpetual Education Fund. This fund is a "revolving resource in which money is loaned to an individual to help pay for training or advanced education. When a student has graduated and is working, he or she then pays back the loan at a low interest rate. Repayments allow for future loans."[35] Available in 63 different countries, the Perpetual Education Fund has helped tens of thousands of Church members enhance their education when they could not have afforded to otherwise. On average, students spend two to three years in the program, which increases their income by 200 to 300 percent. You can contribute to this fund by writing "Perpetual Education Fund" in the "Other" category on the contribution slip.

Temple Patron Assistance Fund. This fund is a "way to provide a one-time visit to the temple for members living outside of the United States and Canada who otherwise would not be able to go."[36] Though today there are more temples throughout the world than in previous generations, there are still many members who cannot afford to make a trip to receive their endowments, be sealed, or both. Since 1992, the Temple Patron Assistance Fund has been entirely sponsored by member contributions, providing the means for thousands of families to receive their temple blessings.[37] You can contribute to this fund by writing "Temple Patron Assistance Fund" in the "Other" category on the contribution slip.

The Church provides these and other opportunities to effectively share your financial resources to bless God's children. There are two significant advantages for contributing through the Church. First, 100 percent of your donation goes to help those in need. All administrative and overhead costs are paid by the Church. Second, your contributions are tax deductible, which enables your money to go further. For example, if you donate $1,000 to the Perpetual Education Fund and you have a 25 percent marginal tax rate, it means that your $1,000 contribution will result in a $1,000 itemized deduction, giving your family an additional $250 refund on your taxes.

Look for Other Ways to Share Your Resources and Bless God's Children

Outside of formal channels, there are many ways to use our means in anonymous and ad hoc giving. Sister Mary Ellen Smoot related an inspiring story of a young couple that budgeted a portion of their income each month to helping others. She then counseled, "Make unselfish investments that will produce spiritual dividends. In my personal life I have found that what you give to others always pays dividends. Service to others is a wise investment."[38]

If we watch for opportunities to be of ad hoc service to others, we will find ways to serve with our resources. Let me share a personal example. One day Tammy was in line at the supermarket with a boy about ten years old just ahead of her. He had a shopping cart with a few staples: milk, bread, eggs, potatoes, vegetables, etc. After the cashier rang up the purchase, the boy handed her a wad of money. She counted it out and told him that he was short about $10. Tammy said the boy looked very distraught. When the cashier asked what he would like to put back, Tammy stepped forward and said, "I'll cover that." The boy looked up at Tammy and said, "You don't have to do that." Tammy responded, "I know I don't have to, but I want to." The boy's eyes filled with tears as he responded with a meek "Thank you." Then the cashier's eyes welled up with tears, and Tammy started to tear up too. Tammy said it felt so good to have been in the right place at the right time to share a $10 bill.

Throughout our marriage, Tammy has taught me to be more generous. For example, she was a waitress earlier in her life and is very aware of how much work servers do. She has encouraged me to stop being stingy and to be generous in my tipping when we go out to eat.

I have to tell you, it feels so good to give an unexpectedly large tip. I appreciate Tammy's generous spirit.

Share Your Resources Anonymously with Friends in Need

There are several advantages to sharing financial resources with others anonymously. The first is that there is not a burden of reciprocity. Another advantage is that if the recipient of your generosity does not know the source, that person may think positive thoughts about any number of people.

Our family has a Christmas tradition of sharing several significant financial gifts anonymously with those who could use Christmas cheer. The whole family gets involved, bringing the spirit of the season to our home in abundance. Tammy seems to have a sixth sense about the needs of others, often selecting families that I would never have guessed would need some help. And it always turns out that she was right on. It can be quite the challenge to get the money safely to someone without revealing your identity, but that's a story for another day.

Share Yourself Along with Your Resources

Serving anonymously with your resources is great in some circumstances. In other circumstances, it is important to share yourself along with your resources. President Gordon B. Hinckley taught:

> Let us now in our time, each one, reach out more generously to love those around us in the spirit of the Christ. It is not enough even to give alms to those in need. For as important as that is, it is as Sir Launfal, worn and old, learned from Him who shared his crust, "the gift without the giver is bare; / Who gives of himself with his alms feeds three, / Himself, his hungering neighbor, and me."[39]

Bless Your Family and Your Extended Family with Your Resources

There are many opportunities to use your resources to bless the lives of immediate and extended family members. We can bless parents and children, uncles and aunts, and grandparents and grandchildren. I will always remember the way my father-in-law, Irving J. Ray, blessed my life. Irving grew up in the Depression, was a salt-of-the-earth World War II veteran, and supported his family as a small-time farmer and a building and plumbing contractor. He was also the most frugal person I've ever met.

In the early 1980s, Irving visited Juanita and me at our home in Marietta, Georgia. I was working for IBM at the time, in the early days of the personal computer. IBM offered a 50 percent discount to employees, and I was debating between buying an IBM PC for $1,500 or an IBM PC Jr. for $1,000. My father-in-law took a great interest in my decision. He asked me which I was going to buy, and I told him that I would probably buy the less-expensive PC Jr. He asked, "Which computer is better?" I told him that the PC was much better than the PC Jr. Then he asked, "Will you use this for your work?" I told him that I would. He then looked at me very seriously and said, "You know, son, I am known for being a tight-wad, but when it comes to buying a backhoe, I always buy new, and I always buy the best. You can't take chances when you are supporting your family. I think you should buy the PC." I thought about it

and slept on it but decided we just couldn't afford the PC.

In the morning, Irving asked what I had decided. When I told him, I could tell he was frustrated with me. After a morning of work at IBM, I took my lunch hour to go buy the PC Jr. at the IBM Store. When I put on my pin-striped suit coat, I felt a lump in my inside pocket. I pulled out an envelope stuffed with twenty-five well-worn $20 bills. There was a note scrawled in Irving's nearly illegible handwriting: "Get the new, good backhoe." With tears in my eyes, I stepped up to the counter and bought a gleaming IBM Personal Computer (complete with no hard drive, one 256k floppy disk, and 128k of memory). I will never forget that unselfish act of sharing by my frugal father-in-law. Forever after that experience, I loved that man with all my heart.

Summary

Finally, ponder these words by C. S. Lewis about sharing our resources. He said, "I am afraid the only safe rule is to give more than we can spare. . . . If our charities do not at all pinch or hamper us, I should say they are too small. There ought to be things we should like to do and cannot do because our charitable expenditure excludes them."[40]

To close this tome, let me bear my testimony. I have a testimony that when we understand that money matters and take the time to budget, eliminate debt, be wise in paying taxes, protect our families through insurance, invest wisely, and share our resources, we receive both material and spiritual blessings. I testify that we must build our financial homes upon the rock of the gospel of Jesus Christ. If we do this, when the rains of recessions descend, floods of layoffs come, and the winds of high interest rates blow and beat upon our homes, they will not fall, for they will be founded upon the rock of Christ.[41] I invite you to live joyfully within your means for the rest of your life, so that on judgment day you might give a good report of your financial stewardship.

Notes

1. Spencer W. Kimball, "The False Gods We Worship," (June 1076), https://www.lds.org/ensign/1976/06/the-false-gods-we-worship?lang=eng.
2. See Helaman 5:12 (adapted).
3. Moses 1:39
4. John 14:6
5. D&C 72:3–4
6. I Timothy 6:10 (emphasis added)
7. "The Family: A Proclamation to the World," Liahona, Oct. 2004, p. 49; Ensign, Nov. 1995, p. 102. Retrieved from https://www.lds.org/topics/family-proclamation.
8. David O. McKay, "Conference Report," (April 1935), https://archive.org/stream/conferencereport1935a#page/n0/mode/2up.
9. Matthew 16:26
10. Psalms 24:1
11. John 1:3
12. D&C 93:10
13. Job 33:4
14. Moses 7:32
15. Mosiah 2:26
16. Mosiah 2:21
17. D&C 82:3
18. Matthew 25:14–16, 19–21 (adapted)
19. David O. McKay, "Conference Report," (April 1950), https://archive.org/stream/conferencereport1950a#page/n33/.

20. D&C 72:3
21. Glenn L. Pace, "Principles and Programs," (April 1986), https://www.lds.org/general-conference/1986/04/principles-and-programs?lang=eng.
22. Luke 12:16–21
23. 2 Nephi 28:21
24. Spencer W. Kimball, "Welfare Services: The Gospel in Action," (Nov. 1977), https://www.lds.org/ensign/1977/11/welfare-services-the-gospel-in-action?lang=eng.
25. D&C 130:20–21
26. Leviticus 27:32, D&C 119:4
27. Malachi 3:10
28. Jeffrey R. Holland, "Like a Watered Garden," (Oct. 2001), https://www.lds.org/general-conference/2001/10/like-a-watered-garden?lang=eng.
29. See note 25.
30. Carl G. Pratt, "The Lord's Richest Blessings," (April 2011), https://www.lds.org/general-conference/2011/04/the-lords-richest-blessings?lang=eng.
31. Thomas S. Monson, "Welcome to Conference," (April 2013), https://www.lds.org/ensign/2013/05/welcome-to-conference?lang=eng.
32. Jacob 2:17–19
33. https://www.lds.org/topics/humanitarian-service/help?lang=eng
34. https://www.ldsphilanthropies.org/humanitarian-services/funds/humanitarian-general-fund.html
35. https://www.lds.org/topics/pef-self-reliance/perpetual-education-fund?lang=eng
36. Heather Whittle Wrigley, "Fund Helps Members Worldwide Receive Temple Blessings," (Jan. 2012), https://www.lds.org/ensign/2012/01/fund-helps-members-worldwide-receive-temple-blessings?lang=eng.
37. http://www.ldsphilanthropies.org/temple/funds/temple-patrons-fund.html
38. Mary Ellen Smoot, "Everything Money Cannot Buy," (Feb. 2002), https://speeches.byu.edu/talks/mary-ellen-smoot_everything-money-buy/.
39. Gordon B. Hinckley, "Words of the Prophet: Forget Yourself and Serve," (July 2006), https://www.lds.org/new-era/2006/07/words-of-the-prophet-forget-yourself-and-serve?lang=eng.
40. C. S. Lewis, Mere Christianity (1952), 67.
41. See Matthew 7:25

Glossary

401(k)
A defined-contribution (DC) retirement plan offered to employees in which a specified amount of money is taken from both the employer and the employee on a regular basis and invested.

After-tax return
The return on an investment after the impact of federal, state, and local taxes has been taken into account.

Accountability
The obligation to account for one's actions or to accept responsibility.

Actively managed funds
Funds that are managed by professional investors who constantly "buy low" and "sell high."

Adjustable rate mortgage (ARM)
A loan which allows the interest rate to rise or fall with changes in mortgage interest rates.

Adjusted Gross Income (AGI)
The first step of calculating your federal income tax, determined by subtracting your adjustments to income from your gross income.

Agency
The ability to choose.

Amortization
The amount and frequency of equal payments that will gradually repay a loan (including principal and interest) over the length of the loan.

Annuity
The disbursement of money on a periodic basis—a series of equal payments which are made at a specific time.

Asset classes
A group of financial assets with similar risk and return characteristics.

Assets
The monetary value of what your family owns that could be turned into cash.

Automobile insurance
Insurance against damage to your vehicle, damage to another vehicles, bodily injury, or damage to property resulting from an accident involving a vehicle.

Automobile loans
Short-term loans that are secured by the automobile the loan is paying for.

Balance
The total amount owed on a credit card at a specific time.

Balloon mortgages
Mortgages where all remaining principle is due a certain number of years into the contract.

Benchmarks
Passively managed portfolios of financial assets that indicate how well your financial assets are performing by comparison.

Beneficiary
The recipient of life insurance who benefits in the event of the death of the insured.

Blend stocks
Stocks that include components of both value and growth stocks.

Bond
A loan with a set interest rate purchased from a government or company.

Bond mutual funds
Diversified funds in which you buy a share in thousands of different bonds in a changing portfolio.

Budget
A spending plan in which family income is allocated to specific categories of expenditures.

Capacity
Your ability to repay the debt from your family's income.

Capital
The worth of all your assets.

Capitalization
What you could buy the company for if you bought all of its stock.

Cash inflow
Family income.

Cash management
How to effectively manage your family's monetary assets.

Cash outflow
Family expenditures.

Cash value
The total account value that is available to the life insurance policy owner while he or she is alive.

207

CD
Certificate of Deposit. Pay a fixed interest rate for keeping your funds in the account for a fixed period of time.

Character
The amount of integrity you demonstrate.

Co-insurance/Co-payment
The portion of expenses beyond the deductible that the insured person pays, up to an annual maximum.

Collateral
An asset that can be pledged against a loan.

Collision coverage
Auto insurance that pays for damage to your car when it is involved in an accident, regardless of who is at fault.

Compounding periods (N)
The frequency with which interest is applied to an investment.

Compound interest
Interest earned on interest.

Comprehensive coverage
Auto insurance that protects from risks other than vehicle collision.

Conditions
The economic state of the nation or community at the time of a loan request.

Consumer loans
An amount of money lent to an individual for personal, family, or household purposes.

Convertible loans
Loans in which the interest-rate structure can change.

Coordination of benefits
Multiple insurers coordinating insurance claims medical payments so as to avoid double paying.

Corporate bonds
Bonds issued by corporations.

Coupon bonds
Bond purchaser receives regular interest payments until maturity date.

Credit
A contractual agreement in which a borrower receives something of value now and agrees to repay the lender at some date in the future, generally with interest; the term also refers to the borrowing capacity of an individual or company.

Credit bureaus
Private companies that collect and report your financial information from creditors, public records, and various institutions.

Credit card
A form of open credit that allows you to borrow money up to a specific limit with no collateral, with the expectation that you will pay back the money at a specific interest rate and with specific terms.

Credit evaluation
The process of turning the information in your credit report into a three-digit number to determine whether or not you deserve to be given credit.

Credit-holic
Someone who is addicted to credit and whose financial life is out of control.

Credit limit
The available credit given to a specific account holder.

Credit reports
Files of information that credit bureaus compile about specific individuals.

Credit score
A three-digit number that is used by banks, insurance companies, and other financial institutions to determine how likely it is that you will be creditworthy and pay your debts on time.

Current market value
The price at which your family's asset could be sold in the present market environment.

Debt
Something owed to someone else.

Debt-elimination calendar
A debt-elimination strategy in which you plan out all debt repayments, paying all minimum payments but focusing mostly on one until it is paid off, then using the amount of money previously paid toward that debt to pay off the next most important debt.

Deductible
A specified amount that you must pay to cover an expense that could qualify for your insurance coverage before your insurance begins paying for eligible expenses.

Deductions
IRS-allowed reductions to your adjusted gross income that are used to calculate taxable income.

Defined-benefit plan (DB)
A type of retirement plan in which all contributions are made by the employer and the benefit is guaranteed for life and based on the number of years of service and the final salary.

Defined-contribution plan (DC)
A type of retirement plan in which contributions are made by both the employer and the employee, but the investments are chosen by the employee; the contribution amount is specified by a formula, but the benefit amount varies according to payment amounts, the market, and the management of the employee.

Depreciate
To lose value over time

Disability insurance
Insurance that provides payments to insured individuals in the event that regular income is interrupted by illness or an accident.

Dividends
Money paid to shareholders on a regular basis.

Emergency Fund
Liquid financial resources to meet unexpected and immediate needs; this should total at least 3–6 months of living expenses.

Equity
Hypothetical amount of money you would have left if you sold your home and paid off your mortgage today.

Estate
The money, property, and other assets owned by a person at the time of their death.

Estate taxes
A tax charged on the value of a person's estate upon his or her death if the estate is sufficiently large.

Excise taxes
A tax levied against certain specific products or services (such as fuel, liquors, and cigarettes) on a per unit basis.

Exclusions
Specific conditions or items that are not covered by the standard insurance policy.

Face value (bonds)
Value of the bond when redeemed on the maturity date.

Face value (insurance)
The basic benefit the life insurance company will pay the beneficiaries upon the death of the insured.

Family loans
Borrowing and lending between family members.

Fast Offerings
The term used in The Church of Jesus Christ of Latter-day Saints to denote money or usable commodities donated to the Church, which are then available to provide financial help for those in need.

FDIC
Federal Deposit Insurance Corporation. The government agency which insures deposits at most commercial banks for up to $250,000 per depositor. Joint depositors are insured for up to $500,000.

FICO score
The most common type of credit score.

Financial Reserve
Cash or other liquid assets held to cover 3–6 months of emergency expenses.

Fixed expenses
Expenditures that your family has little direct control over and that do not often change from month to month.

Fixed-rate loans
Loans that maintain the same interest rate for the duration of the loan.

Fixed rate mortgage
A loan which has a constant (or fixed) interest rate throughout the life of the contract. Monthly PI (principal and interest) remains fixed the duration of the loan.

Future value (FV)
The monetary value of an investment at some point in the future.

Geometric return
The compound interest rate of an investment.

Global funds
Funds that contain a mixture of US and foreign holdings.

Grace period (credit cards and loans)
The period of time between a payment due and penalties, interest, or cancellation.

Grace period (insurance)
The period of time between the payment due date and the cancelation of your insurance.

Graduated payment mortgages (GPM)
Mortgages with lower initial payments that increase over time.

Growth stocks
Companies whose earnings are expected to grow very rapidly.

Guaranteed renewable
An option that gives an individual the right to continue insurance at the end of each premium period

HALT principle
Avoid making purchases or financial decisions when you are
Hungry
Angry
Lonely
Tired

Health insurance
Insurance for expenses relating to health and medical procedures.

Health savings account (HSA)
An account that is created by an employer on behalf of an employee to save money toward medical expenses.

Home equity loan
A loan which uses the equity in your house to secure your loan (to be avoided!).

Homeowners insurance
Insurance that covers a personal residence combined with other personal protections for the owner(s).

Income and expense statement
A record of your family's past cash inflows and outflows over a specified period of time.

Income taxes
A tax levied directly against the earnings of workers; this tax is one of the main sources of government funds.

Individual Retirement Account (IRA)
A tax-advantaged retirement plan that is managed by the individual who owns the plan. Maximum contributions are $5500 per years until age 50. Money may not be withdrawn without penalty until age 59 ½.

Inflation
Decrease in the purchasing power of money.

Inflation protected securities
Securities whose yield is linked to the rate of inflation as measured by a specific inflation index.

Inheritance taxes
A tax on money and property received by heirs.

Installment loans
Loans that are repaid at regular intervals.

Insurance
A contract in which an individual receives financial protection or reimbursement against losses from an insurance company.

Interest
Remuneration for investing or loaning money.

Interest rate (I)
The rate you will receive for investing at a specified compounding period for a specified period of time (generally expressed in percent per year).

Intermediate-term bonds
Bonds with a maturity of about four to seven years.

International stocks
Stocks of companies based entirely outside the US or throughout the world.

Investment
A current commitment of your money in the expectation of reaping future returns.

Investment Plan
A detailed road map of your investment risk and return, investment strategy, constraints, and reporting and evaluation methodology.

Itemized deduction
The sum of the possible deductions from AGI that you qualify for.

Junk bonds
Bonds with high yields issued by companies in distress.

Large-cap stocks
Stocks from companies with a capitalization of more than $10 billion.

Lease
Long-term renting with a number of conditions.
Notes

Liabilities
Synonymous with debt, calculated by adding up the outstanding balances on any current and long-term family debts.

Liability coverage
Auto insurance that pays for losses related to bodily injury, property damage, lawsuits, and defense costs.

Life insurance
Insurance against the financial loss resulting from the death of the insured.

Liquidity
The immediate accessibility of money.

Loan contract
A document which describes what the lender requires of your family once you are granted the loan.

Long-term bonds
Bonds with a maturity of about seven or more years.

Long-term care (LTC) insurance
Insurance that covers the costs of nursing home facilities and long-term home health care.

Lump sum
One payment at a specific time.

Mad money
A certain amount of funds allocated to each spouse, for which they are not responsible to the other spouse.

Marginal tax rate
The rate at which the next dollar earned is taxed.

Maturity date
Date at which a bond is redeemed at face value.

Maximum annual co-payment
The most you can pay towards co-insurance in any given year.

Maximum annual out-of-pocket cost
The most you can pay towards medical care in any given year (insurance premium + annual deductible + maximum co-payment).

Medical payment coverage
Auto insurance that pays for accident-related medical costs and funeral expenses incurred by you or your family members within three years of an accident.

Mid-cap stocks
Stocks from companies with a capitalization of $2 billion to $10 billion.

Miscellaneous
One of your budget's most important, but often neglected, categories; a generous catch-all category for those unexpected expenses which find the holes in your budget.

MMA
Money Market Account. This is similar to a savings account, but instead of having a fixed rate of interest, its interest rate varies with the current level of market interest rates.

Monetary assets
Financial resources that are legal tender (cash) or can be converted to legal tender very quickly.

Mortgage
A loan in which the home serves as loan collateral.

Municipal bonds
Tax-free bonds issued by state and local governments.

NCUA
National Credit Union Administration. Government agency which insures deposits at credit unions for up to $250,000 per depositor or $500,000 for joint depositors.

Net worth statement
A snapshot of your family's total assets minus your total liabilities on a particular day.

Nominal return
The return on an investment before the impacts of inflation and taxes are taken into account.

Non-cancelable
A type of policy in which your premium cannot be raised nor your policy canceled prior to age sixty-five

Opportunity cost
The potential loss or gain that occurs when one financial option is chosen over another.

Ownership
The right to possess or own something.

Passively managed funds
Funds that are managed by professional investors who invest money using a "buy and hold" strategy.

Payday loans
Short-term loans of one or two weeks which are secured with a postdated check.

Payment (PMT)
A periodic amount invested or received during the life of the investment (e.g., monthly payment, annual disbursement, dividend, etc.).

Personal exemption
A specific amount of money that can be deducted from AGI for each qualifying person in the household.

Personal property taxes
A state and local tax against certain personal assets.

Plastic surgery
Cutting up a credit card, making it unusable, but still keeping the account open.

Point
Equal to one percent of the mortgage loan value, points are paid to the lender in exchange for a lower interest rate.

Policy owner
The individual or business that pays for and owns the insurance policy.

Portfolio
All of your various investments.

Premium
A specified amount paid regularly (usually monthly or annually) to an insurance company in exchange for coverage.

Present value (PV)
Current value of money.

Principal
The original amount of money borrowed or invested (generally synonymous with present value).

Property taxes
A tax levied against the assessed value of land and buildings.

Purchasing power
The value of monetary funds based on the amount of goods or services that one unit of money can buy.

Real return
The rate of return on an investment after the impacts of taxes and inflation are taken into account.

Refinance
To finance a home again with a new loan and a new interest rate, must pay off old loan and closing costs.

Roth IRA/401(k)
A type of retirement plan in which contributions are taxed before they are put into the account and money is not taxed when it is withdrawn.

Sales taxes
A percentage tax applied to the purchase price of taxable goods.

Secured loans
Loans which use one of your assets as collateral to guarantee that the lending institution will get the amount of the loan back even if you fail to make payments.

Short-term bonds
Bonds that mature in less than about four years.

Single-payment loans
A type of short-term lending repaid in one lump sum that may be used to temporarily finance a purchase until permanent, long-term financing can be arranged.

Small-cap stocks
Stocks from companies with a capitalization of less than $2 billion.

SMART principle
Family goals should be
Specific
Measurable
Attainable
Relevant
Time-bound

Social Security taxes
A tax levied against the earnings of workers to fund the Social Security system.

Speculation
The practice of engaging in risky financial transactions, often promising greater than market-rate return, in an attempt to profit from fluctuations in the market.

Standard deduction
The dollar amount set by the government that any tax filer may use as a reduction to AGI; the amount differs depending on filing status.

Stewardship
An ethic that embodies the responsible planning and management of resources.

Stock Exchange
A market in which securities (bonds, shares, and notes) are bought and sold.

Stock mutual funds
Funds that pool investor money to purchase many different stocks in groups or types of companies.

Student loans
Loans which are often used to pay for higher education and have federally subsidized interest rates.

Taxable income
The second step of calculating your federal income tax, determined by subtracting your deductions and exemptions from your AGI.

Tax credits
Dollar-for-dollar reductions from your tax liability.

Tax-deferred accounts
Accounts which allow you to invest without first paying taxes on the principal; you then pay taxes on both the principal and the earnings when you withdraw money at retirement.

Tax due/Tax refund
The final step of calculating your federal income tax, determined

by subtracting tax credits from your tax liability.

Tax-eliminated accounts
Accounts which require you to pay taxes on the principal before you invest it, but you do not have to pay any taxes on the capital gains or future earnings.

Tax Freedom Day
The day of the year on which you have earned enough money to pay for all of your taxes for that year.

Tax liability
The third step of calculating your federal income tax, determined by multiplying your taxable income by government-set tax rate(s).

Term life insurance
A policy in which the face value is paid to the beneficiaries when the insured dies.

Time value of money (TVM)
How the value of money changes over time due to inflation and interest.

Timing the market
The attempt to obtain greater than market-rate returns by buying when the market is low and selling when the market is high.

Tithing
The act of paying a tithe, which is a portion (in the LDS Church, a tenth) of a person's income, to support religious institutions.

Traditional IRA/401(k)
A type of retirement plan in which contributions are not taxed and constitute an income adjustment when they are put into the account and money is taxed when it is withdrawn.

Truth in Lending Act
A law which requires that all lenders provide the consumer with certain information before they sign the credit contract.

Uninsured/Underinsured motorist coverage
Auto insurance that covers your costs if you are injured in a hit-and-run accident, or injured by an uninsured motorist or a motorist whose insurance is insufficient to pay for your expenses.

Unsecured loans
Loans which do not require collateral and are generally offered only to borrowers with excellent credit histories.

US Treasury Bonds
Bonds backed by full faith and credit of the United States.

Value stocks
Companies that are inexpensive in terms of the underlying fundamentals of the market.

Variable expenses
Expenditures that your family controls and that may vary from month to month.

Variable-rate loans
Loans which have an interest rate that is adjusted at different intervals over the life of the loan.

Waiting periods
A stated length of time that must elapse before certain types of coverage are available to the insured

Waiver of premium
An option that pays your premium for you in the case of disability, thus keeping your policy in force

Whole life insurance
A policy in which the premiums are divided between death protection and safe, relatively low return investments.

Zero-coupon bonds
Bonds purchased at less than face value then sold at face value at the maturity date with no interim interest payments.